OVERSEAS DEVELOPMENT ADMINISTRATION

APPRAISAL OF PROJECTS IN DEVELOPING COUNTRIES

A GUIDE FOR ECONOMISTS

LONDON: HMSO

Front Cover: Nursery workers tending seedlings in the Karnataka Social Forestry Project in India.

Contents

iii

PART II   Illustrations of Project Analysis

Preface

i. The purpose of this Guide is to provide practical assistance to economists assisting in the preparation and appraisal of projects to be submitted for public sector funding. The economic appraisal principles outlined are based on those developed by I. M. D. Little and J. A. Mirrlees (henceforth Little–Mirrlees) for OECD and aims to translate these into methods that can be used within the time constraints which invariably apply in the field. But the Guide aims to cover a somewhat wider area than the economic appraisal itself and therefore includes guidance on other areas of project preparation where the economist can contribute usefully.

ii. The Guide should therefore help economists working in ministries and public sector agencies in developing countries whose work includes advice on the design and acceptability of projects competing for investment funds. Its further purpose is to provide a standard for the Overseas Development Administration (ODA) itself. The Guide outlines the approach used by ODA economists and economic consultants commissioned by the ODA in their project work.

iii. This third edition of the Guide retains the same basic principles for economic appraisal as the second edition published in 1977. It assumes that public sector investment is aimed at the greatest possible increase in the standard of living of the population over time and that this objective is best furthered through the operation of competitive markets. The opportunity cost valuation principles therefore take full account of the advantages to be gained from trade. The numeraire – the unit of account – is expressed at world prices.

iv. ODA experience over the past ten years has resulted in changes of emphasis in this edition, however. It is now widely recognised that the success of a project depends on the economic environment in which it operates, the institutional arrangements for its operations and its financial viability. The chapter on financial planning has therefore been expanded and a new chapter added on institutional considerations.

v. Environmental and social issues – the latter including the role of women – are also given greater weight in considering development options now than they were in the mid-seventies, not least because of their effect on long-term economic prospects. Detailed treatment of these areas is outside the scope of this Guide but the measurement and valuation principles proposed allow for the inclusion of their effects.

vi. The investigations and analysis currently underway in these areas may result in changes in their treatment in project appraisal in the future. It was not possible to anticipate these in the Guide, which aims simply to reflect current best practice. The reader is advised to watch out for developments in technique.

vii. A further innovation is to draw widely from ODA experience in financing projects in developing countries by including, as Part II of the Guide, a range of case studies. These are in three categories: two detailed case studies which provide precise illustration of how the principles of the Guide can be applied; fifteen briefer case studies which illustrate the different problems presented in different sectors; and four methodology studies which illustrate particular valuation issues. These case studies have been distilled from ODA records from the 1970s and early 1980s. They do not fully reflect current ODA practice – the newer preoccupations with environmental and social aspects are under-represented for example – but they show how economic appraisals were undertaken by ODA staff and consultants commissioned by ODA in real world situations, where approximations and short-cuts are usually necessary.

viii.   The case studies in Part II are linked to the exposition in Part I through the device of *boxes*, each of which identify case studies illustrating particular aspects of appraisal. Space has been made for them by omitting the sector checklists which were annexed to the 1977 edition as similar (but improved) checklists were provided in 1983 in the ODA publication *Planning Development Projects* (see Selected Bibliography).

ix.   The main author of this edition is John MacArthur, Deputy Director of the Project Planning Centre for Developing Countries of the University of Bradford. ODA advisers also contributed significantly to ideas, material and drafting of the text. Considerable benefit was gained from a seminar attended by about twenty development economists from British Universities, other institutions and consultancy firms in November 1986.

J. M Healey
Chief Economist

PART I

PRINCIPLES AND METHODS

1
The Framework for the Economic Appraisal of Projects

The Role of Economists in Project Appraisal

1.1   The central role of the economist in project appraisal is to undertake the economic appraisal itself. But economic principles are relevant to other aspects of project appraisal also. The 'project cycle' runs through various stages – identification, feasibility study, design, commitment, implementation, operation and evaluation – and economic appraisal can contribute to every stage. It is as important to identification and design as it is to final decisions whether to implement, modify or cancel projects.

1.2   At every one of these stages other kinds of appraisal must be undertaken in association with economic appraisal. Technical appraisal is an obvious pre-requisite to economic appraisal because the original ideas and estimates of engineers, natural resource specialists, doctors, public health experts, architects, educationalists and others provide the raw material for the economist's measurements of costs and benefits. Financial appraisal is also closely related to economic appraisal and the forecast accounts for an enterprise are another important source of data for the economist. What may be less apparent is that environmental and social analysis can also contribute to the economist's work, by drawing attention to wider project effects, non-financial issues and long-run sustainability.[1]

1.3   The reason for this close relationship between economic and other forms of appraisal is that the distinctive feature of economic appraisal is its concern with national costs and benefits. Economists seek to identify and measure all the effects of a project and to value them in national resource terms. Their canvas is therefore wider than that of others involved in the project – sponsors, technical advisers, financiers, tax collectors, etc. – and there is a corresponding need for them to draw on the skills of others in undertaking economic appraisals. The counterpart of this is that economists can contribute usefully to the work of other specialists if they are concerned with national rather than particular interests.

1.4   Economic appraisal is most frequently applied to public sector projects and the reasons for using it in the private sector may not be fully appreciated. Private sponsors are mainly pre-occupied with their own interests and less concerned with national effects, but the principles and procedures set out here can be applied with equal validity to private sector projects. Where private sector investments need government support, either as financial contributions or through administrative procedures such as protective tariffs or restrictive licensing, economic appraisal to estimate national costs and benefits should be applied.

---

[1] The Overseas Development Administration is preparing an environmental assessment manual and a social appraisal guide. These will provide detailed guidance on these important areas of project appraisal.

Project Definition

1.5   The aim in economic appraisal of measuring national costs and benefits is normally approached by defining 'with' and 'without' project situations. This detaches the project definition in economic appraisal from the concepts of project sponsors and physical planners. For example, while they can confine their attention to the manufacturing plant or agricultural scheme, the economist must consider effects on imports and exports, other local production, social infrastructure, transport facilities, consumer prices, the government budget and so on. Gains to some members of the community can be losses to others and only net effects should be measured in estimates in national resource terms.

1.6   In principle the economist can 'internalise' all these wider aspects in the economic appraisal by simply defining the project along 'with/without' lines. However, conventional practice distinguishes between 'internal' and 'external' effects. Internal effects are those experienced by parties directly involved in the project. In most cases analysis can be simplified and improved by defining the project so that all major, direct effects are automatically included in the arithmetic of economic analysis with less direct or tenuous effects analysed separately as 'externalities'.

1.7   The definition of the project in this sense calls for skill and judgement. In many cases it will have significant effects on the appraisal but there are no simple rules of definition. The range and size of project effects will depend on the nature of the project and the economic and physical structure into which it is fitted. Situations in which a project is likely to have economic effects well beyond its physical boundaries include the following.

a.   The project is large in relation to the sector or economy in which it is located. It may therefore change trading and employment patterns as well as affecting economic (transport, power, water) and social (housing, schools, hospitals) infrastructure.

b.   It is part of an interconnected system (for example, electricity grid, railway network, telecommunications system).

c.   It will have significant off-site physical effects. Examples are a manufacturing plant with harmful effluent, a hydropower investment which will create a lake and therefore resettlement, a mining development with large transport requirements and landscape effects, etc.

d.   It will be a monopoly supplier or customer, therefore having widespread economic powers over consumers or producers.

e.   The project is new to the country or region in which it is located and may therefore affect technology, management, working practices and social habits in ways which are uncertain.

1.8   A special category covers projects which involve replication of a basic model. Cases include agricultural developments in which smallholders agree to follow a particular cropping pattern, installation of minor telecommunications exchanges, village water or power supplies and so on. The key characteristics of such developments are that each individual case will have relatively low costs and the pattern of supply and demand will be similar in all cases. In this situation the appraisal can be carried out for the model – the individual

4

smallholding or telephone exchange – and the results multiplied up to obtain total project costs and benefits.

1.9   Firm adherence to the with/without project discipline combined with a sense of what is practicable with the time and resources available for appraisal are essential. The case studies illustrate how economists chose to define projects with characteristics similar to those listed above in ways which allowed them to measure effects well enough to produce valid results.

The Broader Project Framework

1.10   How does the project appraisal fit in with the rest of economic management in the public sector? The national budget is a crucial element in economic policy. The ways in which it raises revenue often affect private incentives and allocation decisions; the deficit and its financing are important in determining inflation and thus the real exchange rate; and the pattern of public expenditures reflects the role which the government is intent on playing in the supply of goods and services in the economy. Expenditures are conventionally divided into recurrent and capital: capital expenditures are in theory defined as relating to the creation of physical assets which last at least one year; the rest are labelled recurrent. In practice recurrent expenditures in agricultural services, infrastructure maintenance, social services etc. may be bundled up into 'projects' to make them attractive to outside donors and financiers. Project appraisal is concerned with seeking to optimise the capital budget, including the choice of 'projectised' recurrent services: it helps in choosing the best project design, the best set of projects within the capital budgets of individual ministries and, in principle at least, the best set of projects among those proposed by different ministries. It can also be used to choose the level of maintenance expenditure to plan for and to decide on the timing of rehabilitation, replacement and expansion programmes.

1.11   Resources available to finance the capital budget are drawn from the surplus of revenue receipts over recurrent outlays, foreign grants and loans and such domestic borrowing as is compatible with macro-economic stabilisation objectives. Foreign borrowing may be limited by the need to avoid excessive external debt. Annual resources for the capital budget will therefore generally be limited. The public investment programming process allocates these resources between on-going and new projects.

1.12   In the budgetary process there is active competition between spending ministries for resources. Within spending ministries project ideas emanate from departments and sponsored outside bodies. The ideas are not always well thought through. Undertaking new projects is often regarded as more prestigious than devoting adequate resources to routine maintenance, even if the end result is a less cost-effective provision of public services. Project concepts are frequently advanced without adequate consideration for the means of meeting the consequential recurrent costs. Planning or Finance ministries are supposed to instil order, method and discipline into investment programming through the application of project appraisal techniques. The same techniques should be applied by the planning departments of spending ministries. It has to be recognised, however, that political pressures may override the application of these procedures. Many projects, moreover, have outcomes which are hard or impossible to measure in monetary terms. Such projects are difficult to rank in order of preference alongside the project ideas of competing ministries. In these cases the potential role for project appraisal is more limited.

1.13   Governments which draw up multi-year (usually 3 year) public expenditure budgets are better able to clarify the trade-offs between capital and recurrent expenditure and between different project proposals. These budgets also help to determine the timing of project starts which is compatible with the overall policy requirement of respecting annual public expenditure limits. One procedure for reconciling the objectives of accelerated development expenditure and consistency with current annual expenditure limits and future recurrent budgetary capability is to divide projects into three categories:

Group 1:   projects which are on-going together with new projects which have been fully appraised and which are also guaranteed to receive full internal and external capital and recurrent funding. These projects should go into the multi-year budget.

Group 2:   projects which have been fully appraised and meet the criteria of acceptance but which are not yet fully funded. These should remain on hold until funding is assured.

Group 3:   projects which have been proposed but not yet appraised by all the relevant authorities.

If the status of project proposals is clear it is easier to make public investment budgeting more orderly.

1.14   In all cases economists will need to take account of the macro-economic management which actually exists and not what they would like it to be, recognising that in some cases a new project can itself help to correct economic distortions. Where projects are likely to perpetuate or extend macro-economic distortions – through pricing, monopoly, foreign exchange or other effects – these should be highlighted in the economic appraisal.

Project Objectives

1.15   Project objectives are not always self-evident and they can evolve during the preparation process. But clear definition of the objective will help preparation and appraisal and the procedure adopted by the Overseas Development Administration (ODA) may be a useful guide in this respect.

1.16   Appendix 1.1 gives the format used for applications to the ODA committee which considers major project proposals, and attached to it is an outline of the 'project framework' used throughout project preparation. The format illustrates the breadth of the issues relevant to project preparation. The purpose of the project framework is to ensure that objectives are defined as clearly as possible at an early stage and that the link between inputs and outputs is registered.[1] As preparation proceeds the framework is revised and refined and it is a useful starting point for evaluation following project implementation.

---

[1] This concern with measurable, timebound objectives is a reflection of government policy throughout the public sector in Britain.

Valuation Principles

1.17   Where markets function in a relatively unrestricted fashion and the distribution of income is not considered to be unsatisfactory, the prices resulting from the interaction of supply and demand in those markets should be a good guide to resource costs. It will be necessary to eliminate transfers such as indirect taxes and subsidies but further adjustments to market prices will not generally be necessary. These conditions do not hold in many developing countries, however, and valuation issues are therefore a major concern in economic appraisal. The objective is to determine prices which reflect national costs and benefits and for this purpose the 'opportunity cost' principle is adopted. This is the value to society of the good or service in its best alternative use (other than the project under examination).

1.18   Detailed valuation principles are covered for three different situations in chapters 3, 4 and 5. Chapter 6 then explains how to extend the analysis to take account of risk and uncertainty. This further step should not be overlooked, because economic appraisal involves forecasting which is always uncertain. The results of an appraisal should never be presented as a single figure: a range should be shown reflecting the forecaster's best estimate of the errors attached to each component of the appraisal.

1.19   The numeraire used in this Guide is expressed in world prices and the separation of inputs and outputs into 'tradeables' (ie entering into international trade) and 'non-tradeables' is a fundamental analytical technique. This leads to three layers of valuation complexity: tradeables, where the principles are simple even if the practice may present problems; non-tradeables, where the difficulties multiply as the opportunity cost principle is traced through the domestic markets where the goods are exchanged; and the layer which poses maximum problems for the economist, non-tradeables which are not sold. This last group includes services such as primary health care and education, general government administration, roads, broadcasting and other components of the economic and social fabric. The inability of the economist to value the outputs of such sectors (which are sometimes the inputs of other sectors) does not rule out economic appraisal, however. The important point is that resources are needed to produce the service, that the normal valuation principles can be applied to these resources, and cost-effectiveness analysis will usually assist in design and decision.

Limitations of Economic Appraisal

1.20   The scope of economic appraisal and its relationship with other types of analysis make it difficult to limit the content of a manual on economic appraisal. A first step in preparing this Guide was to exclude any attempt to provide instruction on the enormous body of knowledge that contributes to technical appraisal. It assumes that engineers, agriculturalists, environmental specialists, sociologists and any other technical advisers will have drawn on their disciplines appropriately in detailing the technical parameters of project implementation and operation. The economist can question the standards and assumptions adopted by technical specialists but ultimate responsibility for them must rest with these specialists. For example, it is the engineer who must determine the maximum output of a manufacturing process, frequency of shut-downs and wastage rates; the agriculturalist (working with a sociologist) who forecasts the viability of new agricultural practices, rate of take-up and yields; the public health expert who forecasts demand for domestic water supplies and effects on water-borne diseases.

1.21   Environmental questions also need to be addressed to technical specialists but their impact on economic results, defined widely and in national terms, require particular attention. This aspect is outlined in this Guide under the general heading of project externalities with the qualification that expert advice will be needed whenever a project seems likely to have significant environmental effects.

1.22   Gender factors also need special consideration. Gender bias has been eradicated from the text of this Guide as far as possible. It has been assumed that technical specialists will have taken account of the gender factor in their preparation work; for example, that agricultural advisers will realise that farmers are often women and that technical designs will take this into account. Neutral terms such as 'consumers', 'producers' and 'labourers' are intended to cover women and/or men as appropriate but specific reference is made to gender features where these seem to need particular consideration.

1.23   Financial, institutional and manpower (including women) questions are also given some attention here because of their important bearing on economic performance. Again the qualification should be noted that the economist cannot substitute for a specialist adviser in determining important aspects of project design in these fields, although he can contribute to the work.

1.24   The presentation of material in the Guide is geared to preparation of a cost-benefit analysis. This conventional tool of the economist provides a valuable framework for the analysis but it is frequently misunderstood. It will be apparent from this introduction that the narrow concept of a comparison between 'sales' and 'costs', with important externalities and non-quantifiable effects ignored, is not the approach adopted here. Cost-benefit analysis should incorporate all the national effects which can be identified, including the effects which can be quantified but not expressed in financial terms and those which cannot be quantified at all. In some cases international effects should also be measured. Often the appraisal will comprise a numerical, value-based cost-benefit analysis supplemented by qualitative description of those effects not captured in the basic calculation; in other cases the output will have to be expressed in physical terms and only the costs valued according to the principles set out here. The results will need to be presented and interpreted in different ways but the cost-benefit principle can be retained.

Appraisal in the Project Cycle

1.25   Project design is an iterative process involving initial concepts, examination and comparison with similar projects and alternative concepts, refinement, redesign and so on. In the natural resources sector a flexible approach is sometimes adopted, incorporating initial proposals, pilot projects and substantial redesign before full-scale implementation goes ahead in successive stages. The full project cycle in all sectors implies drawing on the post-implementation evaluations of previous projects as part of the iterative procedure.

1.26   Economic appraisal should be integral to all stages of the cycle because decisions are taken at every stage. Wherever possible the nature of

8

these decisions should be explicit and options should be kept open as long as possible. A common error is to settle for a particular design and level of service at an early stage because it is standard practice, and thereby exclude viable options from full appraisal. The value of technical standards should not be under-estimated – they are usually the result of rigorous testing and evaluation – but they cannot be expected to provide the correct solution in every set of circumstances. Non-standard solutions and non-conventional concepts should be sought and appraised whenever this is practical.

1.27   The terminology for the various stages of project preparation and implementation is not rigid but the following definitions may help in using this Guide.[1]

Identification
The earliest phase, when a development opportunity is conceived (for example, available land with crop-bearing potential or a market for a particular product) or a problem requiring a solution arises (such as a traffic bottle-neck). Identification implies outline of an investment concept in a crude but reasonably comprehensive manner. Provisional objectives for the project should be established at this stage.

Feasibility
There are often several feasibility stages during which the initial concept is explored in various depths to determine its technical, economic, financial, etc. viability.

Commitments and Negotiation
There are often a series of commitments – particularly when projects are staged – and they are followed by invitations to tender and negotiations with contractors, potential financiers, suppliers, future customers and so on. At the early commitment stages there are still considerable uncertainties.

Design
Preliminary design and feasibility are often simultaneous but detailed design, which can be very costly (up to 15% of project costs) usually follows provisional commitment to the project. As noted above, numerous decisions which will affect economic performance are taken throughout design; and economic appraisal often results in redesign.

Implementation
The stage when capital investment takes place, staff are appointed, trials are conducted and the plant is commissioned.

Operation
The period when the benefits are realised: production and sales occur, long-term employment is created and repair and maintenance undertaken.

Monitoring
Project sponsors and technical staff monitor progress during implementation. It requires the collection, analysis and utilisation by management of information to ensure that work plans are being achieved and objectives obtained as planned or that adjustments are made.

---

[1] An extensive glossary of the terminology in common usage and employed in this Guide is at page 229.

Evaluation
This is a systematic examination of a completed (or sometimes on-going) project with the aim of determining its efficiency, effectiveness, impact, sustainability and developmental value. This will yield the most useful results when the asset has been in operation for some time so that the lessons learned from all stages can be incorporated into similar investments in the future.

1.28   This sequence is equally applicable to investments of a less tangible nature than a discrete investment project. A programme of expenditure designed to raise capacity in a sector – such as an expansion in the number of agricultural extension officers or an in-service training programme for teachers – can benefit from the disciplines of project appraisal in the same way as conventional projects such as power generators and fertiliser factories.

Appendix 1.1
The ODA Format for Project Submissions

Both the format for ODA project submissions and the project framework which are attached are outlines to be filled in according to the specific characteristics of the project under consideration. All sections need to be completed, although entries may be minimal in some cases.

This completed project submission is a comprehensive and usually substantial document. The project framework needs to be limited to a single page, however. Its purpose is to provide a simple overview of the project's main characteristics and objectives and this will be frustrated if it spills over to several sheets.

The Format

(a) **Summary**

(b) **Project Description**
 — A description of the main components and objectives. Attach a project framework (see attachment).

(c) **Background**
 — An explanation of the origin of the proposal and how it fits in with the UK aid programme.

(d) **The Project and the Development Programme**
 — The relationship with the recipient government's development programme, with the recipient government's priorities, and with other donors' activities.

(e) **Technical Appraisal**
 — The conclusions of assessments by relevant advisers (eg engineering advisers or medical advisers), including results of pre-feasibility or feasibility studies which may have been undertaken by consultants.
 — Particular issues addressed under this heading include the appropriateness of technology choice, including cost-effectiveness.

(f) **Labour, Inputs and Services Required**
 — Arrangements for manpower, raw materials and other inputs (eg power, water) and other necessary services not part of the project itself.

(g) **Economic Justification**
 — Conclusions of economic appraisal and financial analysis.

(h) **Social and Environmental Aspects**
 — Conclusions of assessments by relevant advisers.
 — Questions addressed include: Who are the major beneficiaries? Will any groups be disadvantaged? What will the effects be on employment? What changes in social patterns are expected?
 — The major beneficial and detrimental effects on the physical environment are described, including upstream and downstream effects.

(i) **Financing the Project**
 — Cost estimates, in cash and constant prices, broken down into offshore, local and recurrent costs.

— Special attention is given to intended source and availability of finance for local costs, and for recurrent costs.
(Detailed financial analysis to appear in section g.)

(j) Arrangements for Implementation
— Obligations and capability of implementing agency.
— Procurement.
— Arrangements for technical monitoring and supervision during implementation.

(k) Arrangements for Operation of Completed Project
— Obligations of agency responsible.
— Special measures required (eg tariff studies or revised tariff structures).
— Arrangements for training staff, including management.
— Arrangements for technical assistance.

(l) Monitoring of Project
— A statement of the criteria established for measuring progress in achieving the objectives of the project and arrangements made for collecting necessary data.

(m) Risks
— A statement of the main potential causes of failure, either to achieve the objective or disburse the aid.

(n) Evaluation
— A review of relevant evaluation studies.

(o) Special Conditions
— Any special conditions to be agreed with the recipient government or authority, for example on cost recovery measures, or institutional change.

PROJECT FRAMEWORK

PROJECT TITLE:
BRIEF DESCRIPTION OF PROJECTS

PERIOD OF ODA FUNDING:
TOTAL ODA FUNDING: £
DATE FRAMEWORK PREPARED/REVISED

Project Structure	Indicators of Achievement and Value	How indicators can be quantified or Assessed	Important Assumptions for success (and conditions attached to aid)
WIDER (ie SECTOR OR NATIONAL) OBJECTIVES What are the wider objectives or problems which the project will help to resolve?	What are the quantitative ways of measuring, or qualitative ways of judging, whether these wider objectives have been achieved?	What sources of information exist or can be provided cost-effectively?	What conditions external to the project are necessary if the project's Immediate Objectives are to contribute to the Wider Objectives? What risks have been considered? Are any conditions attached to ODA's aid to improve the prospects of success?
Immediate Objectives; Project Purpose What are the intended immediate effects on the project area or target group? What are the expected benefits (or disbenefits) and to whom will they go? What improvements or changes will the project bring about?	What are the quantitative measures (including the realised internal rate of return), or qualitative evidence, by which achievement and distribution of effects and benefits will be judged?	What sources of information exist or can be provided cost-effectively? Does provision for collection need to be made under Inputs–Outputs?	What are the factors outside the control of the project authorities which, if not present, are liable to restrict progress from Outputs to achievement of Immediate Objectives? What risks have been considered? Are any conditions attached to ODA's aid to improve the prospects of success?
OUTPUTS What outputs (kind, quantity and by when) are to be produced by the project in order to achieve the Immediate Objectives? eg teaching institution, miles or road built or rehabilitated, irrigation system and associated management installed, persons trained.		What are sources of information?	What external factors must be realised to obtain planned Outputs on schedules? What risks have been considered? Are any conditions attached to ODA's aid to improve the prospects of success?
INPUTS What materials/equipment or services (personnel, trained etc.) are to be provided at what cost over what period by – ODA – other donors – recipient?		What are sources of information?	What decisions or actions outside control of ODA are necessary for inception of project? What risks have been considered? Are any conditions attached to ODA's aid to improve the prospects of success?

2
Fundamental Aspects of Economic Appraisal

Levels of Economic Appraisal

2.1   The key elements of economic appraisal are well-known: identification and consistent valuation of all costs and benefits, appropriate allowance for their phasing over time and application of some decision criterion to determine which projects are acceptable. The main principles adopted in this Guide in relation to each of these three elements are outlined in the following paragraphs of this chapter. The following three chapters then explain the detailed application of these principles according to different assumptions or judgements about the character of the economy in which the projects will be located.

2.2   The alternative sets of assumptions on which these chapters are based are as follows:

Chapter 3
This describes the basic economic analysis for allocative efficiency. Such an analysis would be sufficient in countries where savings are regarded as roughly optimal and where there are no concerns about the distribution of income. It might be considered that these conditions are fulfilled in countries where the government has sufficient policy instruments at its disposal to achieve an appropriate balance between consumption and savings, and between different groups or individuals in society in the distribution of income, without using project selection and design for these purposes.

Chapter 4
Where national savings are considered to be sub-optimal, in the sense that other policy instruments do not result in a level of savings sufficient to support the level of investment deemed necessary by the government, project choice can be weighted in favour of savings and against consumption. This chapter explains the appraisal techniques needed to accomplish this.

Chapter 5
A further dimension is added if it is assumed that the government cannot achieve an appropriate distribution of income between the country's inhabitants by its fiscal and other policies. Project selection and design can be used for this purpose also and the techniques for doing this systematically are explained in this chapter.

2.3   The basic economic analysis for allocative efficiency described in chapter 3 provides important information on national resource flows and it is recommended that this kind of analysis should always be undertaken. Whether the further analysis of chapters 4 and 5 should also be prepared, either sequentially or together, will depend on the characteristics of the economy in which the project will be located. But this decision cannot be taken project-by-project: if an economy is considered to fulfill the conditions of chapters 4 or 5 then the techniques described must be applied to *all* projects.

Valuation Principles and the Numeraire

2.4   In economic appraisal all costs and benefits should be valued at their opportunity cost to the country in which the project will be located. Detailed guidance on how to do this for the different types of costs and benefits which are encountered are given in the following chapters, but the first step is to choose a unit of measurement – the numeraire.

2.5   The recommendation of this Guide is that the numeraire should be un-committed government income measured in terms of foreign exchange of constant purchasing power. This specification contains several components. The first, 'uncommitted government income', means income available to the government to use at its discretion for consumption or investment. This has a bearing on the different levels of appraisal. In an analysis conducted under the basic allocative efficiency principles of chapter 3, all forms of income and costs have the same value but the introduction of a savings premium or distri-butional weights (chapters 4 and 5) will change this. In such appraisals, the different cost and benefit flows may be scaled up or down according to the value attributed to them against the numeraire. For example, income flows which result in extra consumption by affluent individuals might be valued in chapter 5 terms at one-half of an equivalent flow as uncommitted government income.

2.6   The second component of the specification requires opportunity costs to be measured in international prices. It allows discretion on whether these are denominated in local currency units or in some specific convertible currency, for example sterling or US dollars. The final component, constant prices, is designed simply to remove the distortionary effects of price inflation. Detailed guidance on this aspect is given in chapter 3.

2.7   This valuation basis generally follows the Little-Mirrlees approach.[1] The rationale for the use of international prices is that they are a better measure of opportunity costs than domestic prices. For most developing countries, inter-national trade is of great significance, and many investment projects have a high content of imports and exports, especially those that attract donor finance. Several factors make domestic prices unsuitable as indicators of relative opportunity costs without a lot of adjustment. Import tariffs, indirect taxes, overvalued exchange rates, subsidies, overstated labour costs, monopoly prices and other forms of administrative intervention affect the market prices of very many products and services.

Time and Discounting

2.8   Even after the effects of price inflation have been eliminated it is neces-sary to allow for the fact that £1 received (or spent) in the future is valued less than £1 received now. This reflects the commonplace observation that real

---

[1] UNIDO have developed a well-known system for economic appraisal which follows the same fundamental principles as Little-Mirrlees in its approach but adopts a different numeraire. Main texts are listed in section E of the bibliography.

interest rates are generally positive, so £1 received now can be invested to yield more than £1 at the future date after allowing for inflation.[1]

2.9   In economic appraisal this principle is accommodated by discounting. A discount rate is the reciprocal of an interest rate and its application allows future costs and benefits to be expressed in terms of (lower) 'present values'. The choice of the discount rate to be used in appraisal is of some consequence because costs and benefits are not usually spread over time symmetrically: typically the main costs occur early on with the main benefits flowing several years later. The higher the discount rate the lower the present value of benefits compared to discounted costs and the more likely that the benefit-cost comparison will be unfavourable.

2.10   A fundamental principle of discounting is that the rate used should be the same for all sectors. This implies that the rates of return from the marginal projects in each sector will be equal and therefore that the return from the total investment programme is maximised. If different discount rates were used for different sectors, a higher average return could be obtained by shifting investment funds from the low rate sector to the high rate sector.

2.11   A second principle is that the discount rate is specific to the numeraire and the valuation principles used in the appraisal. But it has been noted above that valuations vary with the form of appraisal undertaken (paragraph 2.5). It follows from this that the actual discount rate used will differ according to whether the appraisal is carried out under the approaches of chapters 3, 4 or 5.

Decision Criteria

2.12   It must always be recognised that decisions on projects cannot be determined by economic appraisal alone. Accepting this, the test of acceptability in economic appraisal rests on a comparison of costs and benefits measured in terms of a consistent numeraire. For an analysis conducted in terms of basic allocative efficiency (chapter 3) it is recommended that the test of acceptability should be simply a positive net present value (NPV): the present value (PV) of benefits should be greater than the present value of costs.

2.13   This rule underlines a further standard principle for the discount rate, that it should be set at a level which allows acceptable projects to just absorb all the investible resources available to the economy within a given time period. This principle is called into question, however, when a savings premium is used, as outlined in chapter 4. Nevertheless the decision criterion that NPV should exceed zero can be maintained after making adjustments to the discount rate and other parts of the economic appraisal as described in chapters 4 and 5.

2.14   The Internal Rate of Return (IRR) is often used as an alternative to the NPV criterion. The IRR is simply the discount rate which results in an NPV of zero and its use requires comparison with some minimum rate considered to be acceptable. Theoretical objections to its use are the assumption contained in the calculation of the IRR that net flows are reinvested, as they occur, at

---

[1] Negative real interest rates can be observed, but usually in conditions of capital rationing or for relatively short periods.

exactly the IRR, and the possibility that the IRR will not be a unique number.[1] NPV is therefore a preferable criterion on theoretical grounds and it also has the practical advantage that the trade-off between economic and other aspects of a project can be more readily approached through the NPV. For these reasons this Guide recommends the use of NPV as the decision criterion in economic appraisal.

---

[1] The higher real value achieved by investing £1 over time arises from compound interest. This compounding principle applies to discount rates because they are simply the reciprocal of interest rates (see paragraphs 2.8 and 2.9) and implies investment of net returns at the IRR. If the sign of the net benefit flow changes once only (commonly from negative in the early years to positive later) there will be a unique IRR but if the sign changes more than once there may be more than one IRR.

3
Basic Economic Analysis for Allocative Efficiency

Opportunity Cost and the Numeraire

3.1   The economic appraisal of a project requires the valuation of all effects in particular terms, namely opportunity cost to the economy of the nation in which the project will be situated. On the input side, this 'opportunity cost' is the loss in the value of net output in the national economy that will arise through applying resources to a particular use (the project), which takes them away from another use. On the output side, the 'opportunity cost value' of the new production is either the value of the costs saved by not having to obtain the supply from alternative sources; or the value of the net revenue obtained by selling extra output abroad; or the value that consumers place on any increased domestic supply that is created.

3.2   In a statement of costs and benefits projected for each year from the start of expenditure, all inputs and outputs will be counted in the years in which the opportunity cost effect occurs. Comparison of the cost and benefit values allows the estimation of net benefits each year, some negative, some positive. These annual values can be discounted to allow present values and rates of return to be calculated.

3.3   Prices which reflect opportunity costs are called Accounting Prices[1] and valuation in these terms allows the economic efficiency of the project to be assessed in a consistent way. For the reasons explained in paragraphs 2.7 and 2.8 opportunity costs are measured in this Guide in terms of international prices. The unit of measurement – numeraire – should be uncommitted government income measured in terms of foreign exchange of constant purchasing power. This may be expressed either in terms of a specific convertible currency, or in units of local currency, convertible to any foreign currency at the official exchange rate. Use of this numeraire does not imply that uncommitted government income is worth more than other forms of income. As was explained in chapter 2, in the first stages of appraisal, all forms of income are regarded as having equal value, irrespective of whether they arise in the public sector or to individuals; whether they are received by high income people or by the poor; and whether they are used to increase savings or for consumption.

3.4   This substantial chapter discusses how project effects (in both the 'with' and 'without' cases) may be valued in opportunity cost terms, to indicate the economic efficiency of allocating resources to a project. It begins with a discussion of how inflation effects should be handled. The basis for valuing traded and non-traded goods is then established. Conversion factors to change market prices to accounting prices are next outlined in general terms and in a few specific cases, after which the valuation of domestic factors is

---

[1] Technical terms used in Economic Analysis are defined in the Glossary, between pages 229 and 233.

discussed in some detail. The treatment of unquantifiables, externalities and environmental effects is then taken up. The final section considers estimation and use of the Accounting Rate of Interest, the discount rate appropriate for cost-benefit and cost-effectiveness calculations.

Inflation and the Price Base for Valuing Costs and Benefits

3.5   Projecting input and output values in the year in which the opportunity cost is expected to occur runs into the problem of inflation, the change in unit prices that occurs with time. This problem is usually overcome by expressing all valuations in units of constant real value; that is, the relative values of items at a particular time, the Base Period for valuation. The discount rate will then be expressed in constant price terms also. In principle, economic analysis should take account of changes in the relative values of inputs and outputs over time. If there were no price changes (no inflation), or if all prices changed at the same rate (inflation with no relative price changes), there would be few problems in valuing project items from the economic viewpoint. Both costs and benefits would be subject to equivalent changes, everything could be valued in terms of the prices applying on a particular date, and the decision criteria would not be affected. It is only because particular prices change over time at different rates that there is a risk that inflation will be associated with changes in the relationship between the values of some cost and benefit items. While all prices may change with inflation, not all may change at the same rate.

3.6   Frequently this problem has no practical significance. In the uncertain area of forecasting, there may be no reason to suppose that changes in the prices of the main inputs and outputs will be significantly different from changes in the general price level. In these circumstances it is possible to conduct economic analysis as if there were no inflation, using Base Period values throughout.

3.7   Whether the prices of outputs and the main inputs are expected to vary in real terms over the life of the project should be apparent from the special studies of demand and input supply that are major features of sound project preparation. These projections will be required for use in making forecast accounts in revenue projects, but they are essential also for economic analysis. This is because the pattern of the future prices of output and the main input(s) is often of the greatest significance in relation to decisions about the economic worth of proposed projects. Where one or two outputs and inputs dominate, the assessment of economic viability is often more sensitive to forecasts about the future course of prices than to any other single item.

3.8   If it is thought that some prices will change at a rate different from the general inflation rate, analysis in real terms should take account of long-term changes in relative values. It will be necessary to have some idea of what is meant by 'the general price level' during the life of the project, and to forecast divergencies from this (positive or negative) for the prices of exceptional item. In this context only long-term effects should be allowed for, not short-term variations that may last only a few months, or for one season. Long-term changes to be recognised might include the development of a synthetic substitute which would undermine the market for a commodity, requiring price

19

forecasts to show a decline; or a general tendency for production to increase more rapidly than demand in the long term (like oil output in the mid 1980s), so that prices of that commodity would rise more slowly than average for some time. Other factors might be the development of new, cheaper forms of energy and transport; the exhaustion of particular sources of input supply; and changes in the availability of certain types of labour.

3.9   The most relevant indicators of changes in price level of traded goods will be the indexes of international trade prices for some commodities that are published by international agencies.[1] For non-traded items, historic changes in different price indexes of the country, and known planned developments, can be used to estimate whether any significant relative price changes can be expected. In practice price forecasting is only an approximate business, so precise projections of the general price level and all deviations from it are not essential.

3.10   In some cases it may be easier to conduct the economic appraisal in current prices which means that the discount rate must be expressed in current prices also. In principle this adjustment is simple[2] and the comments above (paragraph 3.8) about price relativities still apply, but most price forecasts for international trade are expressed in constant terms.

Valuing Traded Goods and Services

3.11   Goods and Services produced or consumed in projects are of two basically different types from the viewpoint of valuation.

(1)   *Traded* and *Tradeable* items are those which are, or could be, imported or exported. International trade in these items takes place, and import/export valuations can be obtained.

(2)   *Non-Traded* and *Non-Tradeable* items are those which either are not, or could not be, imported or exported. If they are inputs, the source of their supply will be in the country itself. If they are outputs, the products will be used or enjoyed only within the country, and only domestic users can indicate their value.

The approach to valuation from the economic viewpoint is quite different for the two categories.

The general approach to valuing traded goods
3.12   Traded goods are valued on the basis of their marginal international (border) prices, cif for imports and fob for exports. To arrive at the project value, the border prices are adjusted for the resource costs of internal transport and distribution costs that are saved or incurred.

3.13   Traded Goods feature in many of the illustrative cases included in Part II of this Guide – the two Detailed Cases (DC); the fifteen shorter Case Studies (CS); and the four Methodology Illustrations (MI). Particular aspects of

---

[1] IBRD, FAO, ITC, UNIDO, etc.
[2] For example, if the constant price discount rate is 10% and inflation is forecast at 8%, the derivation of the current price discount rate is:

$$\frac{110}{100} \times \frac{108}{100} = 1.188 \text{ (ie 18.8\%)}$$

the valuation of Traded Goods in the project illustrations are mentioned in Box 3.1.

3.14   The usual convention is to assume that the project will not by itself change the international price, so that the marginal price equals the average price. This must be assessed realistically. The marginal price could differ from the average. As a major producer or consumer, a project might change the terms of trade and international market conditions for a good, though it would be exceptional for an individual project to have this effect. Alternatively, international trade in this good may be subject to quota arrangements, and not all the project's output will fall within the quota.

3.15   The United Nations Revised System of National Accounts (which many countries follow) provides explicitly for recording imports and exports at their border prices. The commodity flow statistics which form an important part of this system of national accounts may therefore provide a useful guide in arriving at 'border prices' in countries where this system has been adopted.

Some valuation complications
3.16   The pricing of traded goods may not always be straightforward. Goods are seldom homogeneous. It is common to find that the home-produced commodity is of a significantly different kind or quality from the imported one. Where the output of a project is of non-standard type, the cif price of the imported good with that name could be an inappropriate basis for valuing domestic production. The analyst must decide whether to make an adjustment to the border price, to allow for quality differences, or to treat the output as non-tradeable if the difference from a traded item is great. However, if it is a minor item, or if it could in some circumstances be substituted for imports, a reasonable approximation is given by taking the cif price of the imported good and multiplying that by the ratio of the domestic market price of the home variety to the domestic price of the imported variety.

3.17   Care will be needed in valuing traded final consumer goods where they are sold at a discount or a premium because of quality differences, strong consumer preference, or for other reasons. The crucial question here is how much foreign exchange is saved or earned per unit of product. When a domestic product is selling at a discount, its accounting price is less than the foreign exchange value of the imported variety: where an imported product is selling at a discount, the accounting price of the domestic product will be greater.

3.18   It may not always be possible to find a unique international price for a particular product. There is always difficulty in determining the marginal price of some goods, especially manufactured goods that are supplied only against quotations. Special circumstances may influence a particular price, like a foreign government subsidy scheme, or foreign firms making sales at abnormally low prices. In these cases, specific price quotations may have to be obtained before a project or design alternatives can be appraised with precision, although estimates may be adequate for preliminary appraisals.

3.19   Furthermore, a particular good may in the past have been imported from different sources at different prices. Which will be the supply relevant to the project under review? In all these circumstances, making the price estimates must be left to the experience and judgement of the appraiser. He will

Box 3.1   Border Price Parity Values for Traded Goods

Traded goods are major items in most projects, especially donor-assisted investments. Their proper valuation is often the major factor in economic analysis. Capital goods, recurrent inputs and project outputs may all be traded.

Outputs, the most important group, are very likely to be increased exports or import substitutes. Accurate pricing can be especially important in agriculture. Methodology Illustration 1 shows in detail how border price parity values at the project level were calculated for two import substitute crops and one export, starting with the cif and fob values. Very similar methods were used to calculate the value of the traded farm outputs in The Basin Irrigation Scheme, DC 2. In the Rock Phosphate Project, DC 1, the single product is a direct import substitute, though of a different quality. Its valuation is examined in detail, because it is so important for appraisal. The valuation of imported capital inputs is also demonstrated in full in the two Detailed Case Studies.

CS 1, on fertiliser production, refers to the valuation of three important traded recurrent items used – the output, an import substitute; gas, the main cost, another import substitute replacing oil; and coal, an export to be diverted to this domestic use. In that project, the main traded items could be easily identified, but some Case Studies mention that the specification of traded goods was not known, so no revaluation could be made apart from the removal from market price of known import taxes.

A particular traded good valuation problem is illustrated in the Special Steels Project, CS 2, which involved the production of a new intermediate product (the special steels) of a kind not previously imported by the country. Valuation was approached there by starting right back at the ex-works price of likely alternatively foreign suppliers, adding shipping costs (firm quotes for both could be obtained), and adjusting for expected discounts, to get an estimate of the cif price. Such innovative approaches must be adopted for the valuation of tradeable products not previously available in the country, though, because of quality differences, it may be difficult to know if the derived values are 'correct'.

have to try to decide what will actually happen at the time, if the project goes ahead. When the output is a traded good, the product will be valued at its world price – that price which, in the best judgement of the appraiser, will actually have to be paid by or to the country. Where the world price will be affected by the output produced or used by a single project (for example, if the country is a major exporter of some agricultural commodity) the fall in the value of the output of existing domestic producers should be regarded as part of the cost of the project.[1] The time that the appraiser should devote to these calculations will depend on the sensitivity of the project to variations in these variables, as explained in paragraphs 6.14 to 6.17.

---

[1] This would be a strong external effect – see paragraph 3.76 below.

3.20   It does not matter which currency is used in the analysis. Although border prices are the basis of valuation, these can be expressed in the domestic currency (the usual practice), or in sterling, or in any other convenient unit. The currency conversions that always have to be made are usually carried out at the official exchange rate. However, in some cases it can be appropriate to use a parallel exchange rate, if one openly exists and it will apply to trade in the item in question. Where more than one exchange rate applies, it can be most convenient to conduct the analysis in sterling or another international currency. The only rule is to be consistent in the use of the currency chosen for the analysis, and in the rates used for converting values originally expressed in other currencies.

Goods that are tradeable but not traded

3.21   Tradeable goods and services include both goods which are actually imported or exported (or very close substitutes for such goods) and domestically produced goods which would be imported or exported if the country were following policies which took fully into account the possibilities of international trade (ie the country's long-term comparative advantage). Which goods featured in a project are and will be Traded (ie imported or exported) will usually be easy to see or predict. However, occasionally items crop up that are Tradeable but not Traded.

3.22   It is not unusual in some countries for imports of some goods to be banned, as a means of protecting domestic production. In these circumstances the real world situation is that the goods are not traded. This poses an appraisal problem. If one of the inputs of a prospective project is a good falling in this category, and it is produced domestically only at a very high marginal cost, it can be argued that the project should not be allowed to fail on this account. The opportunity to import should be considered, with the input valued as a traded good. To rely on the costly local source would push the pattern of investment still further from that which would be consistent with long-term comparative advantage. However, if it is known that imports will not be permitted, and that the good will in fact be supplied from local sources for a considerable time (albeit at a real resource cost higher than the cost of equivalent imports) it should be treated as non-traded. The production conditions effectively make it so. Opportunity cost principles require, however, that outputs which are tradeable but not traded should be valued at the price of the imported alternative.

3.23   The judgement as to whether goods falling within this category should be treated as traded or non-traded can be of critical importance in some manufacturing projects. Judgement on this question will need to take a view of the length of time the prohibition is likely to last in relation to the lifetime of the project. It might be sensible to delay the project until the prohibition is removed.

Valuing non-traded Goods and Services

3.24   Non-traded goods and services can, like traded goods, be both inputs and outputs. They include things that cannot be imported, like water and other utilities, construction, internal transport and land. Certain other items, like bricks and power, could in principle be traded, but may best be consi-

23

dered as non-traded goods, because their transport costs may be such that they seldom enter into international trade. A list of Non-Traded Goods and Services that commonly feature in projects is given in Table 3.1. Asterisks mark those for which centrally-prepared estimates of Conversion Factors[1] would be especially valuable to project analysts.

Table 3.1

COMMON NON-TRADED GOODS AND SERVICES

*Construction – if possible, divided between; modern buildings
                                     'typical' buildings
                                     traditional buildings
                                     roads of different grades

*Rail transport of goods
*Road transport of goods – bulk quantities
                                   – small loads

*Port operation

*Retail merchandising
*Wholesale merchandising
Import and Export Administration
Commodity storage
Stockholding

*Electricity generation and supply
*Water supply – if possible divided between; main urban supply
                                           rural water

Treatment of solid and liquid waste

Posts
Telephones
Telex and telegraph services

*Production of bulky and low quality subsistence foods and vegetables
Production of low quality slaughter livestock
Milk sold unprocessed
Draught animals

*Skilled workers
*Unskilled workers in different occupation types, and different regions
Land

---

* Conversion Factors for these common Non-Traded items should preferably be estimated by a central national agency (eg Central Planning Office) for use in all projects. They would not then be estimated by the analysts of specific projects.

The general approach for valuing non-traded inputs

`3.25 Since traded goods are valued at world prices, non-traded goods and services must be valued in units of similar value, to ensure that everything is valued in terms of the same numeraire throughout. Ideally, the accounting price of a non-traded good which is used as an input in a project (either an investment item or a current input) should be calculated on the basis that more of it will be produced to meet the needs of the project. For valuation, we need to know the composition of the marginal production costs. This means finding out the direct and indirect inputs which go to make up the good, and

---

[1] See paragraph 3.35.

separating them into four main categories: taxes, labour, traded goods and non-traded goods. Taxes would be ignored, as transfer payments that are not resource costs. Labour is valued according to the procedures set out in paragraphs 3.49 to 3.65. Traded goods are valued on the basis of border prices, as explained in paragraphs 3.12 to 3.20. Non-traded inputs should (to the extent possible) be further separated into the four components of taxes, labour, traded and non-traded goods, and the last group broken down again, until virtually everything has been accounted for in terms of taxes, labour and traded items.

3.26   This time-consuming process calls for a lot of data. Frequently economists will have to settle for more approximate methods in carrying out appraisals, but wherever possible this detailed approach should be followed for major non-traded inputs.

3.27   Illustrative materials in this Guide make several references to the valuation of Non-Traded Goods in practice. Box 3.2 draws attention to some of the main instances and paragraph 3.39 gives an example.

Box 3.2   Valuing Non-Traded Goods in Practice

Non-traded items are recurrent inputs in every project. Sometimes project outputs are non-traded, and some capital items may be. The Basin Irrigation Scheme, (DC 2) included several non-traded crops which, being sold in free markets, were revalued simply by applying the Standard Conversion Factor (see paragraph 3.41). Both Detailed Case Studies show how detailed cost composition data was used for revaluing several items. The Village Electrification Project, CS 9, refers to a major non-traded capital item, concrete poles for electricity distribution. Absence of cost data again prevented a full revaluation, though it was noted that the shadow price used was consequently on the high side.

Electricity was a non-traded input whose valuation frequently caused difficulty, because the sale price is less than the marginal production cost. Methodology Illustration 2 gives a very full account of how the Long Run Marginal Cost of electricity was calculated in one case. Upwards revaluation of power inputs are features of the Special Steels Project, (CS 2) and CS 9, Village Electrification. Where electricity was the project output, (CS 7 and 8), its valuation involved the estimation of consumer surplus, as described in Box 3.3.

Valuing non-traded outputs

3.28   When the non-traded good is the output of a project, there can be problems of valuation. Sectors with non-traded output (social services, utilities, subsistence agriculture) are significant, particularly in relation to the distribution of the fruits of economic development. Typically half of GNP is not traded, but these areas can be handled with skill and ingenuity. The techniques of economic appraisal can be applied as a universal tool.

3.29   In principle non-tradeable outputs can be placed on the same footing as tradeable outputs which are valued at border prices. Non-traded outputs are valued on the basis of their marginal social benefit to consumers. If the item is sold in a free market, actual prices will reflect marginal willingness to pay by those buying. However, to get these consumer values into units of value equivalent to foreign exchange, a conversion factor needs to be applied to these consumer prices that reflects the general divergence between border prices and domestic prices that is caused by the factors listed at the end of paragraph 2.7. This is the Standard Conversion Factor that is discussed in paragraphs 3.41 to 3.45. (Paragraph 3.33 deals with the valuation of non-tradeable outputs that are not sold in free markets.)

Consumer surplus

3.30   Consumer surplus is the difference between what consumers are prepared to pay for a good or service and what they actually pay. It applies to both tradeables and non-tradeables, but is particularly relevant to the latter category because the incidence of subsidy or free provision is usually higher. Consumer surplus estimates – willingness to pay – may be the only means of valuing output.

3.31   In some cases, prices can be expected to change as a result of the project, especially where new or more efficient production methods will be used. The valuation in these cases can be adjusted upwards from the lower 'with-project' price, to allow for consumer surplus. However, if projects have much of their benefits as consumer surplus (representing the difference between actual prices and estimated consumer valuations), they should be treated with caution. If sales are subsidised, or the output is free, consumer surplus valuation can all too easily result in investment in some sectors beyond the level that can be maintained from the recurrent budget, creating big problems that lead to breakdowns in projects for the supply of services.

3.32   Examples of the estimation of consumer surplus in case studies in this Guide are outlined in Box 3.3.

3.33   Where the non-tradeable output is either not sold or is charged for only at a very low nominal price, and where willingness to pay is severely limited by income constraints (examples may be the output of the health and education sectors), the problems of valuing it in marginal social benefit terms are very great. Particular procedures to be adopted in these cases to find the least-cost means of production are suggested in paragraphs 3.123 to 3.130. Measures of the value of non-priced benefits (ie consumer surplus estimates) are difficult to obtain, and may be open to question. The value of cost-benefit techniques is limited in the appraisal of projects of this kind.

3.34   Roads are a special case within the category of output that is not sold and is non-tradeable. The economic appraisal of road projects usually depends on the assessment and valuation of cost savings or output increases in the sectors served. The techniques developed for appraising road investments are susceptible to the economic appraisal approach of this Guide, since all of these savings or output increases can be valued as traded or non-traded goods and services. Box 3.4 draws attention to methods for the valuation of benefits in the road projects that are included in this Guide as case studies.

Box 3.3   Valuation involving Consumer Surplus

Consumer Surplus may be incorporated in the valuation of outputs (usually non-traded) where the price charged is less than the amount that many users are willing to pay. Electricity is a common example, and the point is illustrated in CS 7, CS 8 and CS 9, all of which involve the sale of power. Electricity is both a consumer good and an input into productive and service activities. In all three of these Case Studies, willingness-to-pay estimates were based on the cost of alternatives sources of light or energy that were already in use, and which electricity would displace.

The Coastal Town Water Project, CS 10, looks at the value of water, another utility where charges are often not only less than cost but also less than willingness-to-pay by many users. The approach followed in that analysis was to estimate a value that would cover costs, and then to estimate the cost of water used at this price as a proportion of a typical wage. The basis of this approach is that clean water, which is seldom purchased in specific quantities, is demanded by users so long as the charge is no more than a certain proportion of wage income. The World Bank has suggested that this fraction is about 5%. Consumer Surplus on all water used could then be estimated as the difference between whatever is paid for water and 5% of income.

Box 3.4   The Benefits of Road Projects

The estimation of benefits in road projects is always complex and uncertain. The risk is always present that they may be overestimated.

Three Case Studies in this Guide involve road projects, CS 3, CS 5 and CS 6. The first two involve new or improved roads in rural areas. Estimating the extent and value of benefits stemming from such cases is notoriously difficult; some would say well-nigh impossible, especially with the limited resources available to analyse such relatively low cost developments. The approach adopted in these cases started from the opposite direction. Costs were estimated, and then an estimate was made of what increase in farm output would be required to justify the investment. The likelihood of this increase in production was then assessed.

CS 6 is a project for major improvements to an existing trunk road. Data availability and estimation methods allowed only the two main cost reduction benefits to be estimated, vehicle operating costs and maintenance costs, but these estimates were reasonably reliable. Appraisal was made in the knowledge that other benefits had not been valued, but the project (and each of its six sub-components) looked justifiable on the basis of these two main items alone, so there was no need in this case to estimate these other benefits.

Accounting Prices and Conversion Factors for Goods and Services

The calculation of Accounting Prices and conversion factors

3.35   In many cases it makes sound sense for accounting prices and conversion factors for the most important traded and non-traded goods to be prepared centrally for use in all project appraisals, especially the Standard Conversion Factor (SCF), Shadow Wages, Sectoral Conversion Factors, and CFs for infrastructure, construction and utilities. Several countries and donors have prepared sets of the main conversion factors, and accounting prices for individual commodities.[1]

3.36   The method of successive rounds of cost disaggregation described in paragraph 3.25 can be used to calculate the value in accounting prices of any cost or ouput item. However, the same information and time will allow the calculation of a Conversion Factor (CF) for that same item. The conversion factor is the ratio (usually expressed in decimal terms) between the market price and the accounting price of the good or service concerned. If the market price is higher, the CF will be less than one. The CF for an item is a coefficient by which market price values of that item are multiplied to transform them into accounting price values.

3.37   Box 3.5 discusses further the calculation of CFs, and the illustrations of CF derivation that are shown in Part II of this Guide.

Box 3.5 ˙ Conversion Factors for Specific Goods and Services

The Rock Phosphate Project, DC 1, shows how specific CFs were calculated within a particular project. In DC 2, the Basin Irrigation Scheme, and in those case studies that involved Shadow Pricing, individual CFs were not calculated, nor was a statement of economic costs and benefits prepared at constant market prices. Typically, for the analysis of single projects of the kind that a bilateral donor would undertake, the concern is to move directly to the preparation of a full benefit-cost statement at accounting prices, which can be discounted. However, all major projects should be analysed by the central planning agency in the national government. CFs for particular items are of great value to them, for careful use across a range of projects. That agency should not only estimate and make available to other analysts value of the CFs for main items (like those mentioned in paragraph 3.35 and those asterisked in Table 3.1), but should collect others when data on them is available from individual project analyses. Comparisons of CFs for similar items between different projects can serve as a check on the validity of appraisals, and they can be used as appropriate in the appraisals of other projects.

---

[1] The bibliography on pages 234–236 lists some published sets of national Shadow Prices in Section D.

3.38 Differences between market prices and accounting prices principally occur as a result of five sets of factors: (i) import taxes, quotas and import licensing, usually combined with overvalued currencies, which push the domestic prices of imported items above the levels of their foreign exchange costs; (ii) monopoly power, indirect taxes and subsidies, elements in price that do not represent resource costs; (iii) rapid inflation, which distorts price relativities; (iv) externalities, and (v) the various imperfections in capital and labour markets which prevent interest rates and wages from reflecting the opportunity cost of these resources.

3.39 The procedure for cost disaggregation is illustrated in Table 3.2. This shows how the long-run marginal production cost for a non-traded input item costing Ms[1] 1,000 per ton is broken down into its components, in constant market price values:

Foreign Exchange	505
Taxes	121
Labour	266
Others	108
Total (Market Ms)	1,000

Lack of data (we may assume) prevents the last item being divided further. The amounts for each basic component can now be revalued into allocative efficiency shadow prices. The first element, being in border prices, requires no revaluation. The taxes element would be regarded as a Transfer Payment that does not represent a resource cost, and so is ignored. Labour would be revalued downwards, along the lines of paragraphs 3.50 to 3.62, to give a value of, say, Ms 186. The final cost category has an unknown composition. Using the Standard Conversion Factor that is discussed in paragraphs 3.41 to 3.45, it may be revalued at Ms 92. Accordingly, at accounting prices, the costs would be estimated as:

Foreign Exchange	505
Taxes	0
Labour	186
Others	92
Total (Accounting Ms)	783

The Accounting Price for this input item is thus estimated as Ms 783. The CF is 783/1,000 = 0.78. This factor could be used at any point in project analysis to transform constant market values of this particular item to their value at accounting prices.

---

[1] Ms = Moneys, the domestic currency unit used throughout this Guide.

TABLE 3.2
A HYPOTHETICAL MODEL OF COST DISAGGREGATION
(Moneys per ton of output)

	First Round Disaggregation		Second Round Disaggregation		Third Round Disaggregation		Total Cost Disaggregation			
	Item	Value	Item	Value	Item	Value	F E	Tax	Lab	Other
CAPITAL COSTS	Machinery	200	Foreign Exchange	140			148	23	24	5
			Taxes	20						
			Labour	20						
			Transport	20	Foreign Exchange	8				
					Taxes	3				
					Labour	4				
					Other Inputs	5				
	Buildings	100	Foreign Exchange	35			40	18	28	14
			Taxes	15						
			Labour	20						
			Other Inputs	30	Foreign Exchange	5				
					Taxes	3				
					Labour	8				
					Other Inputs	14				
RECURRENT INPUTS	Raw Materials	350	Foreign Exchange	175			189	42	80	39
			Taxes	35						
			Labour	70						
			Other Inputs	70	Foreign Exchange	14				
					Taxes	7				
					Labour	10				
					Other Inputs	39				
	Energy	150	Foreign Exchange	80			88	23	22	17
			Taxes	20						
			Labour	15						
			Other Inputs	35	Foreign Exchange	8				
					Taxes	3				
					Labour	7				
					Other Inputs	17				
	Labour	80							80	
	Overheads	60	Foreign Exchange	10			17	7	17	19
			Taxes	5						
			Labour	10						
			Other Inputs	35	Foreign Exchange	7				
					Taxes	2				
					Labour	7				
					Other Inputs	19				
	Other Inputs	60	Foreign Exchange	15			23	8	15	14
			Taxes	6						
			Labour	9						
			Other Inputs	30	Foreign Exchange	8				
					Taxes	2				
					Labour	6				
					Other Inputs	14				
TOTALS		1,000		1,000		1,000	505	121	266	108

In the Second Round Disaggregation, each item is divided between the four main categories.
In the Third Round Disaggregation, only the last item in each group is further disaggregated.

Sectoral conversion factors

3.40   While it is most desirable to obtain and use individual CFs for each item in a project, this is seldom possible because of data and time limitations. Aggregate CFs for sectoral groups of similar commodities may be derived, from crude estimates of the content of border prices and taxes, with labour and other inputs revalued by only the general adjustment of the SCF, which is explained in the next section. If good input–output data exist for the economy, this national accounts table will often be a useful source of input proportions for estimation by a central agency of conversion factors for sectors and aggregated types of activity. When available, the sectoral CFs would be used in appraisal when the calculation of an individual CF was impossible or when it was not justified, because the item values were small. An analagous Consumption Conversion Factor can also be derived for use whenever general consumption has to be revalued in numeraire units.

The standard conversion factor

3.41   Frequently in project analysis no information on cost composition is available, and no relevant sectoral CF exists. In such cases, a general adjustment must be made, by using a Standard Conversion Factor (SCF) for inputs and all non-traded outputs. This allows for the general distortion between international and domestic prices that is caused by import duties, taxes and tariffs, subsidies and other price-distortions to trade. The value of this most general conversion factor is estimated from a representative selection of traded goods for the whole economy. Even though this approach is crude, it may well be adequate where the SCF is applied to minor inputs only, like the residual 'other' category in the paragraph 3.39 illustration, where a value of 0.85 was used.

3.42   A crude estimate of the historic value of the SCF can be made by calculating the ratio between the total cif value of all imports and their value inclusive of all tariffs and other taxes on imports. The basic expression is:

$$SCF = \frac{\text{Border Price Value of all Imports, without Taxes*}}{\text{Value of all Imports } plus \text{ all Tariffs and Taxes on Imports } minus \text{ subsidies.}}$$

  * (ie cif cost only)

Information for this question is usually obtainable from published statistical sources, the Central Bank and the Ministry of Finance. If import quotas and other forms of foreign exchange rationing are also used, the lower part of the fraction will understate the opportunity cost value of foreign goods, so the SCF value obtained will be an over-estimate that could be rounded down.

3.43   The formula for estimating the SCF quoted above is the correct one to use if it is felt that the main effect of future changes in the availability of foreign exchange will fall on the level of imports. The equation looks only at the relationship between the border price and the domestic price values of imports. However, it may be felt that the volume of exports will also vary; more foreign exchange available may allow less exports, and more consumption at home, as well as import changes. In these situations, a different, more extended formula may be used, which incorporates exports and export taxes.

This formula is:

$$SCF = \frac{\begin{array}{c}\text{Border Price Value of all Imports} \\ plus \\ \text{Border Price Value of all Exports}\end{array}}{\begin{array}{c}\text{Value of all Imports plus all Taxes on Imports} \\ plus \\ \text{Value of all Exports minus all Taxes on Exports}\end{array}}$$

Where some imports or exports are subsidised (eg food imports or exports of 'strategic' manufacturers) the lower part of this fraction will need to allow for this also, with a reverse sign (negative for imports and positive for exports).

3.44 The first of these equations will be the most relevant in poor, import-dependent countries. The formulae will allow SCF values in past years to be estimated. They may provide the main basis for deriving forecast SCF values for the project years, but historic values should not always be used without question or modification. Examples are cited in Box 3.6 of the calculation and use of the SCF in case study illustrations presented in this Guide.

Box 3.6   Use of the Standard Conversion Factor

Use of the SCF should be considered whenever any efficiency economic analysis is carried out. Many of the Case Studies refer to SCFs that were used. Values mentioned ranged from 0.8 to 0.9. Methodology Illustration 3 shows how the two formulae were used to estimate the SCF for one country.

One Case Study, the Special Steels Project (CS 2), said that no SCF was used. This was because there was no apparent shortage of foreign exchange. The country had an open policy on exchange rates. These are not by themselves valid reasons for not applying the SCF. Its use is required because taxes on imports affect their prices in a way that does not apply to non-traded goods. Efficiency values of the two are not comparable unless this adjustment is made. Quite possibly taxes on trade were not important in that country, (the project document did not say), but this situation will be very uncommon.

For some items, application of the SCF is the only shadow pricing adjustment made. This is especially true of non-traded farm produce sold in a free market, as occurs in the Basin Irrigation Scheme (DC 2) for several products. However, the SCF is mainly used on the cost side. Failure to use this adjustment will generally overstate the level of costs, thereby underestimating economic net benefits.

3.45 Sometimes in project analysis, the SCF has been mistaken for a measure of the scarcity premium to be placed on foreign exchange. Consequently, if there was apparently no shortage of foreign exchange, the SCF was not used to adjust domestic prices to numeraire units. This is incorrect. The SCF is a correction for the difference in the basis of relative values between international prices and domestic prices that import duties etc. impose. So that internal and international prices can be brought together consistently into numeraire units, the SCF must be applied to all domestic resource costs whenever import duties and other government interventions affecting the prices of imports and exports occur, especially when they are collectively more than a few per cent of the total value of imports. As was mentioned in paragraph 3.42, where a scarcity of foreign exchange is also important, the simple tax-adjustment formulae may understate the general value difference between domestic and international prices.

Some complications

3.46   In estimating conversion factors, particular care must be taken where import quota, rationing and price control arrangements are being operated, since domestic prices in these instances may not be a true reflection of scarcity values. In these situations, it is necessary to try to estimate what in the absence of rationing, etc., the domestic prices of these items would be. Such estimates may be little more than informed guesses in the absence of data such as price elasticities of demand but, as a minimum, the direction and scale of necessary adjustments can be indicated.

3.47   In many cases, there is no information on the quantities of particular inputs or outputs forecast for a project. All that is known is their annual value. Often only general adjustments can be made for specific taxes, but it will, in principle, always be better to adjust by a conversion factor, whichever seems appropriate.

3.48   Wherever the outcome of the project appraisal is sensitive to the value attached to a non-traded input, it will be necessary to avoid the use of the Standard Conversion Factor, or of broad Sectoral Conversion Factors, in favour of a more complete breakdown of the cost of the non-traded inputs into their different components, as illustrated in paragraph 3.39. The extra time and effort required will generally be justified.

The Valuation of Labour

Unskilled workers

3.49   Gains to labour are frequently stressed as part of the justification for projects. Because wages are sometimes higher than alternative incomes, some project benefits arise on the cost side of the project. However, if the concern of analysis is 'allocative efficiency' only, it implies that the authorities feel able to use general economic policy to distribute project benefits according to the Government's goals, and project analysts need not be concerned with who gets the benefits. In these cases, all inputs should be charged to the project at their opportunity cost, (ie marginal productivity in their alternative use), expressed in world prices or their equivalent. This applies to the economic services of all income-recipients such as unskilled and skilled labour, peasant owner-operators and project sponsors. The cost analysis for unskilled labour, a major non-traded factor of production, is explained in the paragraphs which follow.

3.50   With full employment, it would be normal to charge a project the full market cost of the labour it employs; the market wage rate could be assumed to provide a reasonably satisfactory measure of the value of the marginal productivity of labour in its alternative use (after adjusting to numeraire units by use of a conversion factor). In many developing countries there is good reason to believe that not all market wages reflect opportunity cost. There is often considerable unemployment and under-employment. The wages prevailing in the 'organised sector' of the economy are determined to a considerable degree by institutional factors which make them artificially high. Much employment on projects is in this organised sector, even though the sector often accounts for only a small proportion of the total working population.

3.51 Because of this factor, the Shadow Wage Rate (SWR) for unskilled labour – the opportunity cost of employing some types of additional labour in terms of output foregone elsewhere in the economy – is often less than the market wage at which it is employed. However, outside the organised sector, wages are more closely influenced by local market forces than by institutional factors. In small farming and in the informal urban areas, wages may be taken to be an acceptably close reflection of opportunity cost at market prices. The valuation of unskilled labour costs in these less 'organised' and more 'informal' enterprises in the economy introduces no new principles. The value of payments to them needs only to be adjusted by the SCF.

3.52 The key issue in valuing labour of all kinds is the identification and valuation of opportunity cost – the marginal productivity of workers in the sector from which the labour is ultimately drawn. There may be no single SWR for the economy, unless the country is very small. Shadow Wage Rates can vary by economic sector, location, skill and even by season. For simplicity, the SWRs (like most accounting prices) are usually assumed to remain constant over the life of the project. However, if there is good reason to believe that a SWR will change significantly, then the forecast of its value should take this into account.

3.53 It is important that the appropriate SWR is used in appraisal at the earliest stages of project identification and selection, for it is at this stage that it is most likely to be relevant in determining the choice and design of investments to be undertaken.

3.54 To determine the opportunity cost of unskilled labour employed on a project, we must have some idea of the sources from which this labour is drawn. Traditional discussion of the SWR refered to the establishment of a job in modern industry, for which the labour was supplied from 'traditional' agriculture, the ultimate labour-losing sector. The opportunity cost of employing a man or woman in a modern industrial enterprise is related to the marginal productivity of labour in traditional agriculture. This approach has considerable validity, but it is worth spelling out the assumed labour-moving process. In practice, projects outside agriculture may draw their labour in the first instance from an urban occupation (sometimes of an informal type, eg casual worker, street hawker). But there are likely to be repercussion effects, with the occupation relinquished taken up by a member of the urban unemployed, and that group maintained, in turn, by a new arrival from the rural areas. Opportunity cost is thus likely to relate to agriculture in an adjacent area, even though the employees in the project whose wages are being revalued did not themselves come directly from the rural hinterland.

3.55 The marginal productivity of labour in its best alternative use would be zero if the labour ultimately affected would otherwise be totally unemployed, or if the output of the rural area from which labour was drawn would not be diminished by the withdrawal. This is possible where there is severe population pressure on land, but since it may require remaining rural residents to

34

work a little harder it is for consideration whether any value should be placed on the leisure that is lost. In the development circumstances generally postulated – low levels of economic activity generally in the group from which the labour is ultimately drawn – it does not seem unreasonable to value the lost leisure at zero, and that is the position recommended in this Guide for normal use.

3.56 Where these conditions do not hold, and employment on the project does reduce output elsewhere, the marginal productivity of labour could be lower than the average productivity of the sector as a whole. It will, of course, normally be necessary to estimate the marginal productivity of labour over the whole year. Estimates of marginal productivities should not be based on labour activities in either the slack or the busy season alone.

3.57 Some brief comments on agricultural labour will illustrate the major issues in determining marginal productivity in the various sectors. Examination of agricultural labour markets may give a good estimate of the marginal productivity of workers. The wage should approximate this marginal productivity if agricultural labour markets are reasonably efficient. If the markets are working properly, daily wages should vary between seasons. Indeed, seasonal variation may be looked for as a sign of active labour markets. At peak periods – planting and harvesting especially – labour will be in demand and wages high, but in slack periods they will be much lower and some people may not obtain work. The opportunity cost of a worker over a whole year will be reflected by the product of the average number of days worked during the year and the average payment for a day's work. The calculated marginal productivity of employed labour would also apply to labour working on family farms, provided such farms are active in the local labour market.

3.58 However, there may be no local labour market for all or part of the year (eg the agricultural slack season), and wages may be levelled up by leisure preference, bolstered by local customs relating to the types of work which different people will undertake, and family pooling of income. Furthermore, differences between men and women may exist both in relation to market wages paid and opportunity costs. Because of the many possible complications, local knowledge of the labour-losing area will be required to determine the marginal productivity of labour. However, a large effort to clarify this will be justified only where unskilled labour is a major project input, and where the results of economic analysis are sensitive to the SWR.

3.59 Wage-based estimates will indicate the value of the marginal product at domestic prices. A CF must be applied to convert these values to numeraire units. If the ultimate or direct source of labour for a project is the agricultural sector, a general conversion factor for agricultural output may be applied, to adjust to world prices the value of the agricultural output lost. This factor may be rather high, and can exceed 1.0, since the agricultural sector is usually less protected than the industrial sector, and is often subjected to export taxes. If farming in the labour-losing areas is dominated by one or a few main crops, it could be appropriate to adjust the value of the marginal output by the conversion factors for those specific products, if they have been estimated. As a last resort, if specific or sectoral CFs cannot be applied, the SCF should be used. Some conversion must always be made, to measure the marginal output of farm labour in accounting prices.

3.60   One further aspect of opportunity cost in relation to unskilled labour may need to be taken into account. This is the existence of differences in the nature of the employment created by the project and conditions in the sector from which labour is ultimately drawn. Although output foregone may be low or even zero, it may be the case that nutritional standards are so low in the rural sector that a necessary cost of the new employment is better nutrition – without this the workers could not do the job.[1]

3.61   There may be other 'consumption' costs imposed on the economy by the employment creation – extra transport facilities, new housing, and urban overheads generally. In this sense the rest of the economy has to forgo some output in order to make the new employment possible, and this is a material opportunity cost. Such costs may be met by the employer in non-wage labour expenses, or the workers themselves may have to bear all these necessary expenses from their earnings. Whoever pays, this element in opportunity cost is a production cost that has to be met because of the creation of the new employment itself. The cost would exist even if no cash wage was paid (in the unlikely event of labourers being prepared to work without wages!). If the cost is met by the employer, it will appear as a direct project input. If it is met by others, it is one of the external effects that are discussed below.

3.62   The SWR on these principles is simply the marginal product of labour in its best alternative use *plus* this extra consumption imposed on the economy by this employment creation, with both elements expressed in numeraire units by the application of a conversion factor. More explanation of this appears in paragraphs 4.10–4.11.

3.63   The operational use of shadow wages in the different projects referred to in this Guide is discussed in Box 3.7. It is notable that, for different reasons, some project analyses made no adjustment to labour costs. The lowest SWR, which was used only twice, was 0.5. Substantial downwards adjustments to the market price of labour were not common in the analysis of these projects.

Skilled labour
3.64   The general rule for the valuation of domestic skilled labour (including managerial and professional staff) is to take the domestic market rate for such labour and to adjust it only by the Standard Conversion Factor. This approach is justified on grounds that such labour, being scarce, can usually command an equivalent income in other activities, so the market wage reflects its marginal productivity in alternative use. If the market wage is below the opportunity cost, as revealed by an inadequate supply of labour with the necessary skills, it may be appropriate to add a premium to reflect the difference between opportunity cost and the actual wage. Situations are reported, however, where there is some unemployment of skilled workers. Consequently, there may, in some cases, be a need for judgement as to whether the principles outlined above for unskilled workers should apply to some of those who are called skilled. This issue is not likely to be a major concern in the economic analysis of most investment projects, because skilled labour is seldom a large cost item.

---

[1] The cost-effectiveness study by Porter and Walsh (bibliography, section C) contains an example of such a situation. Part of new consumption expenditure on food was counted as a project cost.

36

3.65   Some projects involve the employment of skilled workers from abroad – artisans, managers, professionals, etc. All payments to them are opportunity costs. That portion which goes outside the country (either as direct payment by the project or through remissions by the workers) is a foreign payment, to be valued at its actual cost. The remainder, which is spent within the country, should in principle be revalued by a specific consumption conversion factor, generally the one for high income groups, but the standard conversion factor may be used instead.

Box 3.7   Shadow Wages in Use

Several of the Case Studies, and both Detailed Cases, refer to the use of Shadow Wage adjustments. However, details of how they were derived is very seldom mentioned. This is not surprising. SWRs, like the SCF and the ARI, are parameters that the central planning agency should certainly be responsible for estimating, and for giving to all national or donor analysts.

In four cases studies from a variety of sectors, CS 9, CS 10, CS 11 and CS 15, no labour cost adjustment was made, because it appeared that no distortions were effective in the labour market. CS 14 was especially concerned with workers employed on woodlot work in rural areas, and a SWR of 0.5 was used. A similar distortion was estimated in CS 5 for workers in labour-intensive road construction, though in that case a savings premium (see chapter 4) of 2.0 was also applied, the only instance of this measure in the 18 project cases reviewed in this Guide. SWRs of 0.75 or 0.8 were used in the Basin Irrigation Scheme, CS 2, and in CS 13, the New Ports Project. The analysts of the Fertiliser Plant, CS 1, may have been prepared to use a SWR less than unity, but there was no purpose in doing so in this typically capital-intensive chemical engineering project, since unskilled labour costs were a small element. The same was true in the Natural Gas Project, CS 12.

Analysis of the Land Settlement Programme, CS 4, illustrated a different shadow wage situation – the need to estimate an opportunity cost value for farm family workers that are not normally costed, and who receive no wage. This regular problem in appraising small farm projects is very challenging and always uncertain. Characteristically, adult family workers in this case were valued at the same level as wage employees in farming of the same kind.

Other Domestic Factor Incomes

Land
3.66   Where land is a relatively unimportant input, as in most industrial projects, it should be valued at its market price, and the Standard Conversion Factor applied. Where land is an important element, as in agricultural development schemes, in principle it should be treated as an annual recurrent cost which represents the land's alternative marginal net product each year,

expressed at world prices.[1] For the schemes in which land costs are significant, (agriculture and forestry of course, but also for large roads and urban expansion), estimating this opportunity cost is usually an essential element of the project design team's work to appreciate and forecast the without-project situation. The outputs and inputs would, of course, need to be expressed in accounting prices.[2] In other cases, where all this detail is not available, it may be sufficient in practice to value it at the market rent which would apply in the absence of the project. This annual rent should be adjusted by the appropriate sectoral conversion factor to express it at world prices. The conversion factor to use will apply to the sector in which the land is in its best alternative use, eg agriculture or industry, and several different main types of agriculture might be recognised. Box 3.8 outlines how this resource was valued in the case study projects which called for the valuation of agricultural land.

Box 3.8   Shadow Pricing Land

Given that development projects scarcely ever arise on high value sites such as city centres, a serious need for a shadow price for land arises mainly in agriculture or other extensive uses of land. In these cases one land use system generally replaces another and a value needs to be placed on 'land' to reflect the net value of the to-be-displaced 'without-project' situation on the area concerned.

Three Case Studies involved extensive land use for natural production. DC 2, which concerns an irrigation project, gives fairly detailed treatment to the alternative net output, which is valued at efficiency prices. CS 4, the land settlement project, and CS 14, for woodlot production, did not value land in a similar, detailed way, possibly due to data problems. It is not known what bias this might have given to the appraisal of these projects. Probably it was small. In the forestry case, the land concerned was not likely to have been very productive. Trees are seldom allocated fertile land, and the woodlot areas were to be donated by local communities, who might not be expected to give up for this purpose anything but marginal tracts.

The treatment of land values was not mentioned in any of the other projects, probably because in all cases it was a relatively small cost item. Standard procedure would be simply to apply the SCF to the purchase cost or annual rental value of the land. Projects undoubtedly occur where the value of the land is a key question, including cases where land costs are widely dispersed (through erosion, for example), but the case studies in Part II do not include such a case.

---

[1] Some schemes change land use irreversibly (for example, open-cast mining, road construction) if only because the costs of reversal are prohibitive. In these cases the annual costs will need to be capitalised.

[2] An elaborate illustration of this approach is given in Chapter 15 of Scott, MacArthur and Newbery. (See bibliography.)

Rent and Profits

3.67   Land, capital, entrepreneurship or any other factor of production may be employed in constructing or operating a project, or in producing a major input to the project. Through this involvement, their owners may be able to extract a reward which is substantially above their earnings in the best alternative use. This extra reward (termed 'rent' by economists) should normally be excluded from the reckoning of costs, since it is really a share in the project's benefits. While such rental elements affect the distribution of the income flows, they are not an opportunity cost for the economy.

Allocative efficiency appraisals are indifferent as to who gains from a project, so the value of the private sector surplus, including any private savings from that surplus, is the same in value as any surplus accruing to any other group (including Government). However, where this rental element accrues to a non-resident and will be remitted abroad, it should be reckoned as a foreign exchange cost in the years in which it arises, after deducting local taxes.

Interest, Depreciation and Terminal Value

3.68   All expenditure, including the take-up of working capital, should be entered in cost-benefit analysis in the year in which the resources and inputs are actually acquired by the project. Interest and depreciation charges should not be entered (although they appear in financial analysis – see Chapter 7) because they are accommodated in economic analysis by discounting and the full charging of capital expenditure in the year in which it is incurred. The corollary to this is that any value which the capital assets have at the end of the project's economic life should be credited in the analysis. Working capital, including stocks, can often be entered at the end of the project, at their market value, and fixed assets will usually have some value. In some cases (roads, irrigation works) they will retain their full value if properly maintained and this can be proxied by the initial capital costs; at the other extreme the assets will have scrap value only (for example, ships, manufacturing plant). Decommissioning costs need to be entered in cost streams and can sometimes be significant (for example, landscape restoration after mineral exploitation, waste disposal following nuclear power plant closures). The effects of discounting future events will considerably diminish the weight of these terminal calculations in the economic analysis, and there is seldom a need for great accuracy in their determination, but they can still be a crucial factor in the project decision if the undiscounted value is high.

Unquantifiables, Externalities and Environmental Effects

3.69   In principle, all effects should be identified, valued, and taken into account in project analysis. Preceding sections of this chapter have indicated the approach to be followed in the valuation of those effects that obviously affect the situations with the project and without it which can be identified, measured and valued. Unfortunately, not all of the changes consequent upon a project are easily handled. The next three sections look at some of the less straightforward effects, and how they may be handled.

3.70   A distinction is conventionally made between internal and external project effects. Internal effects are usually defined as those experienced by one or other of the parties directly involved in the project: the project owners, the work force, its financiers, and government. External effects are experienced by other groups in society. Some, like the buyers of output or the suppliers of inputs, are closely involved. Others may experience effects by being located nearby, while other consequences affect groups whom it is very difficult to identify.

3.71 Finance flows are the most obvious internal effects on those directly involved. Opportunity cost valuation, by recognising value effects other than finance flows to the parties in the project, involves taking account of many external effects, especially the benefits implicit in using the Standard Conversion Factor and the Shadow Wage Rate. However, these adjustments are generally applied in the first instance only to resources and outputs directly featured in the project. Yet other effects must be recognised. Three categories of effects (which overlap) are considered in following sections that may not actually or obviously be covered by appraisal of the direct, visible resource and output dimensions of the project. These are:

- unquantifiable effects;
- external economic effects; and
- environmental issues.

Unquantifiable Effects

3.72 The term 'unquantifiable'; refers both (1) to effects that are known to arise but which cannot be measured in physical terms and (2) to effects which cannot be valued. Difficulties in quantification and valuation will often go together.

3.73 Quantification problems often are data problems: a certain effect could be measured, but has not been. Time and resources might allow an estimate to be made. But for many 'aesthetic' factors – good health, literacy, education, cultural experiences – units of measurement are difficult to define, beyond the purely functional factors of days available for work, working life, skills possessed, etc. that health and education can affect. These things have value that may be reflected in market behaviour. However, where there is no market, or not one that reflects willingness-to-pay, consumer surplus estimates can be attempted. These were discussed in paragraphs 3.30 to 3.33, which emphasised that satisfactory measurement is often very difficult to achieve.

3.74 The 'unquantifiables' mentioned can clearly be direct internal consequences of the project. Some 'social sector' projects have the main purpose of creating these effects. However, other unquantifiable effects may occur outside the project. 'Training benefits' are an example. If a project adopts a new process or technique, this can create skills and attitudes that could be of widespread value over the years in many sectors, as experienced workers and managers move elsewhere. Innovative projects could claim such benefits. 'Demonstration effects' can also arise, especially in tourism projects, where the level of facilities provided for foreign visitors may inevitably induce consumption aspirations and styles amongst local people that government may not prefer.

3.75 Other non-quantified effects are environmental, whose nature and treatment is discussed in a later section. Non-quantified effects of this kind must not be ignored: there is always a risk that effects which can be quantified will seem more important than non-quantified effects, but this can lead to serious mistakes. Project reports must mention the significant non-measured and/or non-valued effects, describe their nature, and indicate their extent. Although they cannot be incorporated in economic measures, they can be considered in the comprehensive review of any project. In some instances they will influence judgement and the decision.

External Economic Effects

3.76   Valuation at opportunity cost prices involves taking account of some value effects that are external to the project, in the sense that they impinge on interests other than those directly involved in the project. Some of these effects may be taken account of in the valuation of resources and outputs directly associated with the undertaking as, for example, when labour working in a supplying industry is revalued as part of calculating the accounting price of a project input. Yet a separate set of economic effects may also arise which have indirect consequences that fall on groups and individuals not involved in the project. The nature of these effects, the need for their consid-erations, and approaches to valuation are considered here. The four types encountered most frequently are:

– Linkage effects;
– Multiplier effects;
– International effects; and
– Strategic effects.

Linkage Effects

3.77   'Forward' linkage effects are increased surpluses to industries which process or use a project's output. There is no reason why the mere provision of goods and services by a project will always result in any extra use of them, thus making linkage benefits possible. The project may simply be an alterna-tive source of supply, so users may realise no additional benefits (as profits, taxes and worker incomes) unless the project will sell at a lower price. In the case of traded goods, the possibility of imports without the project will rule out forward linkage benefits, unless the project price is lower. If a project in-creases output, and allows greater activity by users, the analysis of costs and benefits which takes account of effects on non-traded prices elsewhere should not require further modification. All surpluses expected to arise will have been incorporated.

3.78   'Backward' linkage effects might occur in the industries which supply a project's inputs. Where a project's needs are responsible for economies of scale in domestic production, or it allows new domestic production below import cost, this will be an important fact about project consequences. The appraisal should take account of any price changes for inputs or outputs which would result from implementation. But as with 'forward' linkage effects, the proper analysis of costs and benefits should take into account the effects on non-traded prices elsewhere, in the recognition of abnormal profits etc., in the supplying agencies.

3.79   In some cases, there may be close interdependencies or linkages be-tween several new vertically-associated investments. To look at each in isola-tion could be misleading. It is better to widen the project definition to include all the related investments and external effects will then be internalised.

Multiplier Effects

3.80   Benefits from 'multiplier' effects are sometimes claimed when short-run increases in income are generated as surplus capacity in an economy is activated by additional rounds of spending resulting from the investment. Individual projects can claim such effects if two conditions hold:

a.   There are underemployed complementary factors in an economy which cannot be utilised other than by undertaking this particular investment.

b.   Funds for local expenditure on the project under consideration could not be used for any other project which would generate comparable indirect benefits.

These are restrictive conditions and projects which are claimed to fulfill them should be approached with some scepticism.

3.81   The employment 'multiplier' is allowed for by the use of a Shadow Wage Rate where wages exceed the opportunity cost of labour. If the Shadow Wage is below the market wage, employment in the project will increase worker incomes. This will increase consumption by labour, and so lead to 'indirect' employment generation. This effect is fully taken into account in the ordinary calculation of the Shadow Wage Rate. All extra worker income is treated as a benefit, by counting only alternative earnings as the cost. No special premium for 'indirect' employment generation should be used.

3.82   If certain industries will be working well below full capacity, and the commodity in question is sufficiently important as a project input to merit a full calculation of its value, the appropriate valuation is the current production costs (in opportunity cost terms); short-run marginal cost. This valuation would be valid only so long as the excess capacity is expected to continue. New investment may become necessary to supply a project, so incremental capital costs will have to be included in the accounting price, which will reflect long-run marginal cost.

International Effects

3.83   Some project effects may be 'external' to the economy. For example, project output may increase exports or substitute for imports. If the project's output represents a sufficiently large proportion of total world trade, world prices may be affected, harming other exporting countries but benefitting importing countries. A project may also have effects on world prices for the inputs. It may also affect the environment in neighbouring countries, for example through the discharge of waste into rivers flowing through more than one country. In such circumstances the government may wish to consider the international impact of the project, if only because the national interest could be affected by possible retaliatory action from other countries.

3.84   The benefits from external linkage projects may accrue in greater or lesser degree to the nationals of other countries. Examples are ports,[1] international airports and international highways. In some countries the convention is adopted that such benefits should be credited to the project, but this is essentially a matter of national policy. These cases can raise major issues on user charges which financial planning must address.

---

[1] Case Study 13, the New Port Project, illustrates this particular situation.

Strategic effects

3.85 Some unvalued project effects contribute to objectives other than the primary economic objective considered in this chapter, the maximisation of the value of aggregate consumption over time. Effects on the distribution of income and welfare between members of the community are discussed in chapter 5. In relation to another objective, a project might produce goods or services considered to be strategic to the economy, because they would make it independent of foreign suppliers in time of war or near-war conditions, or provide alternative supply routes. If independence or self-sufficiency in certain goods are explicit objectives, their relative importance would need to be assessed by the government in the light of the economic cost of achieving these objectives. Economic analysis can illuminate this assessment, though it cannot show what the worth is in numeraire units of furthering these objectives.

Environmental Effects

3.86 The consequences of projects on the environment require special attention to the design and appraisal stages. Effects on the natural and the human environment can take many forms. Some are direct effects, expected and explicitly allowed for in the formulation of proposals, but others are indirect, bringing changes and implications to environments that may be far removed from the project itself. Not all of the environmental effects of a project can be fully handled through economic analysis, but there are several approaches to the measurement of value that economists can employ and consider as they assist in analysing and appraising environmental effects. The ideas and techniques available are discussed later in this section.

3.87 The concern in project formulation and review is mainly with the actual or possible negative effects that will arise. However, not all investments have negative effects. Many projects have the explicit purpose of improving the environment, to increase the stability, fertility and productivity of land, lakes and sea, and to provide clean air, pure water and effluent disposal. Negative consequences may also arise in these schemes, but not always. Other projects are environment-neutral. Undertaking them may leave the situation neither worse nor better than the situation without them. This will especially be the case with projects for rehabilitation and capital renewal. No charge on the environment need arise in such cases, provided the previous technology is still available, though at times of renewal the opportunity will often be taken of effecting improvement to reduce noise, pollution and ugliness when restoration or replacement takes place.

3.88 The main interest is on negative effects. Avoidance of dramatic environmental disaster may be possible (where they can be predicted) through planning controls, in ways that are discussed in paragraphs 6.33 to 6.36. The concern here is with the cost of negative effects that can be predicted to arise and which escape planning controls. Wherever possible, these effects should be recognised, quantified and valued so that, at both the design and the appraisal stages, judgements can be made on whether they can be mitigated or, to the extent that they cannot, whether they can be accepted in relation to the other net benefits of the development as a whole.

3.89 It is inevitable that not all environmental effects can be foreseen. Ecosystems can be particularly vulnerable, and when new changes are introduced into a stable situation, the consequences may not all be predictable. Obviously guidance is not possible for such situations: all the analyst can do is to ask the specialists to be alert to the possibilities. The results of chemical discharges into air and water, the food chain effects of persistent sprays and dusts, and some hydrological consequences may all be location-specific, but these are things about which more and more is being learned. Seeking to consider and anticipate them is a strong feature of the project agenda now. Recognising and quantifying them (at least giving a sign and estimate of magnitude to each effect) will be the task of technical experts. The economist may also pose some of the searching questions in identifying environmental effects. However, he or she should be ready to show how effects, once recognised, can be calculated and valued in terms comparable to the value units of the rest of the economic analysis, units of the efficiency analysis numeraire.

The Depletion of Natural Resources

3.90   Extractive projects involve using up existing natural resources. Some – like forests, fish populations and wildlife – could be replaced or left to recover with proper management. However, others like mineral ores and especially fossil fuels, cannot be replaced. Any loss of a natural resource to future generations as a result of a project must be carefully considered and fully reflected in the appraisal.

3.91   Valuable products are often obtained at low cost. Where pricing is based on costs, they may be sold very cheaply, and thus used in part by people and activities that put a very low value on them. Yet as they are used up they bring closer the time when alternative, generally more costly, sources may have to be used to meet the supply.

3.92   Where natural resources are renewable, projects for their renewal (like replanting after logging natural forests) can be formulated and appraised. Where renewal is impossible, it is important to ensure that the diminishing stocks are employed in ways that make the most valuable use of them.

3.93   The Depletion Premium is a pricing and valuation tool designed to achieve this rationing effect. Detail of the theory and formula are explained in Methodology Illustration 4 in Part II of this Guide. In broad terms, the approach ensures that the sale price of such products includes not only production costs but also an element to represent the discounted value of the probably much higher cost that will need to be incurred by obtaining supplies from a different source when the present stock is exhausted. As final depletion approaches, the premium will increase quickly, ensuring that low-productivity users give it up; that stocks are preserved, and that what remains goes to those uses that can obtain the most benefit from it. Where the product appears to be irreplaceable it will be impossible to place a finite value on the premium and broader, non-quantified methods may be needed to determine the acceptability of the project.

Approaches to Valuing Environmental Effects[1]

3.94   Many approaches to valuation have been developed or researched. Some are perfectly usable methods that economists could employ with con-

---

[1] A more full account of these methods can be found in the Asian Development Bank Staff Paper listed in Section D of the Bibliography.

fidence. Others represent approaches that have the potential to assist the estimation of values, but which are difficult to operationalise. Some of these methods involve estimating the value of gross or net output lost or gained through project-induced environmental change. Others look only at the cost side. In all cases the limitations should be recognised and explained in the appraisal report: some environmental effects cannot be measured in financial terms.

3.95   *Generally applicable methods that focus on outputs* include these three approaches.

(1) *Changes in Production Elsewhere*
      This basic but widely-applicable approach recognises that environmental effects caused by one project can reduce the productivity of other systems. Chemical discharge into rivers may reduce fishery production downstream or in the sea, for example. In such cases, the loss in gross or net output on the other systems can be estimated and counted as a charge against the net benefits of the project. All of these external changes would be valued in efficiency prices.

(2) *Estimating Loss of Earnings*
      Reductions in production as a result of environmental pollution can be measured in part by noting the reduction in returns to factors of production. The approach outlined earlier reflects the loss in returns to land and other biological systems. Labour may be similarly affected, with measurably lower earnings as a result of such things as air and water pollution, or noise effects. Lower productivity elsewhere may be only one of the effects of such environmental degradation. Increased medical expenses may also need to be noted.

(3) *Replacement Opportunity Cost*
      An alternative basis for valuing the reduced productivity of production systems and resources is to estimate the cost of replacing lost output from another source. If the river is polluted, the fish are lost. But if demand and need are strong they may need to be replaced by supply from another source. The lost output might be valued at the replacement cost of the product or close substitutes.

      The same approach can be used in the reverse way to estimate a numerical value of a non-marketed good. This mainly applies to proposals for creating or preserving benefits of aesthetic value – unique natural resources or historic works. When steps to preserve them are considered, the value can be estimated of lost output through not using the area in the best alternative way. This will not value the preserved asset, but the question can be posed whether their value is likely to be greater or less than the sacrifice incurred by not allowing the productive alternative.

3.96   *Generally applicable methods that look only at costs* include two major techniques.

(4) *Cost Effectiveness*
      In its environmental application, this approach can involve setting goals or targets for maximum tolerable levels of environmental damage, and then finding the most cost-effective way of meeting them. Examples would be

deciding which method of soil erosion control was best; or what is the cheapest way of keeping BOD[1] levels down in waterborne waste discharge. Sometimes, target levels have not been set, or are flexible. Analysis of the cost of meeting various levels of pollution limitation can be estimated, allowing an assessment of whether the marginal cost of additional reduction is justified by the amount of qualitative improvement obtained.

(5) *Costs of Prevention*

An alternative to accepting the occurrence of some external damage and charging it against the project is to insist that no ill-effects should be experienced elsewhere. If a project might cause them it must meet the cost of the necessary preventative or mitigating works that will allow output to be sustained elsewhere. Damming rivers may exacerbate flooding downstream, so new protective works must be built. Soil erosion high in a catchment can spoil irrigation works below, through sedimentation, which must be ameliorated. The cost of these essential measures must be counted as costs against the new development.

3.97 *Potentially useful approaches to valuing outputs* may be based on the logical but risky approach of observing prices of resources that allow 'surrogate' valuations to be assessed. The basis is to compare the cost of something in two situations which are (to the extent possible) the same in all respects other than one environmental factor. The difference may be regarded as the implicit value put on the difference in the environmental factor. Various instances of this approach may be cited.

- House prices or rental differences between polluted or non-polluted locations (smells, noise levels, etc.).
- Wage differentials reflecting the labour supply resistance effect between good and bad work environments.
- Land value differences between plots with different views or other amenities.
- Using travel costs to estimate the demand curve for free amenities which, though seldom the main product of development projects, may be minor effects of multi-purpose investments (eg recreation associated with dams).
- Taking prices in limited markets to assess the value of proposed public amenity projects. Providing free leisure amenities for all that some individuals provide for themselves is one area of application, but the values placed on clean water or regular power supplies can be an indication of the values placed on these things by those able to afford them.

3.98 These 'surrogate market' approaches are means for trying to estimate the consumer surplus value of environmental benefits lost, gained or preserved. Paragraph 3.33 cautions against reliance in economic analysis on consumer surplus estimates. Those remarks relate especially to attempts to estimate the value of education, health and some very basic amenities. In the valuation of environmental and amenity effects, economists must decide whether any plausible estimates can be obtained through these 'surrogate' approaches. Where they cannot, the environmental effects can only be listed,

---

[1] Biochemical Oxygen Demand.

and mentioned in a qualitative way. Although none of the valuation approaches listed might apply, the environmental effects must not be overlooked in appraisal.

3.99 The various environmental considerations that arose in the project case studies covered by Part II of this Guide are summarised in Box 3.9.

Box 3.9   Environmental Effects

Environmental effects are especially important in projects of certain kinds, but not in all. Investments that actually or potentially change the natural environment must seek to create and sustain a stable situation. Where the basic environment is fragile, special design effects have to be incorporated.

The need to take special account of environment preservation in project design is illustrated in two case studies. The Basin Irrigation Scheme (Detailed Case 2) includes provision for sand dune fixation through tree planting, both to provide a barrier to sand innundation and for its micro-climatic effect in reducing the drying effect of winds. Though a minor cost item, it was an important feature of project design. Similarly urgent protection measures were required in the Development Road, CS 5. Parts of the alignment ran up and down steep slopes, where the soil and substrata were very friable and liable to erosion. Both to ensure the stability of the road itself and to protect the surrounding agricultural land, soil excavation and tipping were done with great care, and bare slopes were planted up at once with fast growing, stabilising species.

Environmental damage through noxious discharges or accidents are special risks in large chemical engineering plants. The illustrative Fertiliser Project (CS 1) emphasises the appreciation of the pollution risk during the design of this project, and the provision for environmental monitoring that was made, including the appointment of specialist staff.

Some types of project inevitably cause some environmental deterioration. Irrigation projects always increase the incidence of some diseases. Typically, the Basin Irrigation Scheme (DC 2) includes provision for health control expenditure throughout the life of the project.

Several of the illustration projects were for rehabilitation, where no new environmental issues would be expected, and some of the others genuinely appeared to raise no new problems of this kind. The Natural Gas Project (CS 12) involves the exploitation of a limited non-renewable resource, and the use of the Depletion Premium is illustrated there and in detail in Methodology Illustration 4.

Amenity considerations were not important in any illustrative case except the Island Secondary School, CS 15. Special emphasis was made there that, in this relatively very large building construction undertaking, the new school should be built 'to designs consistent with the local style', to fit it properly into the cultural, aesthetic environment of this small, distinctive community.

Discounting

3.100   The role of discounting was explained in chapter 2. Both costs and benefits need to be discounted to reflect their irregular incidence through time and the appropriate rate for this is the 'accounting rate of interest' (ARI). This is the rate at which the value of uncommitted government income – the numeraire in this Guide – falls over time.

3.101   In economic appraisal conducted under the principles of this chapter the balance between consumption and investment, and the overall distribution of income, are intentionally set aside. In these circumstances the ARI is the opportunity cost of capital in the public sector, which is measured by the marginal rate of return on public sector investments which have been appraised on the principles of this chapter. At this rate the resources available to the public sector for investment will just be exhausted. Technical justification for this equality between the ARI and the opportunity cost of capital is given in chapter 4.

3.102   The application of this principle to derive the opportunity cost of capital in the public sector (the ARI) is not easy in practice. By definition, the rate which clears the market can only be determined empirically. Increasingly, central authorities are attempting to establish a test discount rate, or minimum rate of return, for public sector projects, and this approximates conceptually to the ARI on the principles of this chapter.

3.103   Whenever projects are being analysed, the advice of the national planning authority must be sought. They may have their own estimates – perhaps narrow or crude – of what ARI is appropriate and in use. They are usually derived from three approaches: micro-economic evidence from recent project appraisals; rates for foreign lending or borrowing; and macro-economic analysis.

3.104   Practical guidance will be needed by analysts in countries where there is no centrally determined test discount rate, and by governments seeking to establish an ARI. The analysis of recent project selection decisions may give an impression of what is regarded as acceptable, but in the absence of a national test rate decisions might not have been consistent. One approach is to choose a test rate unsystematically, and to see from experience whether modification is needed.

3.105   The ARI chosen can never be more than the central value of the band within which the 'true' rate may lie. ARI values used in projects that illustrate this Guide are discussed in Box 3.10. Current experience suggests that a discount rate in the range of 8% to 12% applied to costs and benefits in constant prices is a useful operational guide over a wide range of countries. However, each country's ARI is unique. There is no reason why a rate which clears the market in country A, just absorbing all available funds with the marginal project, will do so in country B. Of course, the notion of 'available funds' that good projects will exactly use up is an elastic concept, especially when international borrowing is possible, and the availability of donor funds is likely to be less than fully predictable. Over time, the supply of projects with comparatively high NPVs may also be increased by additional effort on project identification and formulation.

3.106   For these reasons, a simple balance between the availability of resources and projects suitable to absorb them may not arise, so the 'balancing' ARI might vary from one period to the next. If it is found that there are too few projects with a positive NPV to absorb available funds, greater efforts in project identification and formulation may be more appropriate than reduction of the ARI. On the other hand, if demands for investible funds in terms of projects with a positive NPV exceed the supply (including overseas borrowing capacity), there is little alternative to raising the ARI.

3.107   The second approach to fixing limits to the ARI is to look at rates for lending and borrowing overseas. The ARI should not normally be set below the highest rate at which the country could safely lend abroad after taking into account inflation and currency exchange rate fluctuations (ie the 'real' rate of return on foreign 'gilt-edged securities'). Because surplus savings to lend abroad are usually limited, a choice of this character will normally present itself only to less developed countries in unusual circumstances; for example, when countries enjoy very large oil revenues.

3.108   There may, however, be cases where a country is receiving a volume of official funds (which cannot be re-lent abroad) such that an ARI lower than the (real) foreign lending rate would be required if all the funds were to be absorbed on projects with a positive NPV. In such cases, and in all situations where a country borrows from abroad, the ARI should not be set below the real rate of interest payable on the marginal (most expensive) loan to the country. It is important that this principle be followed in determining the appropriate level of the ARI, even when development finance on concessional terms is available.

Box 3.10   The Allocative Efficiency Accounting Rate of Interest

The ARIs used in the case studies and illustrations were allocative efficiency rates. Different project reports quote a range of values between 8 and 15%. In no case is it suggested that the ARI was estimated independently by the project analyst. All were related to the principles of chapter 3.

Case studies using different rates are:

8%	*DC 2, CS 9, CS 10.*
8% to 12%	*CS 2.*
10%	*DC 1, CS 4, MI 2.*
12%	*CS 6, CS 8, CS 13.*
15%	*CS 12, MI 4.*

The quotation in CS 2 (Special Steels) of a range within which the ARI occurs is probably realistic, especially if detailed estimates had not been made. Some of the ARIs used are described as 'customary', suggesting that a central authority estimate was adopted.

No discount rates are quoted for the two projects in very small dependent territories, CS 11 (Water Distillation) and CS 15, the Island School. As has been pointed out elsewhere,[1] productive investment opportunities in these economies are very limited. ARIs for them are difficult to estimate, but are certainly low, below the range quoted above.

---
[1] See the Commonwealth Secretariat reference in the bibliography.

3.109   The third approach to the opportunity cost of capital in the public sector is macro-economic analysis to derive the incremental output-capital ratio. The techniques for doing this will yield no more than an approximate estimate which can be used as a check on the other approaches.

3.110   Rates of interest in domestic capital markets are of limited value for estimating the ARI. Domestic capital market rates are in current price terms, so an inflation adjustment is needed to bring them to the constant price basis recommended for the ARI. Furthermore, capital markets are often fragmented and distorted, with a range of different unassociated interest rates occurring. The shadow pricing concepts outlined in this Guide – national opportunity costs, international border pricing, etc. – can produce radically different price relationships, including the price of capital. Even if domestic capital markets were free and efficient, the rates of interest determined by them (ie the norminal price of capital) might bear little relation to the rate that would use up available resources when shadow prices were applied. Moreover it is common experience that capital is rationed at the ruling (often controlled) domestic rates of interest, so nominal rates are lower than market clearing rates would be.

3.111   These points do not mean that the medium and long-term rates of interest ruling in domestic capital markets may never be used to estimate a minimum value for the ARI, but they will usually require substantial adjustment before the ARI can be related to them. The experience of countries which have made serious attempts to estimate the opportunity cost ARI suggests that it is usually higher than interest rates in formal domestic capital markets after adjustment to constant price terms.

Decision Criterion

3.112   The decision criterion for the economic appraisal is simply that all projects with a positive NPV are acceptable (paragraph 2.12). Whatever the result, it must then be weighed against the results of other types of appraisal (financial, social, environmental, etc.) which may give conflicting signals. The risks and uncertainties inherent in all forecasting will also have a bearing on the decision. They will apply to all types of appraisal and are discussed in chapter 6.

3.113   An IRR which is greater than the ARI should provide an equivalent decision criterion in many cases, but use of the IRR is not recommended, for the reasons given in paragraph 2.14.

Cost-Effectiveness Analysis and the Choice between Mutually Exclusive Alternatives

3.114   Calculation of one or more NPVs for a complete project will give an indication of the likely value of the proposal from the economic viewpoint, when viewed as a whole. However, this is only one of many discounted measures that need to be calculated for most projects. Alternatives usually exist for some or all main elements of design, and choice between the feasible alternatives should be guided by economic measures.

3.115 For example, cost-benefit analysis will show whether investment in the supply of thermal power will be justified. But the question remains, what thermal generating system will have the lowest cost: steam generation from coal, oil or gas; diesel generators; gas turbines? All may give a positive NPV, but which is the cheapest?

3.116 Many analyses of the technical possibilities will look only at the cost side, it being taken that the output of the alternatives will be the same in every case. Analysis to see which alternative is the most cost effective – ie which has the lowest total discounted cost – should follow the same principles as were outlined in earlier sections of this chapter. The inputs should be valued at allocative efficiency prices, and discounted at the ARI. Only the decision criterion will be different. Alternatives with the lowest discounted value of costs will be preferred.[1] (Since only costs are involved, no NPV can be calculated.)

3.117 Illustrations of cost-effectiveness analysis in the case studies are cited in Box 3.11. They show that cost-effectiveness analysis to choose between design alternatives is a major feature of the project formulation process. It is important that all reasonable possibilities are considered at an early stage in identification and planning, and that economic criteria are used throughout to appraise those that are technically feasible.

Box 3.11   Cost Effectiveness Analysis

Several of the illustration projects refer to analyses that were undertaken, generally on the cost side only, to investigate which production method or other production aspect was cheapest or was most satisfactory from a quality or volume viewpoint. The two electricity cases (CS 7 and CS 8) discuss alternative forms of generation, and the second also investigated optimal timing. The two water cases (CS 10 and CS 11) both considered a variety of possible water sources to meet supply needs. Water projects commonly give careful consideration to the optimal size of main pipeline, and CS 11 also considered the timing of investment. CS 15, which refers to the location of the single secondary school on an island, refers to the analysis of alternative locations. Another, different kind of investigation is demonstrated in CS 13, where analysis looked at the size of the project, as reflected in the number of berths that was 'optimal' in the construction of a new port.

In many types of project, such analyses to find least-cost alternatives are obviously standard good practice. A related type of analysis on the output side is seen in CS 14, when alternative sources of supplying the project output (firewood) were investigated at some length.

3.118 Cost analysis between mutually exclusive alternative technologies is an obvious area of design choice that must be investigated early in planning. Other major areas relate to scale of project or activity unit, and location.

---

[1] Where technical alternatives give different outputs then full cost-benefit analysis is necessary.

3.119   An important feature of project appraisal that cost-effectiveness brings out is the need to split a major project into parts which can be analysed separately. Different components may be carried out separately and at different times. It may be positively misleading to treat a project as if it involved a single comprehensive 'take-it-or-leave-it' decision, with no degree of choice as to whether to accept some features and reject others, or as to the phasing of the project.

3.120   In these areas of identifying and analysing alternatives, the careful guidance of technical consultants engaged to prepare feasibility studies is of the greatest importance. If they are not instructed to consider several possibilities, there is a danger of commitment to a particular solution on technical grounds before the costs of alternatives have been adequately examined.

3.121   Where the outputs (and so the benefit values) of alternatives differ, then partial analysis of those factors within a project that differ between alternatives will take the form of a cost-benefit estimation, with NPV the criterion, not the present value of costs.

3.122   The correct timing of a project can also involve a choice between mutually exclusive alternatives. Ideally the NPV of a project should be calculated on different assumptions concerning starting dates, to providing estimates of the effects of delaying it. In principle, the timing should be chosen which gives the largest positive NPV when the net annual benefits of every alternative are all discounted to the same base year, but this rule may not always be practicable. If a project has a high positive NPV and financial and other indicators are positive it may not be sensible to defer implementation. This is another area where future uncertainties should be balanced against present facts.

Cost-Effectiveness Analysis and Social Projects

3.123   The current practice of economic analysis has its origins in the appraisal of industrial projects, where the outputs are tradeable goods. The principles have been expanded to accommodate other sectors and projects where outputs are non-tradeable but sold, for example power and housing projects, and there are useful examples of measurement of returns to investment in 'human capital' which can be applied in education and health. But it has been noted earlier that the valuation of non-traded outputs which are not sold poses difficult problems. Willingness to pay and consumer surpluses are the relevant opportunity cost principles in these situations, but their practical use is limited. Accordingly, the NPV decision criterion is not easily used in the economic appraisal of many projects in sectors such as health, education, social services and the public service. Other criteria must be used.

3.124   Concern with these 'social' sectors has increased in recent years, especially regarding the distribution of income and the fruits of development generally. One way of improving the conditions of the poorest groups is to increase their access to community assets such as pure drinking water, sewerage systems, and health and education facilities. The principles of this chapter can be applied to the inputs of all projects, for the proper valuation of costs, but where benefits cannot be valued, only the cost side can be considered. Cost-effectiveness analysis is an essential part of the economic analysis of projects in all sectors, but it has a special significance for projects in the social sectors.

3.125 Its use with projects of these types requires a clear definition of objectives and needs. Techniques other than cost/benefit and cost-effectiveness analysis may be employed to check them with other objectives in the rest of the economy. These include general supply and demand forecasting; manpower and educational planning; demographic projection; and others.

3.126 When objectives have been established and accepted, the search can proceed for the solution that is most cost-effective at accounting prices. It may be hampered by lack of comparative data on costs in similar activities. In some cases it may be possible to compare the costs of a suggested approach with the costs of existing institutions in the same country, of a similar type and location, updated if necessary for inflation. This may be done by comparing unit costs, eg. costs per bed, per student place, per mile of road. If national statistics of this kind are not available, it may be necessary to use international statistics, with approximate adjustments as appropriate. This comparative approach can indicate unusual features about the costs of the proposal, and whether alternative ways of achieving the stated objectives should be considered.

3.127 For example, the plan may be for a multi-storey hospital, but if the capital cost per bed seems uncommonly high, it will be desirable to consider whether the same facilities and the same number of beds could be provided with a group of single-storey buildings. The latter method may reduce building costs, while increasing the wage costs of attending patients, but unless a Shadow Wage Rate were used, the net resource cost saving may not be evident.

3.128 The value of analysing the cost of alternative designs for major features of social projects depends critically upon its use at a very early stage in identifying the type of investment required to achieve the stated ultimate objective. For example, once there is a commitment to a hospital possibilities for cost minimisation are automatically constrained. It may be that in some circumstances a hospital programme may be an extremely expensive way of achieving public health objectives. A quite different approach might achieve the desired results at far less cost.

3.129 Work on the valuation of human capital, referred to in paragraph 3.123 above, can sometimes be extrapolated to place a value on the benefits of health and education investments. In education one procedure is to determine the higher earnings of a person with particular educational qualifications as compared to people without them and to estimate benefits by applying this earnings differential to the number of people expected to gain the qualification as a result of an education investment. Similarly a health investment expected to eliminate particular diseases from a community can be valued by reference to the earnings capacity of people without the diseases as compared to those with them. In both cases the valuation of benefits will be approximate and partial but they can provide useful guidance.

3.130 Usually the decision criteria for social projects will rely more on assessments outside the accepted field of economic appraisal than is the case for other types of investment. Assistance the economist can provide in the decision process can be summarised as:

a. seeking to clarify overall objectives in the sector, and indicating the precise contribution of the project under consideration to the fulfilment of those objectives;

b. establishing the most cost-effective method for implementing the project, taking account of both capital and recurrent costs, and using the principles for estimating accounting prices and the ARI used for projects in other sectors;

c. identifying the income/consumption groups of the project's principal beneficiaries;

d. indicating the valuation of benefits arising from improved 'human capital'; and

e. forecasting the flow of funds over the project's life, and focusing attention on the need for financial provision to cover recurrent costs (see chapter 7). Shortage of operating funds is frequently the reason why projects in the social sectors fail to live up to expectation.

4
Allocative Efficiency with Sub-Optimal Savings

The Savings Constraint

4.1   The basic economic analysis for allocative efficiency described in chapter 3 should always be prepared. The principles on which it is based are widely understood, they are relatively uncontroversial and the judgements necessary in applying the principles are mainly specific to the project.

4.2   A judgement that domestic savings are sub-optimal in the country in which the project is located raises wider issues. It depends on the common observation that few developing countries can generate the domestic savings needed to finance all the public and private investments which they would like to make. This depends in turn on views about the ability of the government to use other policy instruments to increase the level of savings and the prospects for foreign capital inflows. The latter can compensate for the shortage of domestic savings, particularly if they are provided as grants, but foreign loans impose a claim on future domestic savings to service the debts. Reliance on capital inflows therefore calls for judgements about the inadequacy of savings in the future.

4.3   If careful consideration of these issues leads to the conclusion that domestic savings are sub-optimal, there will be a case for using project selection and design to influence the savings rate. This carries implications for all projects which are described in the rest of this chapter. The issues involved are most readily explained in fairly technical terms and the algebra used may lend a spurious precision to some of the relationships. The reader is therefore warned that in embarking on the extension of a basic allocative efficiency analysis which is needed when sub-optimal savings are postulated it will be necessary to find empirical approximations for a number of the parameters defined below.[1]

4.4   When countries are using their resources reasonably effectively, a savings shortage becomes apparent in a high rate of return on marginal public sector investments. This relates to those public sector investments which have measurable economic returns. About half of the public sector investment budget is typically committed to education, health, law and order, social infrastructure and other areas which undoubtedly contribute to economic growth but in ways which cannot always be measured by conventional economic rates of return. The allocation of investment funds to these sectors depends on political and macro-economic judgements, as outlined in paragraphs 1.10–1.13. This means that measurement of the rate of return on marginal investments depends essentially on a comparison between investment opportunities which can show a measurable economic rate of return and the

---

[1] The terminology and relationships used in the rest of this chapter are derived from Little and Mirrlees and Squire and van der Tak (see bibliography).

funds available for the sectors in which such projects are found after prior allocations to the other sectors.

Integration of a Savings Premium in Economic Appraisal

4.5 The procedure for measuring the marginal rate of return on public sector investment requires, in principle, that rates of return are measured in basic allocative efficiency terms for all projects competing for funds. Investment funds available should be allocated to the projects with the highest rates of return and the rate on the last project accepted – the 'market clearing' rate – is the marginal rate of return. The difficulties in practice of determining this rate have been discussed already (paragraphs 3.102–3.111) and the further problem raised when sub-optimal savings are postulated is: whether the marginal rate of return is considered 'too high'. Also, since this implies that a premium should be placed on savings, what is the mechanism for introducing this into the kind of analysis described in chapter 3?

4.6 The 'savings premium' can be introduced by defining a term v, which is the value of uncommitted government income (the numeraire) relative to additional private consumption measured at border prices at the average level of consumption. In a situation of sub-optimal savings this will have a value greater than 1 and the savings premium is the excess over 1 (ie if v = 1.2, the premium is 20%). The marginal rate of return to public sector investments, measured empirically from basic allocative efficiency appraisals, is denoted by the term q. If this rate of return is thought to be high it implies that it is higher than the rate at which the average person would discount future income as compared with present income, a rate denoted by i and termed the 'consumption rate of interest'.

4.7 Income which is invested at the rate q will yield a future sum greater than the original investment when discounted back to the present at the rate i. It follows that the average person should be prepared to forgo the present consumption implied when making the investment because he or she places a higher value on the future income which the investment will make possible. To illustrate, if 100 moneys can be invested to yield 10 moneys of output per year in perpetuity (ie q = 10%) all of which is consumed, and if the investor's consumption rate of interest i^1 is 5%, then v is simply the present value of 10 moneys per year discounted at 5%, ie

$$v = \sum_{n=0}^{\infty} \frac{q}{(1+i)^n} = \frac{q}{i} = 2.0$$

More complex expressions are discussed at paragraph 4.12 below.

4.8 Most of the valuation procedures explained in chapter 3 are equally applicable to an economic appraisal in circumstances of sub-optimal savings. There are then three steps needed to integrate the savings premium into the analysis.

    a. Income flows need to be divided into uncommitted government income and other types so that they can be weighted.

---

[1] If incremental consumption is measured at domestic prices and the value of i is derived from such measurements it will be necessary to adjust i by the consumption conversion factor.

b. The savings premium needs to be estimated.

c. The discount rate which clears the market needs to be recalculated.

Relative Value of Different Income Flows

4.9   At this level of analysis the essential choices in weighting income flows are:

a. whether incremental private savings should have the same weight as incremental uncommitted government income (the numeraire) which can be used for investment, and

b. how much to scale down incremental consumption.

On the first of these, it is difficult to justify giving a lower weight to private savings (compared to the numeraire) in the absence of the distributional considerations discussed in chapter 5. The costs associated with public administration could even argue for a higher weight for private savings. This Guide recommends that at this level of economic analysis all savings should have the same value.

4.10   A main source of incremental consumption from projects is likely to be through wages. In paragraph 3.64 above it was argued that skilled labour can usually command an equivalent income in alternative employment and in these circumstances there will be no incremental consumption from this income flow. For some unskilled labour, however, there is likely to be incremental consumption and the use of a savings premium will modify the determination of the shadow wage rate (SWR). The new specification (slightly adapted from that in Little-Mirrlees) is:

$$\text{SWR} = \left\{ \begin{array}{c} \text{output} \\ \text{forgone} \\ \text{elsewhere} \end{array} \right\} + \left\{ \begin{array}{c} \text{cost of increased} \\ \text{consumption} \\ \text{resulting from} \\ \text{employment} \end{array} \right\} - \left\{ \begin{array}{c} \text{benefit of} \\ \text{increased} \\ \text{consumption by} \\ \text{wage earner} \end{array} \right\}$$

$$= \quad m \quad + \quad [c' - m] \quad - \quad \frac{(c - m)}{v}$$

$$= \quad c' - \frac{1}{v}(c - m)$$

where c' represents the total resources devoted to consumption as a result of this employment including urban overheads etc. (see paragraph 3.61).

c   is the consumption of the wage earner with the project.

m   is the alternative marginal product of the wage earner (assumed equal to his previous consumption level).

v   is the value of uncommitted government income relative to additional private consumption at the average level of consumption.

Each of these components is measured at border prices (ie in numeraire units).

57

4.11   When there is no premium on savings, as in the assumptions for basic allocative efficiency described in chapter 3, $v = 1$ and the formula above becomes:

$$SWR = c' - c + m$$

This is the valuation of unskilled labour given in paragraph 3.62, because $c' - c$ is the extra cost to the economy of the consumption imposed by this employment creation and m is the marginal product of labour in its best alternative use.[1] When there is a premium on savings, v takes a value greater than 1 and the SWR becomes higher. Similar treatment should be given to any other income flows which result in higher consumption. NPV is therefore reduced with a savings premium as compared with an analysis under the basic allocative efficiency conditions.

Estimation of Savings Premium

4.12   Paragraphs 4.6 and 4.7 explain that for a project yielding q in perpetuity, all of which is consumed, the savings premium is given by:

$$v = \frac{q}{i}$$

where v   is the value of uncommitted government income relative to additional private consumption at the average level of consumption,

q   is the marginal rate of return to public sector investments,

i   is the consumption rate of interest,

and all measurements are at border prices. Extra complexity is introduced, however, if it is assumed that part of q itself is saved and reinvested, resulting in further incremental returns. If, further, v is assumed constant over time, the following formula results:

$$v = \frac{q - sq}{i - sq}$$

where s   is the proportion of q which is in the form of uncommitted government income plus private savings (ie that proportion of the incremental returns which has the same value as the numeraire),

and   v, q and i are as specified above.

4.13   The longer formula in paragraph 4.12 will give a higher value for v than the shorter formula since q is greater than i. The underlying assumption of the short formula, that $s = o$, is probably unrealistic but it can be regarded as a minimum estimate for v.

4.14   At this point the warning in paragraph 4.3 above should be restated. The terms q, s and i must all be estimated empirically. The consumption rate of interest, i, is an elusive concept and q and s can be fairly volatile. Whatever value of v is derived it should be recognised as, at best, an approximation to be used with care.

---

[1] Total extra consumption is $c' - m$ but of this, $c - m$, the extra consumption of the wage earner, is both a cost and a benefit arising from the new employment.

4.15   Empirical estimates of v for Pakistan and India have resulted in values in the range of 1.6 to 1.8 (ie a savings premium in the range of 60% to 80%).[1] These suggest that values of v in the range of 1.0–2.0 would not be surprising, but the reservations outlined above about the nature of such estimates call for extreme caution in using a value of v greater than 2.0.

4.16   In practice the use of v may not have great effects. The savings premium is applicable to additional consumption only, and for most forms of factor income opportunity cost is close to market valuations. Traded goods often form a large proportion of gross project financial flows and the rewards of most factor inputs are no greater than their rewards in their alternative use, so additional income (and consumption) does not arise. The principal exceptions to this are likely to be profits and the wages of unskilled labour, and sometimes consumers generally benefit via lower prices so that income previously committed to purchasing the project's output is released for additional consumption elsewhere. These are the main forms of additional consumption where the savings premium is applicable and there are surprisingly few projects where they are significant. They crop up most often in rural development, where wages accruing to unskilled labour and profits received by peasant operators (or landowners) habitually comprise major elements of capital and operating costs. Otherwise a significant amount of the project surplus is often captured by the government (or is untraceable), as illustrated in the first detailed case study, and this proportion of the surplus is valued at the numeraire rate.

The Discount Rate

4.17   The marginal rate of return to public sector investments, q, is derived from basic allocative efficiency appraisals where this rate of return clears the market for public sector investment funds. The accounting rate of interest (ARI) is the rate at which the value of the numeraire falls over time and the formula for this is:

$$ARI = sq + \frac{(1 - s)q}{v}$$

where all terms are as defined above and are measured at border prices. The first term in this expression gives full weight to incremental income which is available for investment but the second term reduces the value of incremental income which goes to private consumption if v is greater than 1. In basic allocative efficiency analysis, v = 1 and the ARI = q. The formulation of the ARI above assumes that on average the consumption benefits of public projects accrue to people at the average level of consumption. The effect of introducing consumption weights for different categories of consumers is discussed at chapter 5.

4.18   If v is greater than 1 the value of ARI is lower than q. At the same time the net undiscounted benefits of most projects will be reduced because of the lower social value assigned to consumption benefits, while the lower ARI will raise discounted benefits (all consumption benefits are assumed to accrue to people at the average level of consumption). The ranking of projects will also

---

[1] These figures are derived from papers prepared by consultants for the World Bank. The methodology is explained in Squire, Little and Durdag in the bibliography, section C.

change: projects with proportionately high consumption benefits will tend to rank lower vis-a-vis those with high savings benefits.

4.19   The lower bound of the value of the ARI is the consumption rate of interest (i) which is conventionally taken to be about 5% in societies which are 'savings constrained'. However, using a rate as low as this would only be justified if the savings premium ($v > 1$) were assumed to be constant rather than likely to fall over time. Relaxing this assumption would yield values of the ARI lying between q and i.

4.20   The ARI under these conditions corresponds to the internal *social* rate of return on the marginal project and hence clears the market for investible funds by analogy with q under the efficiency conditions of chapter 3. In principle a value for this market clearing ARI can be obtained by analysis of the national investment budget and all candidate projects. However, in practice approximation to the true ARI can be obtained by using the formula in paragraph 4.17 and using estimates of q (probably from past estimates under efficiency conditions), as well as s and i.

General Comments on the Use of a Savings Premium

4.21   There may be a case for using a savings premium in a number of developing countries although the conditions for its use should always be judged very carefully. A vital condition is that alternative instruments for increasing savings are ruled out. There are further points of caution. First, the approach in this chapter must be national and system-wide. It must be consistent and must apply to all projects and the parameters used must be agreed nationally. A savings premium cannot be used *ad hoc*. Second, the empirical estimation of the parameters is not easy especially the somewhat elusive concept of the consumption rate of interest on which the value of the savings premium partly depends. Finally, the ARI is intended to balance the supply and demand for investible funds and use of the formulae provided here is an approximate guide for this. However, it is essential to monitor the figure used in practice and to make any adjustment required.

5
Distributional Issues

Introduction

5.1   If economic appraisal is not confined to basic allocative efficiency, the conventional approach is to introduce interpersonal distributional considerations alongside the use of a savings premium. The reason for taking account of both is that they depend on similar assumptions, namely that governments are unable to secure the distribution of income and level of savings they would like by use of the tax system and other fiscal instruments and that appropriate methods are available to assist in improving income distribution through project appraisal and selection. This argument is valid for most countries: where the circumstances are such that economic appraisal needs to take account of distributional considerations there is likely to be a need for a savings premium also. In the interests of clarity, however, this chapter will focus mainly on issues relating to the interpersonal distribution of the net income from a project. Later sections bring in aspects of the treatment of sub-optimal savings that were raised in chapter 4.

5.2   The main principle in considering the distribution of costs and benefits, and particularly the net income flows, arising from a project is implicit in the numeraire in this Guide, 'uncommitted government income...' (paragraph 2.5). Where governments have difficulty in obtaining the budget revenue needed to meet pressing claims for recurrent and capital expenditure, they are likely to consider increased income for certain sections of the population, notably the affluent, to have a lower value than extra revenue in their own hands. From this position it is a short step to the notion that different forms of income should have different values ('weights') in relation to the numeraire.

5.3   The opportunity cost principle which underlies all valuations emphasises the need to concentrate only on incremental income. It was noted in chapter 4 that many of the goods and services flows in projects do not generate incremental incomes: their cost or value in the project is the same as in their alternative uses. Only net income flows arising from the project qualify for the differential valuations needed when distributional weighting is introduced.

Identification of Beneficiaries and Weighting

5.4   The first step in such an analysis is therefore to identify the net income flows generated by the project. An example of how to do this is provided in the rock phosphate project which is the Detailed Case Study number 1 in Part II. Table I.15 there shows the distribution of total estimated net economic benefits. That example shows how diffuse the net benefits can be, with many different groups gaining. Box 5.1 provides a brief outline of how benefits were distributed in other case studies in Part II. An important point which emerges from these illustrations is that although the distribution of benefits was systematically addressed in almost all of these real-world projects, it was not done in a fully quantified manner in most cases. The reasons for this varied: in some cases the answer was obvious (beneficiaries were all of one type) but in others it was impossible to identify beneficiaries accurately.

Box 5.1   Estimating the Distribution of Benefits

The illustrative case studies reflect several different approaches to ana-lysing this aspect, as well as a variety of outcomes. The question was usually addressed.

Detailed Case No. 1 on the Rock Phosphate Project, contains a particu-larly detailed analysis in table I.15 of where the benefits go, covering both financial benefits and those associated with shadow pricing. Many of the income changes could be attributed to specific groups without difficulty, but some – for example, the ultimate beneficiaries from the lower input cost to the forward-linked manufacturer – could not. In DC 1, as one would expect from a public sector capital-intensive industry, a high proportion of benefits go to government. In the farming projects (DC 2, CS 4), and with rural roads (CS 3, CS 5) the main beneficiaries are identified as farmers. CS 1 and CS 2 both relate to the manufacture of intermediate products, so it is very difficult to say who the beneficiaries would be, apart from very small numbers of unskilled employees. The electricity cases (CS 7 and CS 8) and the Natural Gas Project (CS 12) involve some sales to final consumers but, more importantly, the sales are to other productive agencies. Who receives benefits from the latter type of use is difficult to say. Quite clearly electricity as a consumption good is primarily for the better off. Two utility projects (CS 9 and CS 10) on Village Electrification and Water Supply, were reported as being for relatively well-off areas. Few if any benefits would go to poor people, because there were not many of them! CS 14 – the woodlots case – could claim exceptionally favourable distribution benefits, with its labour-intensive production of fuelwood for use by low income people.

CS 13 raises the interesting question of the distribution of the benefits of port development between foreigners (shipowners) and nationals, and how far tariffs can be adjusted to capture them for the project agency. Of course, who ultimately receives the national component is impossible to assess, as the project is providing an intermediate service to every activity that involves trade through the port. Perhaps this project could claim, as CS 15 does (the single secondary school in a very small terri-tory) that all members of the community would benefit – every single family! But this is exceptional. In surprisingly few of the projects illus-trated was it possible to give a clear indication of which groups (or government) would be recipients of most of the net benefits that these activities might generate.

5.5   How to categorise net beneficiaries is an important preliminary question although the number of different groups to be recognised will often depend on the nature of the project. In most cases interest in categorisation is likely to centre on the income of the beneficiary, on welfare grounds, but the discus-sion of the savings premium in chapter 4 indicates that other possibilities exist.

A brief listing of possible criteria for classifying the different types of net beneficiaries includes:

- income/consumption level;
- propensity to save/consume;
- public/private sector;
- national/foreign;
- gender.

5.6 The importance of distinguishing project beneficiaries by gender deserves a little explanation. Failure to take full account of the role of women has been increasingly identified as a reason for projects not meeting their output goals, particularly in agriculture. In other cases the social effects have been less beneficial than were expected because needs and operations were considered only from the man's viewpoint. Box 5.2 outlines the gender aspects which were apparent in the case studies in Part II. The general message that emerges is that in most countries there is a need to consider the role of women in projects as both agents and beneficiaries. Usually this will require consultation in project design and appraisal, with women who will be involved in the project, and drawing on their views. For this reason a gender classification may be appropriate in considering the distribution of project benefits.

5.7 Once net project benefits have been identified and allocated appropriately to beneficiary groups, the next step is to 'weight' each group according to some generally agreed scheme. Some forms of net income – for example, that received by very poor people – might have a higher weight than the numeraire. Other forms will have lower weights. An illustration of how to derive numerical weights is in Appendix 5.1. An important point is that whatever the weights which are used, they must be applied to all projects consistently if the economic appraisal is to contribute usefully to project selection. Both costs and benefits can be affected (particularly if private capital is used) and this will cause changes in NPVs and the ranks of different projects.

Problems in taking Distribution into Account

5.8 Application of these principles runs into two major problems. The first is the identification of relevant net income streams (positive and negative) that accrue to particular groups. Projects can result in gains or losses to those engaged in them, to suppliers and consumers, and to other external groups. Even in apparently simple projects, the income change ramifications can be extensive. A manufacturing project may displace imports or augment exports and bring gains to employees and sponsors; local suppliers may also gain through increased demand but importers and transport undertakings may lose; consumers may enjoy lower prices or improved quality (consumer surplus); government should gain through direct taxes but may lose import duties; other local manufacturers may lose markets to the more efficient new project. Sorting out how much of the total allocative efficiency benefits going to each of the groups is obviously not easy to calculate unambiguously.

5.9 Infrastructure projects, a large part of investment in any economy, pose even greater identification problems. The output of roads, power developments, telecommunications, etc. are both consumption and intermediate goods or services. The ultimate beneficiaries or losers may be remote, physically and conceptually, from the project and almost impossible to track down. Box 5.1 mentions some of the problems that can arise. The rock phosphate project (Detailed Case Study 1) illustrates an apparently intractable problem – net benefits arising from price distortions, which may be diffused throughout the economy and are taken into account in the conversion factors used in economic appraisal.

Box 5.2   Women as Project Agents and Beneficiaries

It is increasingly recognised that, for reasons of efficiency as well as equity, the position of women must be considered during project design and at appraisal.

Women are the main productive agents in some projects, especially certain kinds of agriculture, so schemes aimed only at men may not work, and there may be no major beneficiaries. Other schemes – like women's literacy and mother-and-child health care – have women as the main targets. Other developments, though more general in nature, will mainly benefit women, though their involvement may be only as users of a facility. Village water supplies, rural electrification (CS 9) social forestry (CS 14) and public health programmes are common examples. In all of these cases, the position of women must be considered at all stages.

The Rural Development Project (CS 16) illustrates a situation where the need to recognise the important role of women was not perceived during design. Later, after implementation began, a specific component was developed to ensure their involvement and the better attainment of objectives. It is now common practice in ODA to take specific account of the needs of women in agricultural extension schemes.

Whereas in many cases women may be expected to be project beneficiaries, or losers, the gender of beneficiaries is frequently not referred to in project design and analysis. In many types of development, the benefits are general to all types of person, and the impact on women or any other particular group cannot be ascertained. Port or power developments may be examples. However, special implications for women were referred to in two of the illustrative cases. The Land Settlement Project, (CS 4) specifically allowed the innovation for women to become settlers holding land permits in their own right, while plans for off-farm earning opportunities for women's groups were included in the 'social infrastructure' provisions. These measures would ensure that some women were among the specific main beneficiaries of the scheme.

The Island Secondary School (CS 15) drew attention to a situation where women could be disadvantaged by the project. Education for both boys and girls would be improved, but in a situation of very limited employment opportunties. Despite attempts to avoid sex discrimination in jobs, there was a danger that, with greater numbers of qualified school leavers, however great the general value to them of better education, girl school leavers' employment prospects in the island could be made worse. This would not lead to rejection of the project, but emphasises the need for creating employment opportunities.

5.10   There will be considerable variation from country to country and from project to project in the problem of deciding who finally receives the net benefits. Only detailed analysis can provide reliable guidance.

5.11   The techniques for 'consumption weighting' described in Appendix 5.1 reveal the second major problem. Although various attempts have been made to derive weights through revealed preference (past government decisions) and other means, the results have all been subject to serious doubts. It does not seem likely that a set of weights can be determined objectively. As a result they are unlikely to command widespread acceptance and may not be sustainable over the longer term.

The Discount Rate

5.12   Incremental income accruing to people at *non*-average levels of consumption will be weighted differently. $v(c)$ is the weight attached to consumption of each beneficiary group while v remains the value of uncommitted government income relative to additional private consumption at the average level of consumption (paragraph 4.12).

5.13   Applying all these distributional weights to projects will change their undiscounted net benefits and alter the rankings of projects. A different project (from that under basic allocation efficiency or savings premium cases) will become the marginal project. The discount rate which clears the market for public sector investment funds will be derived from this project and will represent the consumption-weighted ARI. Suppose that the consumption benefits of the marginal project all accrue to a group of people with the same income. By analogy with the formula at paragraph 4.17 above, the ARI in this case will take the form:

$$ARI = sq + (1 - s)q \cdot \frac{v(c)}{v}$$

$v(c)/v$ is the value of this consumption relative to the public income numeraire. However, it is not realistic to assume that the consumption benefits of public projects will systematically accrue to groups whose consumption is more valuable than public investment. $v(c)/v = 1$ *on average* is a more reasonable hypothesis and the ARI formula then reverts to the form at paragraph 4.17 and q sets an upper limit on the ARI.

Sub-Optimal Savings

5.14   In most cases the use of consumption weights will be accompanied by a savings premium, for the reasons given in paragraph 5.1. The combined effects of consumption weighting and the use of a savings premium are likely to have significant effects on project results, as expressed through NPVs and project rankings, as well as on the rankings of alternative options within projects. The discount rate used will still need to be the market-clearing rate, derived from the marginal project when all appraisals are conducted using both consumption weights and the savings premium.

General Guidance

5.15   The full application of distributional weighting, including a savings premium, has scarcely been contemplated outside the academic literature. The reasons for this are indicated above: data requirements are high, estimation assumptions will border on the heroic for some areas of the analysis and the weighting system applied will always be open to challenge. But distributional issues are important and this Guide does not conclude that they should be ignored.

5.16 The principal advice to project designers and appraisers is that they should always consider the distributional implications of their work in broad terms. They should consider and try to determine which groups will be most affected by the project, how they can be usefully categorised and what will be the orders of magnitude. The decision process can be improved if it is informed by information such as 'The plant will create employment for 300 unskilled and semi-skilled workers, about half of whom will be women. Higher profits will be received by shareholders and consumers will benefit from prices about 10% lower. About 50 local craftsmen will lose their markets and there may be losses to importers of the product'.

5.17 Any attempt to go beyond this to a fully quantified distributional appraisal, in which consumption weighting is internalised, is a very big step. As with the savings premium, if consumption weights are to be used at all they must be used for all projects in a systematic way as set out above.

5.18 A final comment is to repeat earlier guidance on the use of economic appraisal throughout project preparation. This applies equally to distributional analysis, which is as much of a design tool as basic allocative efficiency analysis.

Appendix 5.1
Consumption Weights

1. If economic and fiscal policy is not adequate to promote a desired distribution of income between contemporaries, project choice can be used to contribute to this purpose. The value of the alternative patterns of distribution can be brought out in analysis by the use of a set of consumption weights. The essence of such a system is that the social value (consumption weight) attached to increases in consumption accruing to different people varies inversely with their consumption level. (In practice income may have to be used as a proxy for consumption.) Using a system of consumption weights encourages consistency between investment decisions (and indeed other forms of government intervention in the economy, such as consumption subsidies) and distributional goals.

2. The theoretical grounds for introducing consumption weights are strong. All governments face obstacles to redistribution via fiscal and macroeconomic measures. It may be cost-effective to use project choice, in addition to general economic instruments, to help achieve distributional goals. But the application of consumption weighting that favours high levels of consumption has implications for savings and the growth of consumption in the future. Moreover the effects of project choice may be irreversible in terms of the cost to future growth. Governments will need to consider future effects very carefully, and be certain that macro-economic measures to improve distribution are ruled out both now and in the foreseeable future, before they give prominence in project selection to high weights for the consumption of some groups.

Determining Consumption Weights for Project Appraisal

3.   Little and Mirrlees propose that the government should take a decision on the valuation to be given to extra income accruing to individuals with different levels of income or consumption.[1] They propose that there will be some level of personal income at which an extra unit of income is estimated to yield the same social utility as an extra unit available to the government. The weight given to an increment of income going to someone with this 'base' level of income b is unity, the same as for uncommitted social income. Further, they suggest a form of valuation function in which the weight attached to an extra unit of income declines as income levels rise, since it is assumed that the marginal social utility of income declines with higher income. Thus persons with an income higher than the 'base' level will have a weight less than one, but those with an income less than the base level will have a weight greater than one. How much less or greater than one will depend on the precise values chosen by the government as the weights given to different levels of personal income.

4.   If a parameter e is defined as the percentage increase in the marginal social value of consumption for a small percentage change[2] in the level of consumption – in other words, the elasticity of the marginal utility of consumption – the social value of a unit of extra consumption of people at consumption level c can be specified as v(c).

This will have a form such that:

$$v(c) = \frac{1}{c^e}$$

Also, at consumption level b, the base level,

$$v(b) = \frac{1}{b^e}$$

So

$$\frac{v(c)}{v(b)} = \frac{b^e}{c^e} = \left(\frac{b}{c}\right)^e$$

But we have defined v(b) as unity, so

$$v(c) = \left(\frac{b}{c}\right)^e \quad \text{when c is measured relative to b}$$

5.   This formulation of a function for the social value of incremental income in relation to levels of existing consumption permits consistent use of consumption weighting in appraisal, but it cannot be pretended that all difficulties are thereby removed. It is not always easy to identify beneficiaries, and their income levels, so it cannot be taken for granted that c will be known. A precise or narrow-range estimate of the value of b may not be readily secured, and e is a somewhat mystical coefficient whose estimation has an

---

[1] For simplicity, we make no distinction here between income and consumption.

[2] The case of large increases in income, eg when an agricultural labourer from the peasant sector is hired in the formal industrial sector, is also easily treated, through expanded formulae – see Little and Mirrlees (1974).

obvious political element. However, it can be observed that the higher the value of e the faster v(c) will fall as c rises: a government that is very concerned to redistribute income through project selection to the maximum extent possible will select a high value for e (say e = 2), and a government less concerned about this may use e = 1 (where v(c) falls in the same proportion as c rises), or less.

6. The investigator may be able to approximate to b by choosing an income level in the range between the level at which income taxation begins and the level above which relief, concessional food sales, and other social benefits end, though in practice there is seldom a systematic framework for consumer subsidy and other benefit thresholds. However, the level of the basic critical income level can be below the average income level.

7. The value of the elasticity e has a big effect on the weights. It has been suggested that it may fall in the range 0.5 to 1.5. The value of the weights at different income levels are as follows:

INCOME LEVEL		WEIGHTS			
(c as a fraction of b)	e = 0	e = 0.5	e = 1.0	e = 1.5	e = 2.0
1/4	1.00	2.00	4.00	8.00	16.00
1/2	1.00	1.41	2.00	3.83	4.00
1	1.00	1.00	1.00	1.00	1.00
2	1.00	0.71	0.50	0.35	0.25
3	1.00	0.57	0.33	0.19	0.11

Private Saving and Investment

8. Additional consumption and savings resulting from a private sector project will have to be carefully valued if the appraiser is concerned with distributional issues. As noted, the main additions to private consumption and savings are likely to be the result of profits, unskilled wage payments, reduced prices to consumers, and the availability of free or subsidised benefits.

9. All of these consumption gains may be valued using the method of consumption weights. But private savings are different. Invested, they will yield a future stream of private consumption and savings and taxes. Each element will require different weights. Savings in private hands may thus have a different value from savings in the hands of government. Where profits form a significant element in the incremental income flows resulting from a project, their proper valuation is likely to require particular care, once basic allocative efficiency has been superseded.

Alternative Approaches for Income Weighting

10. The method outlined above faces severe practical difficulties. Government may find it difficult to offer explicit judgements which will enable a set of consumption weights to be constructed. Arbitrary subjective choice is probably unavoidable, so the whole system becomes open to challenge.

11. An alternative method of determining weights was suggested in the UNIDO Guidelines.[1] It postulated that weights for income distribution and

---

[1] See glossary and section E of the bibliography.

regional benefits might be established *ex post*, through analysing the choices that decision-makers made between projects that offered alternative distributions of benefit. However, it has not proved possible anywhere to make this approach work. Decisions are not always consistent, and the relevance of this factor in any project decision may be difficult to assess.

12.   Doubts have been expressed[1] about the validity of applying distribution weights to all increases in consumption where the continuous elasticity equation is used. The objection is that too heavy a penalty is put on new benefits that go to people above the base level b. Extra consumption to very poor people should carry a premium – that is not disputed. But if the net benefits of production are all used for consumption, producers must need to be increasingly efficient the higher above b they are to create net benefits of equal value to those on lower incomes. This argument, which has been called a 'basic needs' approach to weighting, suggests premiums for people below the base income level but no penalties for those above it.

---

[1] See for example the bibliography reference (Section F) to Harberger.

6
Risk, Uncertainty and Sensitivity Analysis

General

6.1   Planning cannot avoid uncertainty. However good the planning, it is never possible to ensure that what is carried out will be what is planned. Unexpected changes can work to the advantage of the project, but often they have adverse consequences. An essential part of the planning, as well as of appraisal, is (or should be) consideration of what could go wrong, causing adverse departure from the envisaged pattern. Analysis can then investigate both the potential seriousness of such an effect and what might be done to avoid it or reduce either its occurrence or the harm it would do.

6.2   Appreciating and appraising individual or composite 'scenarios' of possible adverse effects can best be done by a specialist who is experienced in the type of project feature in view. However, this informed approach can be guided or supplemented by systematic numerical analysis of forecasts for the project.

6.3   Any appraisal requires forecasts of the future behaviour of variables in the cost and benefit streams. Very few project variables – be they physical quantities or prices – can ever be forecast with certainty. This chapter mainly outlines the elements of a systematic approach to assessing and handling uncertainty in economic appraisal. As suggested in chapter 3, it will always be sensible to show the results of a cost-benefit analysis as a range of values, reflecting major uncertainties, rather than as a single figure.

6.4   The approach and techniques outlined here are not relevant to economic appraisal only. They are equally applicable to financial analysis and other forms of appraisal – technical, social and others.

6.5   Underlying the discussion is a distinction between RISK situations, when the values of possible outcomes can be known and the probability of each can be estimated, and UNCERTAINTY, where the range of possible values may be estimated, but no probabilities can be attached. Situations of complete uncertainty in this sense are uncommon in most investment projects, though data problems can make probability estimation very difficult.

Expected Values

6.6   It is of great importance that the main final product of economic analysis calculations, the Net Present Value, should be as close as possible to an unbiased estimate of the expected outcome. This requires that unbiased estimates are used individually in the main calculation of the value of each of the various elements of the cost and benefit streams, through the lifetime of the project. Often the chosen value of a variable is derived through a combination of data and judgement, and cannot be exhaustively explained. However all values used in preparing forecasts for projects should be a consistent reflection of what the planner thinks will be the case. The pervasive and dangerous tendency towards optimism should always be remembered and guarded against. The values should reflect real expectations, not hopes. Wherever possible, the values used should have a basis in recorded experience, either in operations of the same kind or in pilot schemes. The evaluation of past projects and activities is an especially fruitful source of actual performance data, and of where uncertainties may arise. If the values and probability range of any parameter is critical to project selection and is knowable, but is unknown, the decision can be delayed until further time and resources have been applied to getting more detailed and more valuable estimates.

6.7 Technically, the expected value of a variable is the sum of its possible values at any point of time, each weighted by the probability of it occurring. In a limited number of cases it may be possible, on the basis of past experience, to construct a probability distribution of a variable. This will lie around a central value, which may reflect a long-term trend, as in forecasting future prices of a particular commodity, for example. Normally, however, when arriving at the expected value it will be possible to make only an informal assessment of the chance of the actual value falling either above or below the chosen central 'most likely' estimate. The implicit assumption usually is that the probabilities of possible outcomes will be 'normally distributed', in the statistical sense, about the central estimate. In some cases it may be clear that the range of fluctuation in a particular direction is limited, for example possible changes in crop yields. The assumption of a statistically normal distribution will then not hold, and care will be needed to ensure unbiased estimates of expected value.

6.8 The NPV of a project is itself a variable, the product of very many other variables. The NPV calculated on the basis of the chosen set of expected values for each variable is only one of a distribution of possible NPV values, which could cover a wide range. Assessing the riskiness of a project in the sense of estimating the probability of different values of the NPV is clearly an interesting but complex operation. It is discussed later in this chapter.

6.9 What is essential is to realise that the NPV could easily take a value very different from the main estimate – the 'base case' situation for which the main calculation has been derived. It will not be surprising if things work out in practice to be very different from the base case. To some extent, provision should be made through contingency allowances to cope with some departure from the expected cost forecasts. Also, sensitivity analysis should be used to establish what the effect will be on NPV (or any appraisal measure) of changes from their expected levels in the values of some key variables.

Contingency Allowances

6.10 Because we cannot generally be sure that costs will not exceed their expected levels, particularly capital costs, it is general practice to include in the estimates of capital costs of a project separate allowances for contingencies. Three kinds of cost are sometimes included under this heading, one of which is not really a contingency provision.

(a) Allowances are made to cover costs which have not been separately identified but which the project designers know from experience are

71

likely to arise during the construction period. A lump sum 'other expenses' item should be included in the estimates of costs to cover this assortment of small items. These are, however, expected costs. It can be foreseen that the allowance will be used, so these should be regarded as actually budgeted expenses, not as contingency items.

(b) Allowances are also budgeted to cover unexpected costs which may arise because of physical problems that arise during the construction period – for example, if unexpected expenses arise over the foundations of a building. This form of contingency allowance is a money sum which may be used to meet this need, if necessary. Its estimation is usually based on past experience of the probability of unforeseen costs arising and of their probable magnitude if they do occur. If, after careful consideration, the estimate is thought to be reasonable, the allowance should be regarded for appraisal purposes as part of the cost of the project, even though it may not have to be spent.

(c) Allowances are also required to cover price increases during the construction period.

6.11   In practice, a Physical Contingency Allowance, expressed as a percentage addition to total identified capital costs, is usually applied to cover case (b). It is important that this should be shown separately from the Price Contingency Allowance, which could be drawn on to cover price increases during the construction period. When all costs are expressed in terms of constant prices, no allowance for price inflation needs to be made in the economic appraisal, unless inflation produces a change in the relative prices of the project inputs and outputs. For economic appraisal, therefore, the 'other expenses' item should always be included. The Physical Contingency may be, but the Price Contingency should not.

6.12   Price increases will, of course, affect the project's finance flow, and for this purpose a careful estimate of price increases both during and after the construction period will be required. (This is illustrated in Detailed Case Study 1.) In most cases it will be necessary to consider separately the factors affecting the prices of imported items from those affecting the cost of local labour and materials, since inflation rates are likely to differ between world costs and domestic prices. So long as adequate provision for price increases is made somewhere in the cash flow calculation, it is immaterial whether the provision is made in the costing of the individual items, or whether it takes the form of a collective allowance for price increases.

Management

6.13   The supreme importance of good management for the success of a project must always be kept in mind. Beyond its cost, management is not a technical variable in itself that is embodied in project planning calculations. Nevertheless, the quality of management can have a big effect on the actual level of other variables, particularly those affecting performance. It is likely to affect not only the prices paid for inputs, or realised for outputs, but will also have an important effect upon the level of physical output of the project, and the productivity of labour, machinery and raw materials. Assessment of the quality of the management of a project will be one of the most significant issues, and often one that is subject to the greatest uncertainties. Some aspects of this very broad factor are discussed in chapter 8, which looks at institutional considerations.

Sensitivity Analysis

6.14   Sensitivity analysis is the quantitative process of seeing what change in the value of a dependent variable is consequent on a chosen change in the value of one or more of the variables that determines it. In economic analysis it generally involves considering the effect on NPV of plausible variations in some of the assumptions made. An alternative approach, sometimes used, is to calculate what degree of variation in a particular variable would, by itself, reduce the project NPV to zero. The likelihood of such variation occurring can then be assessed.

6.15   In addition to its value as information for project assessment, sensitivity analysis can help to guide project design. Some ways in which it helps are in:

(a) improving understanding of the nature and workings of the project, by seeing more clearly how change in one thing affects others;

(b) increasing expected NPV, by allowing the testing of variations in the design of the project;

(c) reducing risk by suggesting areas where particular precautions should be taken; and

(d) indicating areas needing more investigation to improve knowledge of the values likely to be taken by significant variables.

Changes in project design consequent on these considerations may not only reduce the lower level of the range of possible NPV values, but may also raise the expected NPV.

6.16   Sensitivity analysis is so important and valuable a guide to project design and analysis that it should be standard practice. Key variables whose variation should be studied will differ from project to project, but a number of standard tests will normally be considered, of which these are very common:

 – the price(s) of the main output(s);
 – the price(s) of the main input(s);
 – the volume of demand;
 – the level of capacity attained during the build-up period; and to be sustained in the long run;
 – the cost of investment, either as a whole or of specific items;
 – the duration of the investment period; and
 – the discount rate.

In manufacturing and agricultural projects, sensitivity tests may also cover the life of the main productive assets and variation in technical input/product ratios.

6.17   The use of sensitivity analysis in the illustrative case studies in this Guide is discussed in Box 6.1.

Independent variables

6.18   In some projects it will be appropriate to calculate in a mechanical way the effect on the NPV of an alteration in each of the main variables, taken one at a time. This alteration should represent a 'reasonably optimistic' and a 'reasonably pessimistic' value for each variable, though generally the pessimistic changes will be of most interest where the expected value of NPV is positive.

6.19   A simple and very common way of making sensitivity tests is just to consider the effects of a 10% variation up or down from the expected value of the variable concerned. A more elegant way of determining optimistic and pessimistic values might be to formulate a probability distribution of each variable and to 'truncate' it in such a way as to leave a 20% probability of the value of the variable falling at each end (in each 'tail') of the distribution. The values at these truncation points then become the alternative values to be used in the sensitivity analysis. In practice this could only be done in an approximate fashion – usually the appraiser can only make an informed guess of the probability distribution – but the purpose of this arithmetic is to test the sensitivity of the NPV to realistic changes in the values of different variables. Ten per cent variations are relatively modest for some types of project.

6.20   An alternative approach to seeing the effect of a given percentage change is to estimate how big a change in a given variable will produce an NPV of zero. This approach is the calculation of a 'switching value' of the variable. For example, what value of the main product of a revenue project would, by itself, give an NPV of zero? The likelihood of this level being reached might be assessed in a way that could clarify judgement more clearly than other sensitivity tests would allow.

6.21   In most cases it will be possible to identify crucial variables by a quick inspection of the statement of costs and benefits, but it may be necessary to carry out trial calculations of the effect of variations in the individual items. The number of variables considered must be a matter of judgement, but the aim should be to cover all of those which might influence the overall riskiness of the project's outcome and value. Where they occur, and are substantial, it is essential to give particular attention to assessing the importance of benefits which are difficult or impossible to value accurately, for example consumer surplus and other externalities.

Inter-dependence between variables

6.22 Frequently the effect of variation in one variable cannot be appreciated through a partial recalculation involving changes in that item alone, because of interdependencies. Variables may move together in the same or in opposite directions. Examples might be price and volume of output moving in opposite directions, or a relative rise in the price of labour implying a relative rise in the price of other labour-intensive inputs. Some of these inter-relationships may be relatively mechanistic or technical, but others may be linked in complex ways. The quality of management is often a major factor which can help to make everything go right or can allow it all to go wrong. The capacity level of working assumed will be a key variable for testing the importance of management. The project appraisal should aim to describe the important interdependencies between variables and quantify the effect of changes in them on expected NPV as far as possible. Where it is important, the effect of being 'reasonably optimistic' and 'reasonably pessimistic' about management should be illustrated.

Lack of symmetry in effects

6.23 The movement of a variable to either side of its expected value may have an equal and opposite beneficial or adverse effect on NPV, if the relationship between the variable and NPV is linear. In such cases, a 10% increase changes NPV by the same amount as a 10% decrease. However, the distribution of possible values of a variable may not be symmetrical about the expected value, and the variable may enter the NPV calculation in a non-linear way. Specially careful data preparation must be undertaken when variations in non-linear effects are being studied.

6.24 In other cases variation in either direction may have adverse effects on NPV. For example, if demand for berths in a port is above or below the optimal level, there will be higher total costs, either from more congestion and delay, or in excess capacity. For some design variables, a single least-cost or maximum net benefit level can be defined.

Flexibility in design

6.25 The way a project is designed can have an important effect on the extent of interdependence between variables and lack of symmetry in the distribution of possible NPVs about the expected NPV. If everything works as expected, the NPV may be high or acceptable, but if the plant is very specific and inflexible in design, any variation from the expected might only make the NPV worse. The design choice between flexibility and maximum efficiency often arises.

6.26 Improving the flexibility of design of a project can be a major way of increasing its expected NPV. Seeking to improve the design is part of the 'study of alternatives' which should be carried out from the first conception of the project, when alternative technical designs and possibilities can be drawn up, costed and appraised using the principles of economic analysis. The amount of inherent flexibility in a project is a significant element in its initial description. It is important to identify strategies for avoiding risks of loss or for taking advantage of opportunities of profit beyond the central expectation. If strategies are available for altering the composition of inputs and outputs, or if minor modifications enable unexpected demand to be met at much lower cost than otherwise, the expected NPV of the project may be higher than in the absence of these possibilities.

6.27 Staged development is one such strategy: provision in the first instance to meet demand over the first few years but designed to allow for easy expansion if demand does increase as expected. Standby power generators as back-up to grid supplies; two-stream processes with each capable of independent operation; designs which allow an extra deck to be added to a bridge if necessary; these are all examples of such flexible designs.

Reducing risk

6.28 Sensitivity analysis enables particular risks to be identified. It will generally be useful to consider ways in which the overall risk can be reduced, particularly if a large element of uncertainty is involved. Increased flexibility in design may be one possibility, but there may be situations where nothing more can be done to reduce risk by altering project design. However, the element of gamble in project selection might be reduced through other actions. Further market surveys or technical feasibility studies may, by giving more information, narrow the range of possible variation in key variables that need to be considered, thus allowing better-informed decisions.

6.29 Long-term contracts may reduce risks in input or output items. The incorporation of a contingency allowance for unexpected construction costs converts part of the risk into a cost. Where management is an important source of risk it may be possible to change the design of the project to reduce the requirement for management expertise; or arrangements may be made for particularly skilled management to be associated with the project, eg through technical co-operation with a private firm with experience in the particular field concerned, or by temporarily involving foreign experts and consultants. Each option will normally involve a cost to be weighed against the benefit of risk reduction. Sensitivity analysis will indicate the areas where further attention to reducing risks may be most worthwhile.

Use of computers

6.30 The widespread availability of desk-top computers and of discounting software allows numerical sensitivity analyses to be undertaken easily. Having machines to do the many calculations without arithmetic error means that much more can be attempted. The temptation to present a vast array of NPV values covering every kind of possible variation in variables must be avoided, but it will become increasingly common for this planning and analysis device to be used at all stages in project preparation and appraisal.

Risk Analysis

6.31 Sensitivity analysis is a technique for identifying and evaluating as far as possible the relative importance of the various items entering the cost-benefit stream. It is an essential element of any economic analysis. Apart from the considerations set out above, it will provide a valuable indication of the usefulness of undertaking detailed work on any particular element in the cost-benefit analysis.

6.32 Sensitivity analysis is therefore the first step in establishing the riskiness of a project. In itself it does not necessarily give precise guidance as to the acceptability or otherwise of the risk. Nevertheless it may often arise that the sensitivity analysis gives such a clear indication of the importance of the uncertainties involved that the decision becomes obvious. For example it may be that, taking the worst plausible combinations of assumptions, the project still has a satisfactory NPV. There may be cases, however, particularly with large projects, where the answer is by no means clear cut, and the possibility of large losses cannot be ignored. It may be desirable, therefore, to undertake more detailed anlaysis to provide tests for the acceptability of the degree of risk involved. Generally, this involves trying to assess the probability of a loss being incurred.[1] For these purposes the analysis is rather drawn out, and it is not possible to lay down simple rules. The theoretical background is set out and the procedure is illustrated in texts listed in the bibliography (especially in sections H and I), but the formal technique of 'Risk Analysis' is unlikely to be used often for economic appraisal except in the largest projects.

Avoiding Unacceptable Risks

6.33 Some investments might involve the risk of a catastrophe occurring from technical or operational causes. A dam or bridge could fail. Poisonous or radio-active chemicals may escape into the atmosphere or into rivers and the groundwater system. Buildings might collapse or tunnels cave in.

6.34 Events of this kind are potentially so cataclysmic that they may be regarded as altogether unacceptable, irrespective of when they may occur. If the possibility of such a thing occurring could only arise in the distant future, it might be argued that the discounted value of the cost involved would be so low that it could be disregarded. However, this discounting effect is generally overridden by the feeling that no plan that includes the possibility of catastrophe at any time should be admitted.

6.35 Generally this threat is handled through the establishment of strict design standards. In some situations, technical designs are available so that the possibility of catastrophe is completely avoided. An example would be the choice (possibly at higher cost) of a system of chemical processes under which the existence of highly toxic intermediates was completely avoided. At the other extreme are situations where any possibility of a particular event is seen as completely unacceptable, so activities involving that risk are entirely ruled out. However, in very many other cases, the design approach must be to set standards which, though they cannot eliminate the risk of catastrophe, reduce the probability of it occurring to acceptably low levels. An example might be a one in ten thousand risk of failure during the lifetime of any installation. This will not remove the risk but would reduce it to an 'almost never' possibility.

---

[1] This is the case in economic and financial appraisal but formal risk analysis has many other applications, of course. It is regularly applied in engineering design, and environmental assessment is likely to make increasing use of this tool.

6.36   The responsibility rests with governments for deciding which risks must be avoided entirely and which others call for minimum design standards. The standards must then be set and enforced. Advice on some design aspects is given by international agencies, like the International Atomic Energy Authority, but others are purely engineering matters that must be determined either as general specifications or to meet problems encountered in specific project proposals. The standard should be set and made known before detailed design begins. Assessing whether they have been met is a feature of the technical appraisal. The economic and especially the social and environmental questions arise in setting the standards, not in appraising the projects.

Government and Risk

6.37   It is sometimes argued that public sector decision-makers should not be too preoccupied with avoiding the risk of economic or financial failure by projects which are otherwise acceptable. Guiding economic and social development cannot be made a risk-free process. Individuals and private agencies may be unable to take big chances, because the failure of one activity could threaten the position of the whole unit. However, because of its size, and the large number of investments being made, government need not be so concerned. Losses on some projects are likely to be matched by gains on others. Risk avoidance would become important only when an individual project was very large in relation to the economy as a whole, or any part of it – a region or town, say, a sector or sub-sector.

6.38   Whatever the merit of this 'pooling' argument, it is clear that government must accept some risks in development. But this does not invalidate the need to consider the riskiness of any proposed project. Simply considering the question carefully can help planners to design projects that are valuable but less risky than other alternatives. A design variant or a project that is both better (higher NPV) and less risky (however measured) than an alternative will, of course, be preferred. Difficulty arises where a trade-off has to be made between the level of expected return, and the level of riskiness.

6.39   Ultimately, the real choice must be made by the decision-taker, rather than by a technocrat inflexibly applying simplistic rules, but the good project analyst will ensure that decision-makers have available to them valuation measures and comment that will inform the decision.

6.40   It is inevitable that undesired inconsistencies regarding risk-taking and risk-aversion will appear in project choices. This is particularly so where decision taking is de-centralised, and it may be administratively difficult to ask the opinion of high-level personnel about all projects. Rules can be specified to provide guidelines for decision-making practice. For instance, the rules might specify the size of projects that should be subject to risk analysis. They may also specify that projects should be rejected if the probability of a negative NPV is estimated to be greater than, say 20%, with a different cut-off point (say 10%) for large projects.

7
Financial Planning and Analysis of Projects

Introduction

7.1   Economic appraisal is the primary means of determining whether a proposed investment is worthwhile. It also provides the main basis for recommendations on pricing policy. The main purpose of financial appraisal is to check that the project is financially sustainable and will have sufficient funds to meet its commitments at each stage of its life.

7.2   The bulk of this chapter relates to new, commercial projects such as the rock phosphate project discussed in the First Case Study. Discussion in this chapter is an oversimplification in two main respects. First, in many instances, proposed projects will be undertaken by existing agencies or be extensions to existing activities. Examples are utility projects or expansion of agricultural services. In these cases the financial appraisal will need to consider the expected financial position of the agency as a whole. This particularly applies where the proposed project is an integral part of a larger investment programme and cannot be appraised in isolation, such as with any power systems.

7.3   A second qualification is that many projects are undertaken by non-commercial agencies, reliant on grants or annual budgetary votes for part or all of their revenue rather than on selling goods and services. Where the agency is financially autonomous the commercial type of analysis discussed below can still be used with some amendments. For government departments normal financial analysis will not be appropriate, but there will still be important financial issues to consider; these will include the adequacy of recurrent budget provision and of financial management. Box 7.1 provides references to case studies where the former was an issue; the latter is discussed in chapter 8.

The Framework for Financial Analysis

7.4   This section spells out the framework for making financial judgements on an enterprise. It is followed by a section on the Financial Analysis of projects. This shows whether an economically satisfactory project is likely to be financially viable also.

Financial Statements

7.5   The normal financial statements which are produced by district agencies or companies are:
   - an income and expenditure account;
   - a balance sheet;
   - a cash flow statement.

These will often be supported by supplementary schedules which show how elements of the main statements have been calculated.

7.6   For overall appraisal and, subsequently, to report on financial performance these statements usually show annual figures. For detailed planning of implementation and subsequent operation, however, forecasts are often needed for much shorter periods especially for cash flow. Where liquidity (ie the capacity of the agency to meet its financial commitments as they fall due) is a serious problem, cash flow forecasts may be needed for each month or even shorter periods and will be reviewed and revised frequently.

7.7   Financial forecasts are usually prepared in constant prices, taking into account only relative price changes.[1] Unfortunately, where a project or agency is funded in whole or part by loans, the use of constant prices does not enable the analyst to avoid the complications caused by having to forecast inflation. Loan repayments and, usually, interest will be expressed in current prices and may be payable in a different currency. Conversion to constant prices will require an assessment of future inflation and exchange rates to ensure consistency with other elements of the forecasts.

7.8   Inflation estimates will also be needed in order to forecast the overall cash requirements of the project, as a basis for putting together a financing plan. Many projects run short of funds before they are fully operational.

---

[1] Relative price changes are discussed more fully in paragraph 3.8.

Where this is due to delays in implementation it cannot be guarded against, except by taking a cautious view of the likely speed of implementation. In many cases, however, problems arise because of unrealistic inflation estimates.

7.9 A major complication in assessing historical accounts arises over the convention of preparing financial statements on the basis of historic costs, ie assets and liabilities are valued at the costs prevailing at the time when they were purchased or incurred. This primarily affects the balance sheet and ratios associated with it. Over time the balance sheet becomes a blend of assets and liabilities valued on different bases. Thereby concepts such as a return on capital employed (paragraph 7.27) when applied to the historic costs of earlier investments become meaningless. These difficulties led to much discussion about current cost accounting when UK inflation was high; this involved revaluing the balance sheet onto a common price basis. Practical difficulties and a substantial fall in inflation rates have caused current cost accounting to fall back out of favour in the UK. It is, however, a serious issue in many developing countries which have high inflation rates and rapidly depreciating currencies.

7.10 The form of financial forecasts and accounts will vary according to the type of project. Box 7.2 provides an outline of the contrasting presentations for the two main case studies in Part II.

Box 7.2   Forecast Accounts and Analyses

DC 1, the Rock Phosphate Project, illustrates the full set of forecast accounts appropriate to a revenue project, and additional financial analyses which are useful are also shown there and in Appendix 7.1

Accounts of this kind will be required for all revenue-earning corporate bodies, including agencies like those responsible for power, water supply, gas and port operation that are illustrated in Case Studies 7 to 13. However, in all of those cases except the last, the project is to be undertaken by an existing agency. The preparation of forecast accounts for them must cover, in a single set of statements, all of the agency's activities, not just those affected by the project. Inevitably this creates more complex account-drafting work than is illustrated by DC 1, a brand new, single unit operation.

Financial analysis of a different kind is illustrated in DC 2, the Basin Irrigation Scheme. Cash forecasting there relates to budgets for small farms, hundreds of which will be the separate business units at the core of the production process. In such projects only one or a few specimen 'model' farm plans can be estimated. As well as providing a basis for testing technical feasibility (land use, labour needs and supply, water and draught power available, etc.) they are the basis for budgets that indicate credit needs, liquidity, loan repayment capacity and expected incremental incomes, in each farm, all of which are likely to have a strong influence on the incentives for farmers to join the scheme and to follow the proposed production systems.

The Income and Expenditure Account

7.11 This records income and expenditure over a period, usually twelve months. In commercial accounting, it is prepared on an accruals basis. This means that money earned or due to be paid, for example for electricity supplied or for materials received, is taken into account whether or not cash payment has been made. This contrasts with cash accounting systems, normally used by government department, whereby only cash received or paid is included in the income and expenditure account.

7.12 Accrual accounting gives a better picture of the trading position of a commercial agency because the income earned from the agency's activities is matched with the expenditure incurred and resources consumed in producing that income. Distortions arising from timing differences are minimised. The Income and Expenditure account must, however, be assessed in conjunction with the balance sheet (paragraph 7.21).

7.13 Table I.5 in Case Study 1 shows a typical layout for an income and expenditure account. The first part is the Trading Account. It deducts the cost of goods sold from the value of sales to arrive at a gross or trading profit. The *cost of goods sold* is measured by adding the cost of stock purchased during the year to the opening value of stock and then deducting the value of stock at the end of the accounting period. The difference between the cost of goods sold and sales is called the gross, or trading, profit. This difference is often expressed as a ratio, referred to as the *gross margin*, which is calculated as follows:

$$\frac{\text{Sales minus cost of goods sold}}{\text{Cost of goods sold}} \times 100$$

7.14 Sales forecasts are a key element in any financial appraisal and are based on the demand analysis which forms part of the economic appraisal. In the demand analysis the quantity of goods sold will have been assessed taking into account the expected price as well as other issues such as growth of the economy, incomes, the overall market for the product concerned and competitive conditions. The level of prices, or tariffs, is frequently a political issue in public sector projects where prices are not determined by competitive forces. Box 7.3 refers to examples in the case studies. Where prices are expected to change in real terms, for example in order to meet a particular financial target, it is essential to review the effect such changes may have on quantities. An unsatisfactory financial result cannot simply be remedied by increasing prices in isolation. For large projects, and where adequate data is available, econometric models may be used to assess and forecast price elasticity, ie the impact of changing prices on the level of demand. In many cases, however, the assessment will be a matter of judgement. In either case, the elasticity assumption is an area of uncertainty and merits later monitoring.

7.15 To derive estimates of *operating profit* from gross profit in the profit and loss account, it is necessary for indirect, overhead costs and depreciation to be deducted. In forecasting costs, consideration should be given to the extent to which they will vary with the scale of production or are fixed. Some costs which are fixed in the short term, such as administrative overheads, may increase if the project expands significantly over its life.

Box 7.3   Tariffs and Charges

Autonomous agencies must raise charges from their clients to meet some or all of their financial needs. 'Commercial' agencies like those illustrated in DC 1, CS 1 and CS 2, (mining and manufacturing) fix their sale prices within the limits set by alternative suppliers on a profit maximisation basis. However, utility agencies are usually public monopolies, whose pricing has no competitive limitations but often has a 'social' content. The general objective for these agencies to cover their finance needs from revenue is reflected in the three electricity cases, the two water cases, and in the port project. In some of these projects, it was recognised that tariffs were too low, even without the new financial obligations that the project financing would bring. In some of the utility cases (CS 7, CS 9 and CS 11), tariff policy and levels had recently been revised to an adequate level. In other cases (CS 8, CS 10 and CS 12) new, higher tariff level policies were agreed as part of the project negotiations. Higher charges were needed to cover the cost of project loans but it was recognised that, while they should increase with general price rises, the real burden would decline as the finance cost elements fell.

In two cases, tariff levels had not been fixed. The Port Investment (CS 13) was to be associated with advisers who would recommend specific tariffs consistent with agreed financial objectives. DC 2 involves a high-cost irrigation project where the national level of fees would not cover the recurrent cost of off-farm agencies. Fundamental policy issues were involved, as well as financial questions.

Tariff level concerns of a different kind arise in CS 12, the Natural Gas Project. That development involved the exploitation of non-renewable reserves of gas and a petrol-like condensate in the gas. Production costs were very low, and small charges allowed a very satisfactory cash flow. However, it was recognised that an additional and increasing Depletion Premium should be added to the sale price. This sum, which is based on the cost of the more expensive substitute fuel needed when the reserves ran out, would allow a more economic allocation of the gas (through simple price effects) to those uses that would gain most benefit from it, while it lasts. This increased price would mean the generation of large surpluses in the National Gas Corporation, which gave the project a substantial resource mobilising value additional to its other benefits.

7.16   Depreciation is the value of the fixed assets (buildings, plant, equipment) of the agency which is estimated to have been used up in the course of the accounting period. This treatment contrasts with economic analysis where the whole cost is entered at the time of purchase. It also differs from the cash flow approach where capital receipts and expenditure are shown when received or incurred followed by outflows in accordance with loan repayment schedules. It is usually calculated in historic accounts on a straight-line basis, ie if an asset lasts ten years then one-tenth of its cost is attributed to each year, but there are alternatives, such as applying a fixed percentage to a reducing balance. Where assets are bought at different times and have varying lives, it is often necessary to prepare detailed schedules of expenditure and depreciation (see Table 1.4 in Case Study 1). In forecast accounts, depreciation is shown at the rates allowed by the tax authorities in order to allow realistic assessment of tax liabilities.

7.17 Operating profit may be shown before or after interest and tax. There are uses for each presentation but it is essential to be sure that the appropriate figure is being used (see, for example, the formula for the return on capital employed in paragraph 7.27). Calculation of interest charges often requires iteration of the cash flow statement in order to take into account interest earned or payable on cash balances or overdrafts.

7.18 In some cases operating profit is then adjusted to take account of extraordinary items, such as redundancy or moving costs. These are shown separately because they are regarded as exceptional items falling outside the normal operating activities of the agency. Furthermore the accounts and associated ratios would otherwise give a misleading picture compared with other years.

7.19 The calculation of the tax payable may be a complicated issue, particularly where a project forms part of a larger enterprise. The liability will depend on local law with regard not only to tax rates but also capital allowances and offsets against losses in previous periods or other parts of the business. With the public sector, tax calculations will not be of great importance from the profitability viewpoint and approximate estimates only will be adequate. Cash flow implications, however, may compel more thorough analysis. For private companies, tax considerations may be crucial to profitability, especially where foreign investors are involved.

7.20 The final part of the Income and Expenditure Account is the *Appropriation Account* showing how any profits or losses are to be shared between reserves and dividends. While this is often not included in forecast project accounts it is of importance where the agency concerned is expected to finance part of its investment from retained earnings or where fluctuations in profitability may make it desirable to hold reserves. Excess distribution of profits to shareholders can cause later financial problems. Where institutions are expected to meet part of their investment expenditure, *a self-financing ratio* is often calculated and targets may be set for it. This can be useful in financial analysis and a target may be set to ensure that the institution will meet its investment commitments and their financing.

The Balance Sheet

7.21 The Balance Sheet provides a snapshot picture of the assets and liabilities of an agency at a fixed point in time. A typical format is shown in Table 1.6 of Case Study 1. The main elements are:
- *Fixed Assets:* shown net of accumulated depreciation over their lives thus far;
- *Current Assets:* mainly stocks (raw materials, work-in-progress and finished goods), debtors and cash or short-term deposits;
- *Current Liabilities:* tax due and creditors (where payment is due to be made in the next twelve months);
- *Long Term Liabilities:* loans and other creditors (including tax) due in over twelve months;

– *Capital and Reserves:* share capital (ordinary and preference) and reserves (eg out of past profits or due to revaluation of assets), often known
as shareholders' funds.

7.22 A balance sheet will often refer to *net assets*, which equals *capital
employed.* These are usually defined as:

Fixed assets + current assets − current liabilities = long term liabilities +
shareholders funds.

The Cash Flow Statement

7.23 The importance of this statement lies in showing where an agency's
funds are coming from, how they are used and whether there is sufficient
liquidity to enable financial commitments to be met. It is perfectly possible,
particularly with a fast growing company, for a business to be profitable but to
go bankrupt for lack of cash to finance increased stocks and debtors.
Companies in financial difficulties may need to forecast cash flow even on a
daily basis, since the timing of receipts and payments becomes extremely
important.

7.24 Table 1.3 of Case Study 1 shows a very detailed cash flow forecast. A
more typical case would consolidate all profit and loss account figures into an
operating profit figure for each year. To this would be added depreciation,
which would have been deducted in the profit and loss account because
depreciation is not a cash cost. Figures would then be included for such items
as capital receipts, loan repayments, changes to the level of debtors and
creditors and tax payments.

Ratio Analysis in the Interpretation of Accounts

7.25 Some key ratios may assist in assessing the financial viability of a new or
existing institution or project from projections or from its financial accounts.
Ratios are better measures than simple financial values in overcoming some of
the difficulties caused by changes in price levels or by comparisons of institutions of different sizes. They may be ratios or percentages, and are best used
as trend information or with comparative data for similar institutions. Common
sense and a questioning mind are also essential. Unfortunately, it is not possible to prescribe fixed targets for these ratios as a simple way of judging
success or failure. Most ratios will vary from sector to sector and in different
countries. This presents particular problems in developing countries where
comparators are much less likely to be available than in the UK. Rather than
seeking absolute answers to whether an organisation is performing well, ratio
analysis is better used to build up an overall picture and to identify areas for
closer examination.

7.26 The ratios described here measure the financial position or performance of commercially-oriented institutions, and they are also relevant to
individual projects. There are many possible ratios. The intention here is to
specify a few that relate to key financial features. Limited time will be available for analysis. Use of these ratios will help to identify where further analysis
might be justified. Other useful measures are given in standard texts on
accountancy and financial management.

7.27　These ratios are illustrated in Appendix 7.1 by reference to the Rock Phosphate Project, Detailed Case Study 1 in Part II.

A. Profitability: Return on Capital Employed (ROCE)

The purpose is to measure how efficiently management is in generating funds through the use of its financial capital. The formula suggested is:

Profit (Net Income) before tax and interest payable × 100
Share capital plus Reserves plus Long Term Debt

The historic cost convention (paragraph 7.9) often renders this ratio meaningless because figures for capital employed are so out of date. It is therefore desirable for assets to be revalued regularly in order to arrive at useful ratios. The ROCE should not be presented without explanation on this point.

B. Financial Structure: Gearing Ratio

This demonstrates the relative proportions of debt and equity in financial structure. It provides some indications of scope for further borrowing and the relative importance of interest payments to the financial performance. The formula is:

Long term debt
Equity.

There is no specific level for this ratio, though there are often rules of thumb for particular types of enterprise. Where debt is high relative to equity the risk of financial problems increases, since debt service payments have to be maintained in bad times as well as in good, whereas dividends to equity holders may be reduced. Conversion of debt to equity is one way to strengthen the balance sheet of a company in financial difficulties.

C. Financial Structure: Debt Service Coverage

This shows the extent to which uncommitted (ie after tax) internally generated funds cover annual debt service (interest and principal). The formula is:

Profit (Net Income) after tax + interest on long term debt + depreciation
Debt Service

Clearly this ratio must always be above 1 if debt is to be serviced. How much greater it needs to be is dependent on the perceived risk of adverse fluctuation in results from year to year. It will also depend on the gearing ratio.

D. Liquidity

There are two common liquidity ratios; the current ratio and the quick (or Acid Test) ratio, which assess whether current liabilities can be met when due.

The current ratio formula is:

Current Assets
Current Liabilities

The quick ratio is often preferred because some assets (eg stocks) may not be readily convertible to cash. This is calculated as:

Current Assets — Stocks
Current Liabilities

If the ratio is below one, the institution would theoretically be unable to meet its debts as and when they are due. In practice, however, some companies operate quite successfully on ratios of less than one.

E. Management of Working Capital

i. *Debtors*

Excessive debtors could indicate poor financial management, problems with a particular class of debtor and/or liquidity problems. A common indicator for a business with a reasonably smooth sales profile is:

$$\frac{\text{Year end debtors} \times 365}{\text{Sales}} = \text{Collection Period in days}$$

An analysis of the age of debts will often provide useful additional information.

ii. *Stocks*

Stocks vary from raw materials for a manufacturer to spare parts for a utility or stocks of finished goods. The following formula is most appropriate to manufacturing, but it can assist generally in interpreting all stock levels over time and between like organisations:

$$\frac{\text{Sales for year}}{\text{Stocks at year end}}$$

A low figure may indicate poor management of procurement or of the manufacturing process; it may also be caused by substantial stocks of unsellable goods which are really worth much less than indicated. A low value to stocks could be a symptom of financial difficulties, with insufficient funds available to maintain supplies of materials at an efficient level.

iii. *Creditors*

This is commonly measured by:

$$\frac{\text{Year end creditors} \times 365}{\text{Purchases}}$$

Where an organisation has liquidity problems this figure will be relatively high. The result may be difficulty in obtaining necessary supplies. On the other hand, a very low figure while arguably a sign of financial strength may be an indication of unsophisticated financial management, failing to make use of available credit periods.

7.28   The examples in Appendix 7.1 have comments on the adequacy of each ratio in relation to that particular type of enterprise, a mining company. Different types of enterprise will have different ratios: for example, an agricultural marketing corporation would be expected to have a poorer working capital ratio than a bus company. The interpretation of financial ratios needs to take account of type of institution (or project), the performance of similar institutions (possibly in other countries) and trends over time.

Unit Costs

7.29   Unit cost figures provide a basis of comparison of efficiency between similar activities and over time. They are frequently used with non-revenue

87

projects where output cannot easily be valued. Some simple examples are:

- current cost per child in schools,
- road maintenance costs per mile,
- water supply costs per 1000 gallons.

Where costs include a significant capital element the problem of valuation of capital employed (paragraph 7.9) makes calculation difficult. Annual depreciation costs may be used where capital costs have been revalued.

7.30 The main limitation of unit cost measures, apart from calculation problems, is the difficulty of ensuring that the output is of similar quality. For example, a low cost per child in schools may mean that teachers are poorly paid and little is spent on educational materials rather than mean high efficiency.

Financial Analysis of Projects

Introduction
7.31 Although the economist will rely primarily on economic analysis to assess the case for a project, financial forecasts and analysis will often have an important influence on project design. In extreme cases, financial issues may present such difficulties that a project requires revision or cannot be undertaken at all despite having an adequate economic rate of return. This section discusses the main issues which are likely to arise.

Estimation of Investment Requirements
7.32 The investment required often includes not only capital expenditure but also provision for interest incurred during construction, for working capital and for initial operation or start up costs. Although the project will have been justified on the basis of constant price estimates, it is essential for there to be an analysis of total investment needs in current prices, as a basis for a financing plan. Timing will be important, not only because of inflation (paragraph 7.8) but also to ensure that finance will be available at the time required, and that it will not be drawn down too early resulting in unnecessary financing costs.

Analysis of the Financing Plan
7.33 It has been noted that the balance between equity and loans is an important issue and that excess reliance on loans increases the debt service burden. There may be other reasons for wishing to see a significant proportion of equity. Major equipment suppliers or management companies, for example, may perform better if they have an equity stake in the success of the project.

7.34 Loans for project investment may be available from several sources with different conditions attaching, and each should be tested for financial acceptability. Loans may differ in respect of these aspects:

- the interest costs,
- other charges, eg administration charges,
- the required pattern of repayment,
- the currency of loan and repayment,

- the security and guarantees required,
- the timing of availability of funds, and
- any benefits from grace periods.

7.35   The choice between different methods of feasible finance is an important issue in planning the financing of loan based projects. A number of
standard texts explain how to assess the value of alternative forms of finance.[1]

Assessment of Financial Stability

7.36   Even economically worthwhile projects may have financial problems
due, for example, to:

- financial prices of inputs and outputs differing from economic values
  (eg some inputs are highly taxed or output prices are controlled by
  Government);
- irregularities in the timing of revenue and costs either in the course of a
  year or between years;
- concentration of loan payments;
- increased requirements for working capital.

Short period cash flow forecasts should be prepared in order to identify
whether such problems are likely to arise. This is needed before the project
is approved since it may have implications for the structure and financing of
the project.

Rates of Return

7.37   Estimation of a financial rate of return on a project is illustrated in
Table I.10 in Part II. This is often done as an intermediate stage to preparing
an economic rate of return. It is, otherwise, of limited value, except that where
the project forms part of a larger entity which has financial targets it gives
some indication of whether the project contributes to them or will make them
more difficult to achieve. The rate of return to equity can also be calculated
from the Cash Flow Statement.

Non-Revenue Projects

7.38   Although the range of analysis in non-revenue projects will be much
more limited, it is still important. The primary issue is likely to be the availability of funds to meet recurrent costs. Budgetary problems in many countries
have led to failure to make adequate recurrent provision. This has often
reduced the benefits achieved or even led to collapse of projects after the
end of outside support.

7.39   Recurrent costs should always be estimated in detail so that the expected source of finance, usually government, can see the size and timing of
finance required. Estimates should be discussed with the Ministry of Finance,
from whom assurances that provision will be made in future budgets should
be sought.

---

[1] See for example the book by C. Harvey in Section I of the bibliography.

7.40   Where future recurrent support is uncertain it will in some instances be desirable to review project design to see whether the need for recurrent finance can be reduced. It may, for example, be justified to incur greater capital expenditure in order to reduce future maintenance requirements.

7.41   In many cases individual projects are considered as part of a larger investment programme for an institution. In some of these, projects may be interdependent so that the effect of the project under review cannot be separately identified. In these cases, financial appraisal will include a review of the institution's past financial performance. Financial ratios analysis discussed above will form an important part of this along with the assessment of financial management outlined in paragraphs 8.8–8.25.

7.42   Based on the appraisal and on any comparative performance data, a range of financial performance targets will usually be prepared for the institution as a whole. The range of targets, and the degree and timing of any improvement embodied in them, will be a matter of judgement in each case. Typically, the indicators might include:
- *Return on capital employed* (revalued)* as a measure of overall profitability;
- *Improved working capital management* (debtor days, creditor days, stocks);
- *Increased productivity* (sales per employee, total costs per employee).

It is likely that certain physical indicators of efficiency and effectiveness will also be included in any set of targets. This is particularly important where prices are not competitively determined.

Accounting Arrangements

7.43   While many projects fall naturally into a commercial or government ministry structure, issues do arise over whether proposed accounting arrangements are appropriate. Some activities may be undertaken either as part of a ministry, with accounting integrated with other activities, or be given an independent status through establishing a separate body and simply making the project self-accounting. In small countries even commercial activities such as power supply often start as part of a ministry, and subsequently are made self-accounting as one step on the way to autonomous operation. Choices may be more difficult with such activities as vehicle maintenance or plant pools. Such activities are often run on a self-accounting basis with costs being charged out to users. This has the advantage that users are faced with the costs of the decisions rather than making excess demands on 'free' services. This consideration should be an important factor in reviewing accounting arrangements. Weight should also be given, however, to the size of the project, to local capacity and to the need to avoid each project imposing slightly different requirements on local systems.

---

* See paragraph 7.27A.

Appendix 7.1
Financial Ratios Illustration

Paragraph 7.27 listed seven important financial ratios that can be usefully calculated in the financial analysis of a business. The seven ratios are illustrated here, using figures for Year 4 in the forecast financial tables for the Rock Phosphate Project, the first Detailed Case Study in Part II of the Guide. These figures relate to forecasts for the business, whereas the ratios are more often used to analyse the records for an existing enterprise. However, brief comments are made on the calculated ratio values.

A. **Profitability: Return on Capital Employed**
   Funds Generated:
   Profit before tax and interest payable.
   From Table I.5: Add Interest Paid of Ms 2.168m to
   Profit Before Tax of Ms 7.210m.   Ms 9.378m

   Financial Capital Employed:
   Share Capital plus Reserves plus Long Term Debt.
   From Table I.6: Add Total Equity of Ms 20.945m to
   Loan of Ms 19.396m.   Ms 40.341m

   Return on Capital Employed: $\dfrac{9.378}{40.341} \times 100 = 23\%$

This is a very respectable return at this stage of the project's life, especially when measured in constant prices.

B. **Financial Structure: Gearing Ratio   (Debt: Equity)**
   Long Term Debt.
   From Table I.6.   Ms 19.396m
   Equity.
   From Table I.6.   Ms 20.945m

   Gearing Ratio: $\dfrac{19.396}{20.945} = 0.93$

This is an acceptable result for this type of capital-intensive project at this stage of its life. The figure would be expected to fall significantly in future years, as long term debt is repaid and surpluses taken to reserves increase the value of equity.

C. **Financial Structure: Debt Service Coverage**
   Uncommitted Funds Generated:
   Profit after tax + interest on long term debt +
   depreciation.
   From Table I.5: Profit after tax of Ms 3.605m plus
   interest paid of Ms 2.168m plus depreciation of
   Ms 2.633m.   Ms 8.406m

   Debt Service.
   From Table I.2: Add Interest of Ms 2.168m to Capital
   Repayment of Ms 2.286m.   Ms 4.454m

   Debt Service Cover: $\dfrac{8.406}{4.454} = 1.9$

This is adequate cover to safeguard both lenders' interests and the financial viability of the project, particularly this early in the development.

D. Liquidity: Current Ratio

Current Assets.
From Table I.6, Stocks, Debtors and Cash.   Ms 15.224m

Current Liabilities.
From Table I.6, Tax, Creditors and Royalties.   Ms 4.688m

Current Ratio: $\dfrac{15.224}{4.688} = 3.2$

This is more than adequate. There is no specific desirable level of this ratio – it will vary with the type of business, but it should not fall below 1 over the medium to long term. As a rule of thumb, it should probably be between 1.5 to 2. It requires careful interpretation, eg there may be a high level of very slow moving stocks in the current assets figure, which cannot readily be converted to cash to meet current liabilities.

Liquidity: The Quick Ratio

Current Assets – Stocks.
From Table I.6, Current Assets of Ms 15.224m less
    Stocks of Ms 1.455m.   Ms 13.769m

Current Liabilities.
From Table I.6:   Ms 4.688m

Quick Ratio: $\dfrac{13.769}{4.688} = 2.9$

Again, this is more than adequate. A rule of thumb is that the minimum value should be 1, but it is not unusual to find values that at times are a little lower.

E. Working Capital: Debtors

Year End Debtors.
From Table I.6.   Ms 2.423m

Sales.
From Table I.5.   Ms 24.225m

Collection Period: $\dfrac{2.423 \times 365}{24.225} = 36.5$ days

In this example, this result is to be expected given that we have assumed that credit given to debtors to be one-tenth of the value of sales each year. In other circumstances, a view can be taken on whether the result appears reasonable or excessive in absolute terms; against the standard credit period; against prior year figures; and against the payment period allowed for creditors. Debts owed to a business should be carefully limited.

Working Capital: Stocks

Sales.
From Table I.5.   Ms 24.225m

Stocks.
From Table I.6.   Ms 1.455m

Stocks Ratio: $\dfrac{24.225}{1.455} = 16.6$

This high ratio value is acceptable, especially for a project where continuous operation depends on the constant availability of essential parts
and materials, some of which may have to be obtained from abroad, with
long delivery times.

8
Institutional Considerations

Introduction

8.1 Experience has highlighted the importance of institutional considerations, even where institutional development is not a direct component of a project. Many projects which have appeared sound from technical, economic and financial viewpoints have been partly or wholly frustrated by institutional constraints. This applies equally to non-revenue, mixed revenue and revenue projects. Some examples of common institutional problems are:

- inefficient organisation structures;
- a lack of clear and agreed objectives;
- poor management systems, for example planning, accounting or management information;
- manpower constraints such as overmanning, skill shortages or lack of motivation;
- shortages of finance, typically through Government controls on tariffs for revenue earning projects or recurrent budget constraints for Government departments;
- a lack of accountability for individual performance;
- for bodies outside central government, problems with the institutional framework, for example because of unclear or contradictory Government policies and excess intervention from outside in day-to-day management.

8.2 Assumptions about institutional effectiveness are, unavoidably, embodied in the overall appraisal of any project. The purpose of institutional appraisal is, at the minimum, to make such assumptions explicit in order to assess whether the project is realistic given institutional constraints. Where problems are identified, possible solutions will need to be considered. These may involve additional project components or parallel action by the institution or government. If it appears that problems cannot be overcome, project assumptions will need to be modified adversely, which may in turn undermine the justification for the project.

8.3 Institutional appraisal presents numerous difficulties. The appraiser is unlikely to have expertise in the range of skills involved. Political and cultural issues will be important; and the way the institution works in practice may not be what is formally said and is often obscure to the outsider. It will be essential to work closely with the institution concerned and those to which it is responsible. It will also often be necessary to draw on sources of more specialist advice.

8.4 This chapter summarises the main issues which will need to be considered, while Appendices 8.1–8.3 provide checklists to be drawn on in undertaking institutional appraisal.

Institutional Appraisal

8.5   This should cover both the institution itself and the environment in which it operates.

Internal factors are:

(i)   *Organisation structure:* Types of post; units of organisation; responsibilities; lines of control and reporting; consultation and co-ordination procedures; suitability of work patterns and objectives.

(ii)   *Policy and decision making patterns:* Responsibilities in practice as well as in law; areas of policy and decision making; working of these processes; actual or likely strengths and weaknesses.

(iii)   *Procedural factors:* A diverse area: workflows and communication patterns; organisation 'style'; the utility of office instructions.

(iv)   *Financial resources:* Available resources; likely new resources; patterns and terms of availability; collection and borrowing; financial management and accounting; the uses, effectiveness and efficiency of records.

(v)   *Physical resources:* Fixed assets; critical supplies for the business; accommodation; dispersion of activities; communication patterns; transport; control systems for physical resources.

(vi)   *Manpower resources:* Critical skill needs, sources and deficiencies; training; salary grading and promotional motivation and morale.

(vii)   *Information Systems:* Whether the right information goes to the right level at the right time to facilitate good management.

External factors are:

(viii)   *Economic background:* National and sector prospects; availability of foreign exchange; foreign aid; government budget situation; long and short term planning systems.

(ix)   *Political background:* Difficult to approach but important; political significance of the institution and developments; acceptable types of organisation and ownership; regional factors; government ideology.

(x)   *Social background:* Another sensitive area, including tribal or caste conventions; personal value systems and behavioural conventions; family ties; gender factors.

(xi)   Government policy not only in terms of content but also clarity and consistency;

(xii)   The framework for external monitoring of performance.

8.6   The most appropriate final shape of the institution and the external framework may not be apparent at the outset. Even if they are, resistance to change may require a modest initial approach in implementation of new structures and procedures. Opportunities for further development may occur later, building on achievements. Institutional development will often take a long time with periods of reversal as well as advance. A flexible approach is needed, but this should not become a justification for ducking difficult issues nor does it obviate the need for measurable targets for change and improved performance.

8.7 A checklist of areas to be examined in institutional appraisal is at Appendix 8.1. Two specific aspects are now considered: financial management and manpower.

Financial Management Aspects of Institutional Appraisal

Introduction
8.8 Several basic objectives should underlie the financial management of an institution. These are:

a. to record and safeguard the assets, liabilities, income and expenditure to comply with legal and other requirements;

b. to provide information to management to assist in running activities on a day-to-day basis;

c. to provide a financial framework for planning future activities, in annual budgets and long-term plans;

d. to indicate whether declared objectives are being met; and

e. to ensure that funds are being used efficiently and effectively.

These are valid for all institutions. They are generally achieved through formal systems and procedures.

8.9 This section will assist non-accountants to make a preliminary assessment of how far financial objectives are being met. This may be to assess whether the institution could implement a project successfully from the financial point of view, or to improve financial management of the institution and its general performance. The description and checklists should help readers to assess the effectiveness of institutions in this area.

8.10 The checklists in Appendix 8.2 will assist both appraisal and revision of financial management systems and procedures. More specialist work, like a review of financial accounting systems would require specialist advisers.

8.11 These checklists are very detailed. They are relevant at least in part to all institutions in development work, but not all questions relate to all institutions. Planners and appraisers must decide on the most important areas on the basis of their local knowledge. Questions will vary according to whether the institution is revenue or non-revenue earning, and commercially-oriented or not.

Financial Accounting
8.12 Financial accounting systems record the assets, liabilities, income and expenditure. They should enable production of timely, accurate financial statements and provide a basis for effective control of resources. Cost accounting is a form of financial accounting that determines the cost of a particular job or product.

8.13 The standard period for financial accounts is one year. Accounting information should be updated continuously, enabling accounts to be prepared during the year.

8.14   Financial accounts for each institution are essential. The minimum is a set of annual accounts, normally available six months after the financial year. Annual accounts must be subject to independent external audit. If these two conditions are not satisfied, caution is required in assessing the financial status of the institution. Delay in preparing accounts may indicate poor accounting and financial systems or inexperienced staff. Absence of audit may result in inaccuracies and inconsistencies in the financial statements.

8.15   Well run organisations usually have an up-to-date Accounts Manual, with a chart of accounts, a resumé of the accounting systems and details of the basic accounting routines. A chart of accounts with a coding structure is fundamental as the basis for the classification and collection of information for the financial accounts. Items relevant to an overview of the financial accounting arrangements are in Section A of Appendix 8.2.

Financial Planning and Control
8.16   Financial planning involves assessment of the size and type of funds required to achieve the objectives, and identification of expected financial performance. Financial targets should be set (annually or over five to ten years) for both the institution as a whole and each principal activity. Control is exercised by monitoring actual performance against target. The nature of the target will vary with the type of institution. Some target ratios have been explained in 7.27. Box 8.1 outlines the financial objectives in the case studies in Part II.

Box 8.1   Financial Targets

The financial objectives applying in our illustrative cases varied between and within the different autonomous agencies concerned, reflecting both the different nature of the agencies themselves, and different national approaches. The commercial agencies (DC 1, CS 1, CS 2) were clearly expected to cover all operating and finance costs and make a surplus, possibly a substantial surplus. More modest targets applied to most of the utility undertakings. In the power and water cases, the external funds provided to government for the project would be on-lent to the corporations concerned, to be repaid from tariff income, but additional financial targets were applied. One electricity agency and one water undertaking (CS 8 and CS 10) were expected to earn a return of 8% on the value of assets, and the power agency in CS 9 was required to pay dividends at a minimal level of 7.5%. In the port case, CS 13, a range of financial targets were agreed, covering not only return on investment, but also debt-equity ratio and self-financing. Because of its exceptional nature, exploiting a non-renewable resource, the natural gas authority (CS 12) was expected to generate large cash surpluses, though quite how large they should be was not specified.

8.17   Financial planning beyond one year is generally accepted for capital expenditure but is less common for recurrent expenditure, although that is recommended. A medium term plan (three years) for recurrent expenditure assists strategic decision-making; assists in judging full-year implications of current decisions and non-financial plans; and provides early warning of potential financial difficulties. Micro-computers and software make medium term planning straight-forward and flexible.

8.18 Long and medium term plans do not eliminate the need for annual budgets. Sound budgetary processes are important for control. For the recurrent budget, control consists of:

a. establishing budgets for each area of function responsibility and/or service activity, including allocating responsibility to individual managers for control of budgets;

b. regular and frequent comparison of actual with budgeted results; and

c. action resulting from this comparison, where variances arise between budget and actual.

Budgets should be subject to regular review so that revised plans reflect earlier successes in achieving targets. Annual budgets should be prepared after examination of performance. Budget preparation should not be an automatic updating of previous plans, amended for new spending submissions and accepted without assessment of changing objectives or priorities. The case for continuing existing activities should be reviewed as well as that for new proposals.

8.19 Approval of the annual capital budget does not eliminate the need for individual authorisation of projects. The capital budget should show details of expenditure on projects in progress at the beginning of the year and those expected to start during the year. Details of new and replacement plant, vehicles and equipment should also be included. Sources of funding and the recurrent impact of projects should be identified.

8.20 An important aspect of financial management and control of income and expenditure is the Financial Regulations or Financial Instructions. These relate to authorised cheque signatories, levels of delegated authority, standing orders for tenders and contracts, authorisation of write-offs etc. Whether these are available, up-to-date and implemented in practice is a measure of financial management quality.

8.21 The checklists deal also with the management of working capital. In many parastatal organisations, liquidity will be more important than profit and loss. In all organisations, control of stocks and debtors are as important as is control of annual budgets of estimates. Checklists in Appendix 8.2 B–F cover: Planning, Budgeting; Control of the Recurrent Budget; Capital Expenditure Control; and Working Capital Management.

Audit

8.22 Audit is both external and internal. External audit is primarily to report to shareholders on the accuracy and legality of the annual accounts. In some cases, there is also a responsibility to report on 'value for money' (VFM) issues concerning the economy, effectiveness and efficiency of resource use. The external auditor may be an Auditor-General for government ministries, parastatal organisations and local authorities or a commercial auditor.

8.23 Internal audit provides an independent appraisal; assessing and reporting on the effectiveness of internal systems and controls. This is to safeguard assets, control fraud, maintain accuracy of records and ensure adherence to Financial Regulations and stated financial policies. Internal audit increasingly extends its attention to VFM issues. Internal audit can help external audit in its work. It is undertaken by a unit within the organisation. This should normally report direct to the head of the organisation or the board rather than to the Finance Departments.

8.24   As a minimum, financial accounts of all institutions should be subject to external audit within twelve months after the end of each financial year. Internal audit departments operate a continuous programme of work throughout the year.

8.25   The nature and extent of the audit is shown in the Auditors' work plan. Effectiveness of an audit may be assessed from the findings reported, the recommendations for corrective action and evidence of follow-up action. A common weakness of audit is failure to implement recommendations particularly in Government. Auditors usually report by means of a 'management letter' submitted after their work. Checklist G in Appendix 8.2 covers audit.

Manpower Aspects of Institutional and Project Appraisal

8.26   Although labour, and skilled labour in particular, is a key input to a project, manpower aspects of project appraisal are often overlooked. This section sets out basic questions for both the institutional and the project levels. Available data may be limited, but discussions with individuals who know the organisation, or the development in view, can help.

Manpower Planning
8.27   Manpower is sometimes the largest single cost. Planning which matches available manpower to the achievement of objectives is vital. What practical steps have to be taken in the analysis and planning of manpower aspects for a project?

8.28   An organisation plan is required, of the existing or proposed structure. This provides a model of the overall manpower system, showing posts of different kinds at the various levels. Ideally it will also include the points for external recruitment, and flows between posts through promotion.

8.29   When the structure and posts are clear, existing staffing can be shown and manpower needs, sources and constraints identified. In an existing agency, a stocktake of the current position should be made, including both staff in post and vacancies. Information on staff is available from personnel records or the payroll. Information on educational qualifications and skills of staff may be in personnel records or there may be proxy indications in payroll information, such as bonus payments eg for particular qualifications. Failing that staff surveys may be required. Information on vacancies by grade and department will normally be available, though departmental managers may exaggerate vacancies. It may be possible to check through some independent measure, such as overtime worked or the relation of desired numbers to workload. The stocktake of this type can show current recruitment and training needs. Further replacement needs can be calculated on assumptions on wastage rates, based on information concerning resignations, dismissals and retirements.

8.30   Estimating additional manpower requirements is a feature of project planning. If done by consultants, the terms of reference should include a study of skilled manpower requirements and how far they can be met from existing external recruitment.

8.31   Manpower planning in the feasibility study is likely to be at a general level, indicating the number of posts of different kinds during operations, their costs and possible sources. More detailed planning will be required during implementation, when the project manager specifies core staff requirements for the investment period. If most development work is undertaken by contractors or other existing agencies, the staff required for planning, co-ordination and control will be specialised and small. If direct labour is used in the investment, a manpower planning and recruitment section may be needed from the earliest days, in order that manpower is available when needed.

A Checklist for Personnel Management
8.32   In any organisation decisions about recruitment, retention, training, utilisation, re-deployment, redundancy and retirement have to be taken. Personnel policies, planning and decisions are often taken and implemented without adequate planning or information. Appendix 8.3 presents a checklist of information requirements for the main aspects of manpower planning, covering both the project and the institution.

8.33   Four stages are covered:

A. A manpower stocktake within the organisation and the external labour market.

B. Forecasting demand and supply.

C. Planning to meet requirements of the organisation in contraction and expansion.

D. Monitoring adjustments and feedback for reappraisal.

Appendix 8.1
Institutional Appraisal Checklist

1.   This checklist is for preliminary assessment of main institutions responsible for projects and programmes. More detailed work requires specialists. It is all purpose, not sector-specific, but directed towards public sector institutions, though much is relevant to the private sector.

2.   The questions are comprehensive and apply to typical institutions in development work. Not all questions relate to all institutions. Analysts must decide which are the more important.

3.   The checklist is designed for an existing institution but the same questions can apply to planning and appraising new or changed institutions. Judgement of the points depends on the experience of the appraiser. Standards cannot be provided; they will vary with the type of institution and level of development.

A. External Environment Checklists

(1) *The Legal Framework*

a. What is the constitutional and/or legal status?

b. What are the key features concerning: legal responsibilities; financial and operational performance; constitutional and/or social obligations?

c. Are the responsibilities and obligations actually discharged by the institution?

d. Are changes needed in the legal instrument, or is there sufficient autonomy/protection/obligation/flexibility in the existing framework?

(2) *National Development Objectives*

a. What role is the institution expected to play in national development?

b. Do the internal plans and budgets accord with the national objectives?

c. Does the National Plan provide sufficient resources to enable the objectives to be fulfilled?

d. Does the National Plan provide for necessary policy changes and complementary roles by other institutions?

e. Are there any conflicts of objectives, between specified objectives or between specified and unspecified objectives? How are these seen and resolved?

(3) *The Supervisory Framework*

a. Are there clear reporting lines to Government and to legislative bodies?

b. Are specific quantified objectives set by Government for the institution? Are they set unilaterally or participatively?

c. Where objectives are not quantitative (eg legal obligations) how are they defined?

d. What are the financial and administrative limits: eg approval of capital expenditure; setting tariffs; amending staff terms and conditions of service?

e. How is the institution monitored by Government?

f. Does the institution have the confidence of Government?

g. Will Government support further analysis/development of the institution?

h. Do external agencies work with this institution? Do they have an interest in institutional change?

(4) *The Operating Environment*

a. Are any competitors providing similar goods or services? If so, how good is knowledge of those competitors?

b. Is there an overlap, conflict or competition with other institutions in the fulfilment of responsibilities?

c. Is there a clear understanding of client needs, and response to changes in those needs? How are client needs monitored?

101

d. Are pricing strategies sensitive to competitive and client pressures?

e. What are the main features of the political and social environment?

B. Internal Structures – Checklists

(1) *Organisation*

a. Obtain or draw up:
  i. a chart of the organisation;
  ii. charts of the individual main groupings at middle/senior management level.

b. Are there any multiple reporting lines?

c. Are there any one-on-one relationships?

d. Are spans of control reasonable?

e. Is the number of levels of management/supervision appropriate?

f. Is the balance between line and staff groupings realistic?

g. Are there any regional structures? If so:
  i. are all functions represented?
  ii. what are their reporting lines to the centre?

h. Is there a non-executive body in authority (eg a Board or an elected or appointed Local Council?) If so:
  i. what is its composition?
  ii. does it play a strategic or tactical role?
  iii. what is the formal/actual pattern of political/executive relations?

i. Is there a formal staff establishment for the institution?
  i. Is it appropriate to present or projected levels of operations?
  ii. Is there any inventory of staff and qualifications?
  iii. Are there any key skill shortages, staff surpluses? What is being done to rectify the situation?

j. Are there job descriptions, at least for key posts? When were they updated?

k. Do work units have clearly defined plans, priorities and budgets?

l. Is there a Standing Regulations Operations handbook? Is it up to date and relevant to today's situation? Is it comprehensive?

(2) *Functions*

a. What is the central purpose of the institution?

b. How are the purposes and responsibilities defined? Do the forms and methods of definition create any problems?

c. If there are a number of purposes, are they ranked?

d. Does the allocation of functions between departments appear sensible?

e. Are there any functions which are not essential to the central purpose?

f. Are there any obvious missing functions? (possibly of a non operational kind – eg planning).

g. How is coordination of the various functions achieved? Is it formal or informal? Is it through the Chief Executive Officer or through a corporate process?

h.   Is top management's workload primarily strategic or of a day-to-day nature?

i.   Is there a manpower/job evaluation/organisation review function? Is rigidity apparent?

j.   Does the physical location of different departments/functions present obstacles to efficient management?

C. Internal Management, Systems and Procedures in General – Checklists

(1) *The Management Process*

a.   What are the formal and actual performance criteria, if any?

b.   What are the real goals in contrast to the formal goals?

c.   What are the relative importance of formal and informal communications to the working of the institution?

d.   Are there any major bottlenecks evident in work flows?

e.   Is there recognition of a need for and commitment to change?

f.   Do any cultural or other external factors affect the processes of decision-making or management?

g.   Is structural change likely to be a prerequisite of management/operation change?

h.   Which individuals would be prime movers in institutional changes?

(2) *Delegation*

a.   Are delegated authority limits specified for: financial management; personnel management; operational management?

b.   Does actual delegation correspond to the limits set? Do transfers of resources follow delegation of responsibility?

c.   Do middle managers have the skills/experience and confidence necessary for delegation to work?

d.   Where does executive power really lie?

Appendix 8.2
Financial Management Checklists

Items marked with an asterisk in these checklists are basic issues, essential to the appraisal.

A. Financial Accounting Overview

*a.   Obtain a copy of the most recent annual financial accounts and audit report.

*b.   Is there an Accounts Manual? If so: does it cover all the accounting systems in use? Does it provide system flow charts? Does it specify a chart of accounts? Could it cope with organisation and operational changes? When was it updated?

c.   Are the accounting systems manual, computerised or both? If both, are they run in parallel and, if so, why?

d.   Is accounting the sole user of computing facilities?

e.   Are the accounts and budget control information kept on a cash or an accruals basis? (The cash basis accounts for cash actually received or spent. The accruals basis recognises income as it is earned or expenditure as it is incurred).

f. Are accounting records up-to-date?

*g. For commercial and quasi-commercial organisations, are financial statements produced more frequently than annually?

*h. When were fixed assets last revalued and verified?

*i. Are cost accounting systems used to cost individual services and products?

j. Are those costs compared to standard costs? How frequently are standard costs and charges reviewed? Are the cost accounts and financial accounts integrated?

k. Is there regular reconciliation of different types of accounts?

B. Planning

*a. Is there any planning beyond the annual capital and recurrent budget processes, eg a corporate plan?

b. How are expenditure priorities set within each plan?

c. Are the financial implications of plans clear and in a standard format?

d. What is the planning time horizon?

e. Are the various plans consistent with each other and the annual budget?

*f. Are the plans achievable and the assumptions reasonable?

*g. Is performance monitored and controlled against plans?

h. Are the plans subject to revision during the plan period?

i. Is planning centralised, decentralised or both?

j. Are the plans subject to sensitivity analysis prior to final agreement?

C. Budgeting

(1) *Both Recurrent and Capital Budgets*

a. Obtain copies of the budget documents for the last two years.

b. From a description of the budget process, look for these points:

    i. Is the strategy and assumptions for the budget process clear?

    ii. How is consistency achieved between annual budgets and medium term/corporate plans?

    iii. Are individuals responsible for the preparation of particular budget votes, and are they accountable for commitment and monitoring?

    iv. Is responsibility for budget preparation and control delegated sufficiently?

    v. What is the process for further review and approval of submissions?

    vi. What is the timetable for the budget process? Is it reasonable?

    vii. Are capital and recurrent costs distinguished?

    viii. How is the budget analysed by programme, project activity, geographical area, type of cost, etc.?

    ix. Are cash flow projections prepared, linked to revenue and capital budgets?

x. Are standard costs (ie expenditure norms) used in budget pre-paration? Do they recognise significant differences between cost centres or projects:

xi. How are inflation and uncertainty provided for?

xii. Are unspent year-end funds carried over, or do they revert to central finance?

c. Review major assumptions made for budgeting. Are they realistic? Are working papers adequate?

*d. Have past budgets been realistic? Compare last actual figures against the relevant estimates for major heads.

(2) *Recurrent Budget only*

*e. Is the budget process incremental, or are resource allocations linked to planned activity levels?

f. Are financial figures supported by performance figures?

g. Are value for money exercises undertaken? Do they feed into the budget process?

*h. Are budgets broken down into cost centres of manageable size?

i. In parastatal organisations are discrete activities treated as individual profit centres?

*j. Determine the process for the review of tariffs and prices.

*k. For non-government departments, is there financial support from government? Is it formalised or ad hoc? Have financial targets been set by government?

(3) *Capital Budget only*

*l. Is there a structured approach to investment appraisal? Describe it. Is there adequate documentation?

m. Is there an agreed test discount rate?

n. Who is responsible for investment appraisal and preparation of the capital budget?

*o. How are projects ranked for inclusion in the capital budget?

p. Is account taken of risk? If so, how?

q. Is there a formal structure of delegated authority for capital expend-itures? How does it relate to organisational structure?

r. Is a full assessment made of the project's effect on the financial position of the organisation? Are full projected financial statements prepared?

D. Control of the Recurrent Budget

*a. Does budgetary control information accord with responsibilities and accountabilities? Does it go to those who control resource use and expenditure? Are increasingly summarised forms given to succes-sive levels of management?

*b. Is information provided in regular and timely fashion?

*c. Are differences between budgeted and actual amounts investigated and followed up? Is correcting action taken and amendment made to budget and to cash flow forecasts?

d. What sanctions are imposed on managers for serious adverse variances?

e. Is there provision for virement between budget heads? Is there a contingency allocation? If so, how are transfers controlled?

f. Do monthly budget allocations reflect seasonal differences?

g. What comparative measures are in use? (eg prior period; same period prior year).

h. Are actual revenue and expenditure figures compared to operational performance? Is attention drawn to unexpected results?

E. Capital Expenditure Control

*a. Is control information provided in accordance with responsibilities and accountabilities?

*b. Is information provided in regular and timely fashion?

*c. Are variances from budget followed up?

*d. Is the likelihood of overspend and the consequent need for further finance monitored and followed up?

e. Do changing rates of progress on capital projects lead to revised cash flow projections?

f. Are reimbursement claims and loan drawdown made promptly? Is due account taken of leads, lags and the need for working capital?

g. Are all relevant costs capitalised?

h. Are capital expenditure proposals submitted for approval in a prescribed form at the relevant level of authority?

i. Are the costs of completed projects reviewed against original estimates?

F. Working Capital Management

*a. Are cash, inventory, debtors and creditors monitored on a regular and timely basis? Who is responsible?

(1) *Cash*

*b. Are cash flow projections prepared? For what periods? How frequently are they updated?

c. Are all opportunities taken for minimising idle cash or the level of overdraft?

d. Is cash flow the determining factor in paying creditors and ordering?

(2) *Debtors*

e. Are the credit terms given sufficiently tight and applied consistently?

f. What is the age analysis of debtors outstanding?

g. Are any particular categories of debtor a problem?

(3) *Inventory*

h. What arrangements exist for stock counts?

i. When were minimum order levels last reviewed?

j.　Are obsolete stocks regularly identified and disposed of? When were they last reviewed?

(4) *Creditors*

k.　Are creditors paid on time? Is there any evidence of unwillingness to supply because of slow payment or non-payment by the institution?

G. Audit

(1) *External Audit*

a.　Who audits the annual accounts?

b.　Is the auditor independent of the institution under review?

c.　Do they have a good reputation and adequate experience?

d.　Have they ever qualified the accounts?

e.　Obtain a copy of any management letter submitted by the external auditors on conclusion of their audit.

(2) *Internal Audit*

*a.　Is there an independent internal audit?

b.　If so, does it provide a continuous appraisal of accounting and management procedures?

c.　Is it primarily for checking compliance with procedures, or in reviewing systems and/or VFM exercises?

d.　Does it pay adequate attention to internal checks and control?

*e.　Is there an internal audit plan? If so, obtain a copy.

Appendix 8.3
Manpower Planning Checklist

As with other checklists, this one is designed to cover all eventualities. It should be used selectively: no single institution or project is likely to need to be covered in the full detail listed.

A. Manpower stocktake

(1) *In an existing organisation*

a.　What are the numbers employed, and trends?

b.　Are they analysed by sex, age, location, educational, professional and technical qualifications, practical experience and skills gained on the job inside and outside the organisation?

c.　Is there a vacancy analysis by skills, posts and location that also shows duration and trends?

d.　Is there an analysis of absence statistics? Trends in sickness leave can be an indicator for stress.

e.　Does the age distribution by skill, experience and qualifications highlight any unusual trends? Is the proportion of young employees high and rising, with possible problems for promotion, lack of experience and increased wastage?

f.   Are there signs of an ageing workforce indicating retirement prob-
     lems? Are there trends in length of service distributions and/or
     wastage patterns?

g.   Is there a simple and basic manpower information system? Is it used
     by senior management before decisions?

h.   What is the policy, programme and achievement regarding training
     activities, and in which areas?

i.   What is the capacity for additional training? What constrains training
     – finance, regulations, working methods, production targets or other
     factors?

(2) *External labour market*

j.   What is the external manpower environment? Is it easy to recruit
     people?

k.   Are some skills or types of labour more difficult to recruit than
     others?

l.   What are the likely future trends?

m.   What is happening in the outside labour market? Is the competition
     for labour likely to increase or decrease? Are other organisations in
     the vicinity or in the same business expanding or contracting? How
     would that affect this organisation?

n.   Are outside forces likely to change the supply situation? (eg -
     Government policies, donor activities, education and training estab-
     lishments).

o.   Is the organisation in touch with educational and training establish-
     ments? How can they help?

p.   Can these factors be influenced to the advantage of the
     organisation?

B **Forecasting demand and supply**

The stocktake provides information and data about the situation and
trends. Changes in the supply and demand for people have to be carefully considered, especially when new developments are planned.
Identifying trends is an important part of managing adjustments to meet
requirements.

a.   What vacancies may be created by development in each period in
     terms of numbers, skills, experience and location? Can these be
     filled from within? When will recruitment from outside be appro-
     priate?

b.   How many people may leave in the future? Expected retirements?
     Trends in voluntary losses?

c.   What are the expected trends in losses, in terms of qualifications,
     experience, contribution to the organisation etc.?

d.   What movements do or could result from promotion, career
     development, transfers?

e.   What supplies of skills may come from current or proposed training?
     Are these adequate? Could in-house training provide for future
     needs?

f.   What approaches to external recruitment sources will be requested – to individuals, other employers, education and training establishments, etc.?

g.   Are likely future needs and supplies known? Is anyone trying to find out? Do they need help?

C Planning and adjustment

The next stage is planning and adjustment, during which actions are taken to meet requirements. Experience and expertise in the handling of people can be important, calling for specialist manpower skills and expertise. These may exist within, but sometimes they have to be obtained through consultancy.

(1) *Adjustment in Non-Contracting Situations*

Adjustment in the supply and use of people may require the following:

a.   Recruitment planning: What are recruitments and the internal situation? What does this mean for recruitment plans and actions?

b.   Training plans and programmes: Is there a training plan that identifies and reflects future needs?

c.   Industrial relations planning: Do desired changes have implications for industrial relations? Are employees and/or their representatives involved in planning and introducing change?

d.   Management and employee development: Are promotion and career development patterns satisfactory or in need of change?

e.   Pay and conditions: Are present levels or proposals appropriate? What future adjustments might be necessary, especially to pay structures? How can these be implemented?

f.   Motivation: What incentives do or will employees have to be productive and efficient? Can motivation be improved? How will the changes be implemented?

g.   Manpower costs: Have costs been worked out for other options, as a basis for selection? Is manpower budgeting used in the selection and operating of other manpower patterns and changes? Who is responsible for assessing costs and benefits of other choices?

(2) *Contracting Situations*

Special care is needed in a contracting situation, to which these points may apply.

h.   What are the plans for reducing employee numbers, and how are these to be implemented?

i.   Will natural wastage assist?

j.   How can the manpower reductions be implemented with the minimum social cost, and with minimum economic cost?

k.   How can quality of service be maintained during adjustment, with disruptive effects minimised and managed?

l.   What are the implications for redundancies, training, re-training, recruitment policies and recruitment action?

D Assessment and Feedback – The Monitoring Phase

All organisations need to monitor not only their own manpower information system, but the decisions and adjustments that are made concerning personnel. This feedback and learning from past events helps the planning process to become relevant to needs. Important change questions can arise during project implementation and operation.

a. What are the experiences of seeking to recruit and retain workers of particular kinds?

b. What are the effects of changes that are introduced?

c. Are appropriate yardsticks used for assessing the effects of manpower actions and plans?

d. What costs were involved in making manpower plans and adjustments? Did unforeseen costs arise through the action taken?

e. What does manpower experience mean for future adjustments? Cost criteria may not be the only ones appropriate for such an assessment. What have been the effects of any social disruption caused?

f. Were any economic or financial measures of productivity and performance short-sighted and inappropriate? Were longer term costs incurred as a result of short term savings and other adjustments?

g. How will manpower monitoring information be used to influence decisions on people and on the objectives and role of the organisation?

PART II

ILLUSTRATIONS OF
PROJECT ANALYSIS

PART II

Illustrations of Project Analysis

PART II
Illustrations of Project Analysis

Introduction

1.   This part of the Guide contains material that illustrates very many of the methods and approaches for project appraisal that were described in Part I. Drawn from project papers in ODA, a variety of different projects are described in varying degrees of detail; case studies to illustrate what analysts did in particular situations. Three kinds of material are included.

2.   Section A contains very detailed presentations which show all the stages for financial and economic analysis in two very different types of development. Full exposition of these methodologies accompanies discussion of a host of other considerations that arose in the planning and analysis of these schemes.

3.   Section B contains case study outlines of sixteen projects of very different kinds. Without presenting the data or methods used, each example is described; the analyses used are outlined; and the results of economic analysis are presented and discussed. The importance of different planning and analysis factors naturally varies widely between these projects.

4.   Section C is a specialised section, which contains a full exposition of how analytical methods were actually employed to calculate four important parameters used for the economic analysis of particular schemes.

5.   The derivation of these case studies from ODA experience means that they are biassed towards the later stages of project preparation, when donor assistance is usually sought. This is not ideal – it cannot be stressed too often that financial, economic and other appraisals should be used to guide design throughout the project preparation process – but some of the appraisals were early enough in the preparation process to affect design. The main features of economic appraisal apply at any stage in project preparation. The illustrations should therefore assist economists working with engineers, agricultural specialists and others in identifying, proving feasibility and making the preliminary design of projects.

A. Detailed Case Studies

Introduction

1. The two detailed case studies in this section were selected to provide practical guidance on the sources and detailed manipulation of data in economic and financial appraisal. They were therefore chosen from two different sectors – minerals exploitation and agriculture – and have widely different characteristics. Both cases were taken from ODA records and are therefore real world examples.

2. The first case – a Rock Phosphates Project – is a single product project with relatively heavy capital costs and modern technology production. It illustrates many aspects of shadow pricing but there are few social complexities and the risks are readily identifiable. The second illustration, a Basin Irrigation Scheme, is typical of many agricultural developments, with a range of products and varied marketing channels. It raises questions about financial incentives and social change, and operational factors are crucial.

3. The arithmetic of project appraisal is presented in considerable detail in these two studies because guidance is not available in most textbooks on project appraisal. It should be fairly easy to deduce from these tables how to undertake the calculations necessary in dealing with the other problems in economic appraisal, for example, those outlined in the illustrative case studies in section B.

Detailed Case Study I: The Rock Phosphate Project

1. This case study – the Rock Phosphate Project – is based on a real project developed by technical consultants for ODA. The project is used as the basis for illustrating the different types of analysis discussed in Part I, and reflects the direct relationship that exists between the planning and the analysis of the financial and the economic aspects of a project.

Brief Outline

2. This project was located in an agricultural country where phosphatic fertilisers were manufactured, using imported raw material. Workable quantities of phosphate had been discovered fairly close to the surface and technical appraisal had demonstrated that its quality would allow its use in fertiliser making, as an alternative to imports. No other phosphate mining had taken place in the country, but the relevant Regional Development Authority had sponsored investigations and trial workings, for which some small fixed investment had been made. The present project envisaged establishing a new commercial entity to exploit the deposit, mining the ore and crushing it at the mine to produce a powder that would be transported in one and a half tonne bags by lorry to the fertiliser factory. Most of the ore could be mined on a cut-and-fill method. Use of this method, in preference to room-and-pillar mining, would allow an expected 700,000 tonnes to be extracted, which would allow a plant handling 200 tonnes per day (57,000 tonnes per annum) to be

worked for around 12 years. Electric trains (with battery locomotives) would carry the ore from the mine to the crushing plant, from whence conveyors would transport the material to the crushing, bagging and loading plant. 343 people would be employed when the mine was in full production, about half of them underground.

3.   Substantial capital expenditure would be required to build access roads, offices, and buildings for the crusher and bagger; for mining and ore transport; for the crushing and bagging plant; for electricity distribution and battery charging; for a well-equipped workshop; and for tractors and other vehicles. Power would be purchased from the regional grid. Explosives would be a significant cost item for mining. The new business would take over the small amount of existing plant and the land from the company at no cost. Some of the exising capital items would require replacement after only a few years.

Forecast Accounts for the Rock Phosphate Project

Introduction
4.   These accounts for a 'greenfield' project illustrate the basic accounts and schedules for a revenue project in their simplest form, without the complications of a pre-existing business. A complete set of tables is shown (including a forecast Balance Sheet) in a typical presentation, though reflecting particular features of this proposed investment. The following section shows the tables, generally for the first six years of the project, as prepared using constant prices, which were based on a period around 12 months before major work on investment was expected to begin. A later section shows how inflation was taken into account for the early years of the project. The currency unit is the Money (M). At the time of project preparation, the exchange rate was Ms 18.00 = £1.00.

The constant price accounts
The main accounts are in 3 tables.
    TABLE I.3   Cash Flow Forecasts
    TABLE I.5   Trading and Profit and Loss Account
    TABLE I.6   Balance Sheet
There are 3 supporting schedules.
    TABLE I.1   Capital Costs
    TABLE I.2   Equity and Loan Financing
    TABLE I.4   Depreciation Schedule

5.   Numbering of the tables reflects the approximate sequence in which they would be prepared. However, the timing of the drafting of schedules is not fixed, as in some areas iteration is required, for example between the Cash Flow Forecast and the schedule of Equity and Loan Financing.

6.   Comment on the tables will emphasise aspects of their composition and significance.

7.   The *Capital Costs* statement, Table I.1, shows the main categories for fixed investments, which will be the subject of costs over approximately two years in the pattern shown. Most expenditure is in the first year, with completion, commissioning and trial operation in the second year. Overhead ex-

penses will be incurred in these years in managing the processes of capital acquisition and supply. Replacement begins rather early, as some taken-over items from the preliminary work are scrapped. A major reinvestment in mining equipment will be required in year 11, the tenth year of operations. Exceptionally, this project has no cost for the acquisition of land. The project is based on government land that is all rock with no alternative use. It will be provided free to the project, but government will take a royalty on sales.

8.   Equity and Loan Financing (Table I.2) is prepared in conjunction with the Cash Flow Forecast (Table I.3). The Equity and Loan Financing contains the estimates of funds needed to meet costs until revenue from operations provides sufficient funds. It is estimated that, at constant prices, Ms 40 million will be required for this project. It is suggested that the project should be financed half by equity shares from Regional Development Authority (RDA) and half through a loan from National Industrial Development Bank (NIDB). Finance from each source would be drawn in equal amounts, as required. The Cash Flow Forecast records only expected cash movements. By taking account of cash expenditure on materials for production and stock, the timing of payments to suppliers of other goods and services, and the receipts from customers, the Cash Flow Forecast will provide for the working capital requirements.

9.   As production and sales turnover increase, there is the requirement for extra working capital to support growth. The Cash Flow Forecast balance at the end of a period will show the cash deficit (ie additional funding required) or cash surplus. The specific provisions for working capital are described, *inter alia* in the Notes on the Forecast Accounts that are in the Box on page 125.

10.   Knowledge of the amount and draw-down of the loan allows *Loan Repayment* to be calculated, as shown in the lower part of Table I.2. Negotiations have suggested that interest (due from the day of drawing) might accumulate up to year 2. Thereafter the total amount due would be repaid in 8 equal yearly instalments. The annual sum due is calculated by applying the Capital Recovery Factor (CRF) for 8 years and 10% (which is 0.18744) to the amount outstanding at the end of year 2. The division of the annual payment between interest and capital is shown in the table.

11.   Knowledge of the timing and cost of capital expenditures allows *Depreciation* to be calculated. The figures for this project are in Table I.4. There are various ways in which depreciation can be calculated. The method used in this illustration is 'straight line' depreciation – each year the same proportion of the actual historic cost until total cost has been charged. The depreciation rates used are those relevant to the expected life of each of the different categories of item. For ease of calculation, replacement investments are shown individually, separate from the initial capital. The table also shows the amortisation of Pre-Operating Expenses over the first five years of revenue-earning operations – a process like depreciation of charging expenses incurred before operations against the years which are expected to benefit from the investment.

12.   The *Trading and Profit and Loss Account* is at Table I.5. Trial operations and labour training begin during year 1. All labour will work for only part of that year. As everyone will be learning phosphate mining anew, it is not expected that any saleable production will arise during the few operating

117

THE ROCK PHOSPHATE PROJECT

TABLE I.1

CAPITAL COSTS

Constant Ms million

ITEM	INITIAL CAPITAL			CAPITAL REPLACEMENTS			
Years	0	1	TOTAL	2	3	4	5
BUILDINGS	2.851	—	2.851	—	—	—	—
PLANT AND EQUIPMENT							
Mining and Transport Machinery and Equipment	5.769	2.488	8.257	—	—	—	—
Grinding Machinery	19.015	0.370	19.385	—	0.200	—	—
Electrical Plant	0.200	2.815	3.015	—	—	—	—
Workshop and Equipment	0.523	—	0.523	—	—	—	0.110
Roads, Bridges etc.	0.952	—	0.952	—	—	—	—
Total	26.459	5.673	32.132	—	0.200	—	0.110
VEHICLES, TRACTORS, ETC.	0.299	0.114	0.413	—	—	0.299	0.114
TOTAL	29.609	5.787	35.396	—	0.200	0.299	0.224
Pre-Operating Overheads[1]	1.480	0.289	1.769				

[1] Capital charges arising from preliminary investigations and trial workings.

THE ROCK PHOSPHATE PROJECT

TABLE 1.2

EQUITY AND LOAN FINANCING

Constant   Ms millions

Years	0	1	2	3	4	5	6	7	8	9	10	11
INFLOWS												
Equity	16.000	4.000										
Loan	16.000	4.000										
Total	32.000	8.000										
LOAN SERVICING												
Total loan servicing of which:	—	—	—	4.454	4.454	4.454	4.454	4.454	4.454	4.454	4.454	—
Interest @ 10%												
Unpaid	—	1.600	2.160	—	—	—	—	—	—	—	—	—
Paid	—	—	—	2.376	2.168	1.940	1.688	1.412	1.107	0.773	0.405	—
Capital Repayment	—	—	—	2.078	2.286	2.514	2.766	3.042	3.347	3.681	4.046	—
Amount Outstanding at year end	16.000	21.600	23.760	21.682	19.396	16.882	14.116	11.074	7.727	4.046	—	—

119

THE ROCK PHOSPHATE PROJECT
TABLE I.3
CASH FLOW FORECAST

Constant Ms million

	Year	0	1	2	3	4	5
	Balance B/F	—	0.911	1.059	3.672	5.788	11.346
INFLOWS							
Equity		16.000	4.000	—	—	—	—
Loan		16.000	4.000	—	—	—	—
Sales Revenue		—	—	9.562	16.363	23.502	24.225
TOTAL INFLOW		32.000	8.911	10.621	20.035	29.290	35.571
OUTFLOWS							
Capital Costs							
Buildings		2.851	—	—	—	—	—
Plant and Equipment		26.459	5.673	—	—	—	0.110
Vehicles, Tractors etc.		0.299	0.114	—	0.200	0.299	0.114
Pre-Operating Overheads		1.480	0.289	—	—	—	—
(Sub-total)		31.089	6.076	—	0.200	0.299	0.224
Operating Costs		—	0.761	2.807	4.375	5.821	5.821
Mine Materials		—	0.644	2.437	3.796	5.051	5.051
Grinding Materials		—	0.117	0.370	0.579	0.770	0.770
Mine Labour		—	0.250	1.375	1.375	1.375	1.375
Grinding Labour		—	0.100	0.310	0.310	0.310	0.310
Mine Power		—	0.050	0.413	0.689	0.991	1.021
Grinding Power		—	0.070	0.552	0.927	1.331	1.372
Underground Transport		—	0.030	0.134	0.220	0.316	0.326
Mine Administration		—	0.145	0.313	0.342	0.342	0.342
General Administration		—	0.145	0.212	0.230	0.230	0.230
Overheads		—	0.200	0.437	0.474	0.474	0.474
Selling & Distribution Costs		—	0.025	0.084	0.088	0.088	0.088
(Sub-total)		—	1.015	3.830	4.655	5.457	5.538
Royalties		—	—	0.312	0.563	0.812	0.855
Interest Payable		—	—	—	2.376	2.168	1.940
Tax on Profits		—	—	—	—	1.101	3.605
Capital Repayment		—	—	—	2.078	2.286	2.514
TOTAL OUTFLOW		31.089	7.852	6.949	14.247	17.944	20.497
Cash Balance C/F		0.911	1.059	3.672	5.788	11.346	15.074

THE ROCK PHOSPHATE PROJECT

TABLE I.4

DEPRECIATION SCHEDULE

Constant   Ms million

ITEM	LIFE Years	RATE %	CAPITAL SUMS		ANNUAL DEPRECIATION			
			Purchase	Cost	Year 2	Year 3	Year 4	Year 5
BUILDINGS	20	5	Initial	2.851	0.143	0.143	0.143	0.143
PLANT AND EQUIPMENT								
Mining and Transport Machinery and Equipment	10	10	Initial Year 3	8.257 0.200	0.826	0.826	0.826 0.020	0.826 0.020
Grinding Machinery	20	5	Initial	19.385	0.969	0.969	0.969	0.969
Electrical Plant	20	5	Initial	3.015	0.151	0.151	0.151	0.151
Workshop and Equipment	13	7½	Initial Year 5	0.523 0.110	0.039	0.039	0.039	0.039
Roads, Bridges etc.	20	5	Initial	0.952	0.048	0.048	0.048	0.048
TOTAL					2.033	2.033	2.053	2.053
VEHICLES, TRACTORS, ETC.	5	20	Initial Year 4 Year 5	0.413 0.299 0.114	0.083	0.083	0.083	0.083 0.060
Total					0.083	0.083	0.083	0.143
TOTAL DEPRECIATION					2.259	2.259	2.279	2.339
Pre-Operating Overheads		20	Initial	1.769	0.354	0.354	0.354	0.354

THE ROCK PHOSPHATE PROJECT
TABLE 1.5
TRADING AND PROFIT AND LOSS ACCOUNT

Constant Ms million

Year	1	2	3	4	5
TRADING					
Sales	—	10.625	17.000	24.225	24.225
Less Cost of Sales:					
Mine Materials	0.275	2.215	3.545	5.051	5.051
Grinding Materials	0.060	0.338	0.540	0.770	0.770
	0.335	2.553	4.085	5.821	5.821
TRADING PROFIT	(0.335)	8.072	12.915	18.404	18.404
PROFIT AND LOSS					
Less					
Mine Labour	0.300	1.375	1.375	1.375	1.375
Grinding Labour	0.120	0.310	0.310	0.310	0.310
Mine Power	0.060	0.448	0.716	1.021	1.021
Grinding Power	0.080	0.602	0.963	1.372	1.372
Underground Transport	0.035	0.143	0.229	0.326	0.326
Mine Administration	0.150	0.342	0.342	0.342	0.342
General Administration	0.150	0.230	0.230	0.230	0.230
Overheads	0.210	0.474	0.474	0.474	0.474
Selling and Distribution	0.030	0.088	0.088	0.088	0.088
	1.135	4.012	4.727	5.538	5.538
Royalties	—	0.375	0.600	0.855	0.855
Interest	—	—	2.376	2.168	1.940
Depreciation	—	2.613	2.613	2.633	2.693
PROFIT BEFORE TAX	(1.470)	1.072	2.599	7.210	7.378
Less					
Corporation Tax 50%	—	—	1.101	3.605	3.689
PROFIT AFTER TAX	(1.470)	1.072	1.498	3.605	3.689
APPROPRIATION					
Less					
Dividends	—	—	—	—	—
Other Appropriations	—	—	—	—	—
RETAINED PROFITS	(1.470)	1.072	1.498	3.605	3.689

THE ROCK PHOSPHATE PROJECT

TABLE I.6

BALANCE SHEETS

Constant Ms million

	Year 1		Year 2		Year 3		Year 4		Year 5	
NET ASSETS EMPLOYED										
FIXED ASSETS										
Buildings	2.851		2.708		2.565		2.422		2.279	
Plant & Equipment	32.132		30.099		28.266		26.213		24.270	
Vehicles, Tractors etc.	0.413		0.330		0.247		0.463		0.434	
Pre-Operating Overheads	1.769		1.415		1.061		0.707		0.353	
NET FIXED ASSETS		37.165		34.552		32.139		29.805		27.336
CURRENT ASSETS										
Stocks	0.639		1.021		1.455		1.455		1.455	
Debtors	—		1.062		1.700		2.423		2.423	
Cash	1.059		3.672		5.788		11.346		15.074	
Less Creditors (due within one year)										
Tax	—		—		1.101		3.605		3.689	
Trade Creditors	0.213		0.340		0.485		0.485		0.485	
Expense Creditors	0.120		0.302		0.374		0.455		0.455	
Royalties	—		0.063		0.100		0.143		0.143	
NET CURRENT ASSETS		1.365		5.050		6.883		10.586		14.180
LONG TERM FUNDS										
Less Creditors (due after one year)										
Loan		21.600		23.760		21.682		19.396		16.882
NET ASSETS		16.930		15.842		17.340		20.945		24.634
CAPITAL AND RESERVES										
Called Up Shares		20.000		20.000		20.000		20.000		20.000
Reserves		(3.070)		(4.158)		(2.660)		0.945		4.634
TOTAL EQUITY		16.930		15.842		17.340		20.945		24.634

months of year 1, but sales will begin in year 2. As labour, management and associated firms gain experience from the operation of the business, production and sales will increase so that by the beginning of year 4 production will have reached the fully planned capacity level of 200 tonnes per working day. Variable costs and royalty (a payment in lieu of a land charge) will build up in a corresponding way. Fixed costs and administration costs are recorded, as are interest payments due and the annual depreciation charge to arrive at the Profit before Tax. Tax on Profits is incurred at the rate of 50%. However, losses can be offset as a charge against profits in subsequent years. The loss in year 1 is thus set off partly against all profit in year 2 and part of the year 3 profit, when only Ms 2.201 million is liable for tax. The tax amounts shown are the liability for tax on operations during the year in question. They would normally be paid in the following year. Unless a system applies of paying advances on tax during any year, the liability for tax cannot be calculated and negotiated in practice until after the end of the year concerned.

13. The Trading and the Profit and Loss Account showed that once this mine gets into full production it can be expected to generate quite large profits. On the constant price basis used, the financial provision of Ms 40 million for investment will leave a comfortable balance at the beginning of the operating period proper, in year 2. Thereafter the cash surplus increases steadily. This will be especially pronounced after year 10, when the final portion of the loan is repaid. Calculations not presented here suggest that, by the year 15, when the project is taken to be liquidated, over Ms 66 million would have accumulated. However, it should be remembered that this figure makes no provision for:
- the withdrawal of funds as dividends; and
- interest earned on unused balances held by the project.

This is normal practice. No one would expect that this would be the actual sum held by the project at this remote future date, but the calculation is consistent, and it is not usual for financial planners to forecast dividend payments and interest earnings. Quite clearly, dividends could be paid quite early – perhaps during year 4, when the accumulated surplus is equal to more than 80% of annual operating costs, and set to continue increasing.

14. The final statement is the *Balance Sheet*, Table I.6. These figures show the value of the project at the end of the years referred to. The origin of most of the figures can be easily traced in earlier statements, with additional explanations as noted in the Box I.1.

15. This Balance Sheet reflects a typical pattern for an unchanging project. In the early years, Assets mainly take the form of Fixed Assets. Over time, cash becomes an Asset form of growing importance. On the Liabilities side, long term debt exceeds the value of Equity while interest accumulates unpaid, but by year 5 Equity accounts for more than half of the value of Assets, and debt diminishes steadily thereafter.

Taking account of inflation

16. Tables I.1 to I.6 illustrate the typical form of forecast accounts that may be prepared in planning a revenue project. All of those tables were based on constant prices – the prices in the base period, which is reckoned to be year − 1, about a year before implementation begins. To get a clear picture of actual finance needs, alternative figures must be drawn up that take inflation into account.

Box I.1   The Rock Phosphate Project

Notes on the Forecast Accounts
These notes explain the derivation of some of the figures.

Table I.3   Cash Flow Forecast
This table records receipts and payments of cash, and differs from Table I.5, Trading and Profit and Loss Account, which records amounts due or payable, whether paid or not. The cash flow allows for material stocks held, credit given to buyers and credit received from suppliers. The following provisions for working capital have been allowed for in the cash flow forecast.

Sales Revenue	*– one tenth of annual sales always unpaid.*
Materials	*– physical stocks held of 25% of use expected in the following year: one month credit received.*
Mine Labour	*– Ms 50,000 wages due but unpaid at the end of each period.*
Grinding Labour	*– Ms 20,000 wages due but unpaid at the end of each period.*
Other Operating Costs	*– Credit received equal to 10% of expenses in preceding year.*
Royalty	*– paid 2 months in arrears.*
Tax	*– Full amount paid in the year after the one to which it relates.*

These points allow the Cash Flow forecast to be derived from figures in the Trading and Profit and Loss Account.

Table I.4   Depreciation
A 'straight line' method is used to charge to the accounts the same amount each year for any item. This annual amount would approximately spread the original cost of each capital item evenly over the years of its expected life.

Table I.6   Balance Sheets
The values for the end of each year, like those in Table I.5, are independent of each other, and do not flow from one year to the next, as in Table I.3.

*Net Value of Fixed Assets in any year **equals** Original Cost **plus** Cost of Additions **minus** value of all Depreciation to date.*

Year end values of Current Asset items reflect the stocks and credit provisions allowed for in the Cash Flow Forecast.

*Reserves in any year **equal** the total value of Profit after Tax to the end of that year **minus** the total value of Capitalised Interest **minus** the total value to the end of that year of all Dividends and Appropriations.*

17. Inflation rates are impossible to forecast accurately. For illustration inflation is assumed to take place at the following rates:

	per cent
Year −1 to Year 0	10
Year 0 to Year 1	9
Year 1 to Year 2	7
Year 2 to Year 3	6
Year 3 to Year 4	5
Year 4 to Year 5	5
Year 5 to Year 6	5

It will probably not be necessary to forecast inflation further ahead. By Year 7, the project should be on a rising plane of liquidity; sooner, quite possibly.

18. Estimation of inflation rates allows the calculation of annual factors by which the fixed price values should be raised to show Current Prices (sometimes called Cash Prices) – the actual costs and revenues expected to occur during the years in question. These factors are shown in the second line of Table I.7, in which the important items in Table I.1 to I.5 are shown with inflation adjustments made. Assuming that all prices increase at exactly the same rate as the general levels of inflation (ie no relative price changes), the current price value of any item is found by simple multiplication. Table I.7, however, omits payments of interest and capital amortisation. The reason for this is that in this case study the terms of the loan are fixed and they do not vary with inflation. For a loan of Ms 16 million, the sums to be repaid each year are as shown in Table I.2, irrespective of the rate of inflation. This is normal practice for the terms of most capital loans but some loans do carry variable interest and even, when inflation is high, provision for variation of the capital sum outstanding.

19. It would be possible to draw up a complete set of forecast account tables at current prices, and with a computer this could easily be done. However, short cut calculations can be made. Table I.7 shows how easily this is done for Fixed Capital and Pre-Operating Costs. The same is true of calculating the new values of revenue and different groups of cost item.

20. The annual charge for depreciation can be simply calculated by amortising the original cost over the expected life of the asset. This may be done with the intention of creating a reserve to provide for eventual replacement of the asset, should that be necessary. Pressures of inflation may mean that the reserve is insufficient to finance the cost of the replacement. Calculation of the annual depreciation charge during operations may be based on the current replacement value of the asset rather than the historic cost, thus acknowledging the increasing cost of replacement. From there it is a short step to making an annual depreciation provision to allow for the further effect of inflation on the years past that were not able to be calculated and provided for at the time – a process known as backlog depreciation. However, for the purposes of this exercise, depreciation based on historic costs is adequate and meets the requirements of forecast accounts, especially if (as we assume) the depreciation rates used are those accepted by the authorities for the calculation of corporation tax.

21. In preparing inflated accounts, the main purpose is to consider the adequacy of financing proposals. The original plans for loan and share financing

are retained, and require no adjustment, since interest and capital repayment sums will not vary if the loan carries fixed interest.

22.   The adjusted figures for Operating Margin and Depreciation combine with the earlier values of interest to produce the figures for Profit before Tax, and Taxes on Profit shown at the foot of Table I.7. (It is notable that, under inflation, tax payments begin earlier and are larger.) All of these figures can be combined in a revised Cash Flow Forecast, Table I.8. The revised account shows that the original financing plan was insufficient. The project would be short of funds to the extent of more than Ms 4 million. Early draw-down of shares and loan would allow Year 0 costs to be covered, but not those in Year 1. The project investment would never be completed. This is not just because the cost of Fixed Capital has gone up – in fact, it is still expected to cost a little less than the Ms 40 million available. Increasing the sum for Fixed Capital will not by itself take care of the inflation problem. The financing needs of Pre-Operating Costs, Working Capital and early Operating Losses must also be taken into account. In this case, more finance is needed for the first years. Something like Ms 45 or 46 million should be available. By year 4 the cash position should be comfortable, even with a larger loan, and by year 5 the phosphate mine will be carrying very large cash reserves.

Some Financial Analyses

23.   The main financial analysis – examination of the adequacy of the expected provision of funds – was discussed in the last section. Inflation-adjusted figures showed that the financial provision originally envisaged would be insufficient to launch the project if inflation was at or above the projected rates.

24.   Because of this, additional financing must be secured. In this illustration, the alternative sources and form of extra project funding sources are not looked into. Several possibilities exist – more equity from RDA; a larger loan from NIDB; an additional loan. Investigating the alternatives and sorting between them is the essence of financial planning and negotiation, which can take quite a long time.

25.   The calculation of different cost measures for comparative analysis will be of little relevance for the phosphate mine, since it will be the first of its kind in the country so there is nothing very similar to compare it with. However, some constant price figures could easily be calculated, as shown in Table I.9. These show total production costs, and various sub-divisions, during year 5, when the project has got into full production. The expected efficiency of this mine could be assessed by comparing these values to figures for mining elsewhere, adjusted to the same currency and base period values.

26.   Many financial ratios could be estimated for this project. Single year values for some ratios are presented in Appendix 7.1, so none of the many figures that could be calculated are presented here. It should however be emphasised that the inspection of annual series of key ratio values could give a valuable picture of the financial situation of this project, and of the extent of its riskiness in those early years when indebtedness is at its highest.

THE ROCK PHOSPHATE PROJECT

TABLE I.7

ADJUSTED FIGURES ALLOWING FOR FORECAST INFLATION

Current   Ms million

	Year	0	1	2	3	4	5
Assumed Rate of Inflation		10	9	7	6	5	5
Inflation Factor		1.100	1.199	1.283	1.360	1.428	1.499
Fixed Capital	: Constant	29.609	5.787	—	—		
	Inflated	32.570	6.939	—	—		
Pre-Operating Costs	: Constant	1.480	0.289	—	0.200	0.299	0.224
	Inflated	1.628	0.347	—	0.272	0.427	0.336
Sales Revenue	: Constant	—	—	10.625	17.000	24.225	24.225
	Inflated	—	—	13.632	23.120	34.593	36.313
Materials	: Constant	—	0.335	2.553	4.085	5.821	5.821
	Inflated	—	0.402	3.275	5.556	8.312	8.726
Other Expenses	: Constant	—	1.135	4.012	4.727	5.538	5.538
	Inflated	—	1.361	5.147	6.429	7.908	8.301
Royalties	: Constant	—	—	0.375	0.600	0.855	0.855
	Inflated	—	—	0.481	0.816	1.221	1.282
Depreciation of Fixed Assets	: Inflated[1]	—	—	2.525	2.525	2.553	2.638
Depreciation of Pre-Operating Costs	: Inflated[1]	—	—	0.395	0.395	0.395	0.395
Profit Before Tax	: Inflated[2]	—	-1.763	1.809	4.168	11.108	12.063
Tax on Inflated Profit		—	—	0.023	2.084	5.554	6.032

[1] Using actual (historic) costs of assets and applying depreciation factors in Table I.4 to them.
[2] Sales revenue minus materials, other expenses, royalties, depreciation and interest (all in inflated prices).

THE ROCK PHOSPHATE PROJECT

TABLE 1.8

INFLATION – ADJUSTED CASH FLOW FORECAST

Current   Ms million

Year	0	1	2	3	4	5
INFLOWS Balance B/F	—	(2.198)	(3.687)	0.894	6.122	15.951
Equity	16.000	4.000	—	—	—	—
Loan	16.000	4.000	—	—	—	—
Sales Revenue	—	—	13.632	23.120	34.593	36.313
TOTAL INFLOW	32.000	5.802	9.945	24.014	40.715	52.264
OUTFLOWS Fixed Capital	32.570	6.939	—	0.272	0.427	0.336
Pre-Operating Overheads	1.628	0.347	—	—	—	—
Materials	—	0.948	3.655	6.015	8.381	8.799
Labour	—	0.300	1.764	1.870	1.964	2.061
Other Expenses	—	0.955	3.151	4.442	5.806	6.211
Royalties	—	—	0.481	0.816	1.221	1.282
Interest Payable	—	—	—	2.376	2.168	1.940
Tax on Profits	—	—	—	0.023	2.511	6.018
Capital Repayment	—	—	—	2.078	2.286	2.514
TOTAL OUTFLOW	34.198	9.489	9.051	17.892	24.764	29.161
Cash Balance C/F	(2.198)	(3.687)	0.894	6.122	15.951	23.103

	Constant Ms million		Constant Ms per tonne (57,000 tonnes)
Mining Costs			
Variable: Mine Materials	5.051		
Mine Power	1.021		
Underground Transport	0.326	6.398	112
Fixed: Mine Administration	0.342		
Mine Labour	1.375		
Machinery Depreciation	0.846	2.563	45
Total Mining Costs		8.961	157
Grinding Costs			
Variable: Grinding Materials	0.770		
Grinding Power	1.372	2.142	38
Fixed: Grinding Labour	0.310		
Machinery Depreciation	0.969	1.279	22
Total Grinding Costs		3.421	60
Overheads			
Selling and Distribution	0.088		
General Administration	0.230		
Overheads	0.474	0.792	14
Depreciation		0.524	9
Royalty		0.855	15
Total Overheads		2.171	38

Economic Analysis of the Rock Phosphate Project

Analysis at constant market prices

27. For economic analysis, a year-by-year statement has to be prepared of the cost of all the resources to be applied to the project through individual inputs, all valued at allocative efficiency prices. The same statement should include the value of the output or other benefits that will arise, valued in the same way. The difference between the two parts, the annual Net Benefits, will be discounted at the Accounting Rate of Interest.

28. It has been stressed in Part I that engineering design, financial analysis and economic analysis should all interact in an iterative process. Economic analysis is often introduced as soon as there is provisional knowledge of the physical quantities, which would be valued directly at their own efficiency prices. Alternatively economic analysis can begin from a statement, year by year, of the costs of the project, and the value of output, all valued at constant market prices. Shadow prices are then substituted for the market price valuations of the individual cost and benefit categories in this statement, to allow full assessment of the direct effects of the project when valued in allocative efficiency terms.

29. A basic statement of costs and benefits, valued at constant market prices, is presented for the Rock Phosphate Project in Table I.10. The figures are drawn from some of the basic constant price accounting statements: capital costs are taken from Table I.1; and the figures for operating costs and phosphate sales from the Trading and Profit and Loss account, Table I.5. Only 'real' items are brought in to this table, not any finance payments. In particular, financial working capital is excluded.

30. Table I.10, and the equivalent economic profile of the project, follow typical patterns. During the investment years, Net Benefits are negative, but they become positive as soon as production begins, and quickly reach a high level – about half the value of output. Because the high level of net benefits is sustained for several years, the discounted value of the net benefits stream is high. At 10% discount rate, the NPV of financial net benefits is Ms 33 millions, and the IRR is 20%.

31. This IRR is sometimes called the Financial Rate of Return of the project. It is not the rate of return on any finance in the project. It is given this title because it is the rate of return on real (net) flows when costs and benefits are valued at constant market prices – financial prices as they are sometimes called. It is a measure of limited value because shadow pricing is needed if resource costs are to be measured.

The main economic features of the project
32. From the economic viewpoint, the main features of the project are these.
   – The output – powdered rock phosphate – would be a substitute for imports. The benefits of the project would be the saved cost of the imports, and any difference in transport costs.
   – Much of the machinery and equipment required as capital would need to be imported. Some items would be subject to import duties and sales tax.
   – During the operating phase, main inputs would be (1) materials obtained locally, not specially imported; (2) labour, of which just over 50% by cost is unskilled; and (3) electricity, purchased from the national electricity authority.
Shadow pricing the direct costs of the project concentrated particularly on these items.

National parameters for allocative efficiency valuation
33. These could be estimated for this project only crudely. In the country, taxes on imports were on the whole quite high, with many goods being liable for both import duties and sales tax. Dealings in foreign exchange were strictly controlled, but there were no signs of a very severe shortage of foreign currencies, like cutbacks and physical quotas on a wide range of imports.

34. Consequently, it was felt that the general difference between domestic price levels and world prices was reflected in the level of taxes on imports, which were running at about 25%. Use of the world prices numeraire thus called for a Standard Conversion Factor (SCF) of 0.80 (ie 1.00/1.25) for use where the cost composition of items was not individually considered.

35. Although the mine is located in a small hilly area that is not used for agriculture, it is adjacent to a large farming region that is densely populated.

Several towns and the regional capital are not far away, and local people have experience of industrial work of the kind that this mine will require. No special costs would be incurred for or by workers in this project. Minimum wages in the mine for year-round employment are above the levels obtainable in farming. General enquiry suggested that the wages expected to be paid for unskilled and learn-on-the-job work are about one third higher than the year-round earnings of the many farm employees in the area so, at market prices, the opportunity cost is 0.75 of the actual wage. Nearly all of the agricultural products from this area are consumed within the region. Since farm output carries no special premium, the valuation of the unskilled labour called for a simple SCF adjustment for conversion to border prices. The shadow wage used for unskilled labour was therefore $0.75 \times 0.80 = 0.60$. Although the project will be in the public sector, it will have to compete with the active, diversified private sector in the hire of skilled workers. Salaries will therefore be competitive, reflecting opportunity cost, so the only shadow pricing adjustment for skilled labour will be use of the SCF.

The valuation of output

36.   It is intended that the ore mined in this project will supply one of the three national factories making phosphatic fertilisers. Capacity to produce fertilisers has been expanded in recent years. The three plants are all fairly close to each other, between the mine and the port, and they rely on rock phosphate imported from about 2,700 miles away. All of these factories could handle powdered ore of the kind to be produced by the mine. At the time of project preparation, imports were in excess of 160,000 tonnes per annum, so the whole output of the proposed mine, 57,000 tonnes per annum, could be absorbed. All of the ore output can thus be valued as an import substitute. Valuation of the phosphate produced at the project site is based on the saved cost of importing ore and transporting it to the factories, and the new cost of transporting powdered rock from the project to the factories. Whereas the imports were carried between port and factory by rail, road transport will be used to move the phosphate between the mine and the factories. There is no railway near the mine. Although rail movement would be possible for part of the journey, the extra cost of transhipment at the nearest railhead outweighs any cost savings between rail and road carriage for the rest of the journey.

37.   In calculating the import parity price it was necessary to take account of quality differences between the local product and the imported alternative. The content of soluble P_2O_5 in samples from the mine was only about five-sixths of the average quality of the imported ore. One tonne of locally mined phosphate would thus substitute for only 0.833 tonnes of imports.

38.   Basic figures for the calculations were these:

	MS per tonne		
	Actual cost per tonne of Imports		Saved cost per tonne of Output
CIF cost	620	× 0.833	516
Port handling	45	× 0.833	37
Rail transport	203	× 0.833	169
Insurance, unloading etc.	7	× 0.833	6
TOTALS	875		728

132

Less Road transport		140
Insurance, unloading, etc.		7
Border Parity Value		581

At market prices, the mine output would be valued at Ms 581 per tonne. However, shadow pricing for allocative efficiency must revalue domestic costs at world prices in order to conform with our own numeraire. In this case, only the cif cost is in world prices, paid in sterling or any other convertible currency. The other items are all domestic costs, paid for in Moneys (Ms – the domestic currency).

39.   Revaluing these items was approached in two ways. The first, crude and simple way, was just to apply the SCF throughout, thus:

	Market Price		*Shadow Price*
CIF cost	516		516
Port handling	37	× 0.8	30
Rail transport	169	× 0.8	135
Insurance, unloading etc.	6	× 0.8	5
Road transport	−140	× 0.8	−112
Insurance, unloading etc.	−7	× 0.8	−6
Project value, Ms per tonne	581		568

The shadow price of Ms 568 per tonne can be used to value output quantities in a direct statement of economic values. However, if the shadow-priced statement is to be derived from the market price statement (Table I.10), an output Conversion Factor will be used. The market price of output in the project is Ms 425 so the CF is 568/425 = 1.34.[1]

40.   The alternative approach to valuation was to look more carefully at the two main domestic cost items, road and rail transport. Separate (though limited) studies had shown the composition of costs for these two modes of transport. Information on them is shown in Table I.11. In the first column, the total unit cost of each mode is divided between four major catagories. The composition of each category is presented in the next block of figures. This allows the unit cost of each mode of transport to be converted to its content of Foreign Exchange, Tax, Unskilled Labour and Non-Traded Goods, each of which can be revalued through specific conversion factors. All this is done on the right side of the table.

41.   The calculations show that the specific conversion factor for Rail Transport is calculated at 0.75, not much difference from the SCF, 0.80. Because of the exceptionally high incidence of tax and other transfers in the costs of fuel and vehicles, the conversion factor for road transport is much less, 0.52. Use of these alternative conversion factors in shadow pricing the rock phosphate from the mine gives a Shadow Price of Ms 599 per tonne, CF 1.41. This was regarded as a maximum estimate. The incidence of tax on the large trucks to be used for transporting the rock phosphate from the mine might be less than in the general transport case on which the detailed shadow pricing was based, so the actual CF for road transport may be higher than the estimate of 0.52.

---

[1] Individual conversion factors are not needed if the economic analysis is undertaken item by item but they are shown here and in subsequent paragraphs to illustrate how they are derived for application to summary financial accounts.

THE ROCK PHOSPHATE PROJECT

TABLE I.10

ANNUAL STATEMENT OF FINANCIAL COSTS AND BENEFITS: CONSTANT PRICES

Ms millions

COSTS — Year	0	1	2	3	4	5	6	7	8	9	10	11	12	13	14	15
FIXED CAPITAL																
Mining and Transport Machinery	5.769	2.488	—	—	—	—	—	—	—	—	—	—	—	—	—	—
Grinding Machinery	19.015	0.370	—	0.200	—	—	—	—	0.200	—	—	3.500	—	—	—	—
Buildings	2.851	—	—	—	—	—	—	—	—	—	—	—	—	—	—	—
Electrical Plant	0.200	—	—	—	—	—	—	—	—	—	—	—	—	—	—	—
Vehicles, Tractors etc.	0.299	2.815	—	—	0.299	—	—	—	—	0.299	—	—	—	—	—	—
Workshop and Equipment	0.523	0.114	—	—	—	0.114	—	—	—	—	0.114	—	—	—	—	—
Roads, Bridges etc.	0.952	—	—	—	—	0.110	—	—	—	—	0.110	—	—	—	—	—
Pre-Operating Expenses	1.480	0.289	—	—	—	—	—	—	—	—	—	—	—	—	—	—
Total Capital Costs	31.089	6.076	—	0.200	0.299	0.224	—	—	0.200	0.299	0.224	3.500	—	—	—	—
WORKING CAPITAL																
Unused Materials	—	0.638	0.383	0.434	—	—	—	—	—	—	—	—	—	—	—	—
Work in Progress	—	—	0.213	0.127	0.145	—	—	—	—	—	—	—	—	—	—	—
Unsold Output	—	—	1.063	0.637	0.723	—	—	—	—	—	—	—	—	—	—	—
Total Working Capital	—	0.638	1.659	1.198	0.868	—	—	—	—	—	—	—	—	—	—	—
OPERATING COSTS																
Labour	—	0.420	1.685	1.685	1.685	1.685	1.685	1.685	1.685	1.685	1.685	1.685	1.685	1.685	1.685	—
Administration	—	0.300	0.572	0.572	0.572	0.572	0.572	0.572	0.572	0.572	0.572	0.572	0.572	0.572	0.572	—
Selling and Distribution	—	0.030	0.088	0.088	0.088	0.088	0.088	0.088	0.088	0.088	0.088	0.088	0.088	0.088	0.088	—
Overheads	—	0.210	0.474	0.474	0.474	0.474	0.474	0.474	0.474	0.474	0.474	0.474	0.474	0.474	0.474	—
Materials	—	0.335	2.553	4.085	5.821	5.821	5.821	5.821	5.821	5.821	5.821	5.821	5.821	5.821	5.821	—
Power	—	0.140	1.050	1.679	2.393	2.393	2.393	2.393	2.393	2.393	2.393	2.393	2.393	2.393	2.393	—
Underground Transport	—	0.035	0.143	0.229	0.326	0.326	0.326	0.326	0.326	0.326	0.326	0.326	0.326	0.326	0.326	—
Total Operating Costs	—	1.470	6.565	8.812	11.359	11.359	11.359	11.359	11.359	11.359	11.359	11.359	11.359	11.359	11.359	—
TOTAL COSTS	31.089	8.184	8.224	10.210	12.526	11.583	11.359	11.359	11.559	11.658	11.583	14.859	11.359	11.359	11.359	—
BENEFITS																
Phosphate Produced	—	—	10.625	17.000	24.225	24.225	24.225	24.225	24.225	24.225	24.225	24.225	24.225	24.225	24.225	—
Return of Working capital	—	—	—	—	—	—	—	—	—	—	—	—	—	—	—	4.363
Salvage Values	—	—	—	—	—	—	—	—	—	—	—	—	—	—	—	11.844
TOTAL BENEFITS	—	—	10.625	17.000	24.225	24.225	24.225	24.225	24.225	24.225	24.225	24.225	24.225	24.225	24.225	16.207
NET BENEFITS	−31.089	−8.184	2.441	6.790	11.699	12.642	12.866									16.207

134

THE ROCK PHOSPHATE PROJECT

TABLE I.11

CALCULATING SPECIFIC CONVERSION FACTORS FOR RAIL AND ROAD TRANSPORT

	% of the Market Price	Composition of Each Item (%)				Composition of Market Price (%)			
		Foreign Exchange	Tax, etc.	Unskilled Labour	Non-Traded Goods	Foreign Exchange	Tax, etc.	Unskilled Labour	Non-Traded Goods
RAIL TRANSPORT									
Traded Goods	45	65	25	—	10	29	11	—	5
Non-Traded Goods	3	—	—	—	100	—	—	—	3
Labour	3	—	—	100	—	—	—	3	—
Capital Costs	49	77	23	—	—	38	11	—	—
Totals	100					67	22	3	8
Conversion Factors						1.00	0.00	0.60	0.80
Shadow Price						67	0	2	6
								TOTAL: 75%	
ROAD TRANSPORT									
Traded Goods	25	23	77	—	—	6	19	—	—
Non-Traded Goods	12	—	—	—	100	—	—	—	12
Labour	17	—	—	100	—	—	—	17	—
Capital Costs	46	48	40	—	12	22	18	—	6
Totals	100					28	37	17	18
Conversion Factors						1.00	0.00	0.60	0.80
Shadow Price						28	0	10	14
								TOTAL: 52%	

Capital costs

42. In this project, specification of the capital equipment was such an important aspect of project design and costing that almost all items were individually costed. Almost two thirds (by value) of the total cost of plant and equipment was the cif cost of imports, for which tax and transport costs were individually calculated. For the main locally-supplied items, at-project price estimates were obtained.

43. The availability of these data allowed quite specific conversion factors to be calculated for many of the capital items. The relevant figures are in Table I.12. The level of taxes on these items of imported equipment are high. Because of this, CFs for each item are less than the SCF, when calculated by applying the CFs for each type of cost (in the bottom line) to the percentages.

THE ROCK PHOSPHATE PROJECT

TABLE I.12

COMPOSITION OF THE PROJECT PRICE OF SOME CAPITAL ITEMS, AND THE ESTIMATION OF CONVERSION FACTORS FOR THEM

Capital Item	CIF Cost of Imported Component	Taxes on Imported Component	Transport of Imported Component	Local Component	CF for the item
Mining and Transport Machinery	58	22	0.4	20	0.74
Grinding Machinery	73	27	0.3	0	0.73
Vehicles, Tractors etc.	43	15	1	41	0.77
Workshop Equipment	9	12	2	77	0.72
CF for the type of cost	1.0	0.00	0.80	0.80	

44. For locally supplied capital items, the SCF was mainly used. However, some local data did exist on the cost composition of construction, drawn from an Input–Output table. This information, and the derivation from it of a conversion factor, is shown in the top half of Table I.13. The figures indicate that quite high profit margins appear to be earned in the construction industry. This factor particularly accounts for the estimation of a conversion factor for construction from this generalised data of 0.64, significantly less than the SCF. This was regarded as a slightly low CF, though the construction required for this project might carry margins as high as the general case.

Operating costs

45. With the exception of explosives, locally obtained material inputs were a diverse group. Their cost composition was not investigated for economic analysis. In Shadow Pricing the SCF was applied to them throughout.

46. Power generation costs were not covered by the electricity authority's tariffs, and subsidies were about 23% of all costs. Revaluing this non-traded input thus called for an upwards adjustment of 1.30 to allow for this factor. The crude CF for electricity was thus calculated as 1.30×0.80 (SCF) = 1.04.

136

THE ROCK PHOSPHATE PROJECT

TABLE I.13

CALCULATION OF SPECIFIC CONVERSION FACTORS FOR CONSTRUCTION AND ELECTRICITY

	% of the Market Price	Composition of Each Item (%)				Composition of Market Price (%)			
		Foreign Exchange	Tax, etc.	Unskilled Labour	Non-Traded Goods	Foreign Exchange	Tax, etc.	Unskilled Labour	Non-Traded Goods
CONSTRUCTION									
Traded Goods:									
Direct	16	80	20	—	—	13	3	—	—
Metals	26	74	26	—	—	19	7	—	—
Non-Traded	19	—	—	—	100	—	—	—	19
Labour	20	—	—	50	50	—	—	10	10
Capital	4	83	17	—	—	3	1	—	—
Profits	15	—	100	—	—	—	15	—	—
Totals	100					35	26	10	29
Conversion Factors						1.00	0.00	0.60	0.80
Shadow Price						35	0	6	23
								TOTAL: 64%	
ELECTRICITY									
Traded Goods	9	80	20	—	—	7	2	—	—
Non-Traded Goods	29	—	—	—	100	—	—	—	29
Labour	30	—	—	50	50	—	—	15	15
Capital	62	77	13	2	8	48	8	1	5
Totals	130					55	10	16	49
Conversion Factors						1.00	0.00	0.60	0.80
Shadow Price						55	0	10	39
								TOTAL: 104%	

47. Detailed cost information for electricity generation was also available from a general country study. Its use to calculate a specific CF is shown in the lower part of Table I.13. It was an interesting coincidence that this detailed analysis gave the same CF (1.04) as the crude approach.

48. The categories 'Administration' and 'Selling and Distribution' consisted very largely of the costs of employing Skilled Workers, so the SCF was applied to them. However, three-quarters of the cost of the item 'Labour' in Table I.10 was for Unskilled Workers, the remainder Skilled. The CF for this item was calculated as

$$\underbrace{\text{Unskilled Labour}}_{(0.75 \times 0.60)} + \underbrace{\text{Skilled Labour}}_{(0.25 \times 0.80)} = \underbrace{\text{CF Labour}}_{0.65}$$

Applying the shadow prices: results of economic analysis

49. The Shadow Price CFs used to value the project at allocative efficiency prices are summarised in Table I.14. The first column shows the simple CFs that would be used by applying the SCF to all non-labour locally purchased inputs. The second column shows the alternative values of CFs calculated from the more detailed cost composition data presented in Tables I.11 and I.13. They are significantly different in the case of Building and Phosphate. Whether such differences would have applied in other cases where the SCF was used is not known, because detailed cost data for them was not available. Most of them are not large items and so crude use of the SCF does not matter, but in view of the importance of the operating cost item Materials, it could have improved the analysis technically if more detailed cost information could have been obtained for some or all of the main components of this item.

THE ROCK PHOSPHATE PROJECT

TABLE I.14

SUMMARY OF SPECIFIC CONVERSION FACTORS FOR USE IN ECONOMIC ANALYSIS

	Simple Conversion Factor	Alternative Conversion Factor
Phosphate	1.34	1.41
Mining and Transport Machinery	0.74	—
Grinding Machinery	0.73	—
Buildings	0.80	0.64
Electrical Plant	0.80	—
Vehicles, Tractors etc.	0.77	—
Workshop and Equipment	0.72	—
Roads, Bridges etc.	0.80	—
Pre-Operating Expenses	0.80	—
Unused Materials	0.80	—
Work in Progress	0.80	—
Unsold Output (in Working Capital)	1.34	1.41
Labour	0.65	—
Administration	0.80	—
Selling and Distribution	0.80	—
Overheads	0.80	—
Materials	0.80	—
Power	1.04	1.04
Underground Transport	0.80	—
Working Capital Returned	1.10	1.14
Salvage Value	0.80	—

However, (not untypically) time and data were not available for this aspect of the analysis to be taken to the fullest extent.

50. It is notable from Table I.14 that the CF for most inputs is less than unity, whereas the CF for the product is substantially above 1.00. Shadow pricing will make the project look much more attractive than the constant price figures of Table I.10. The economic costs and benefits are obtained by re-valuing each figure in that table by the use of the 'simple' individual CFs. The total net economic benefits per year are shown in the final column of Table I.15 (the full results are in a worksheet that is not shown here). The national authorities have calculated that the appropriate real accounting rate of interest (ARI) is 10%. (This opportunity cost of capital is not to be confused with the financial interest rate on the loan to the project, which just happens to be the same number in this case.) Taking the net economic benefits and discounting at the ARI of 10% gave an NPV of Ms 101 million. The IRR is 40%. Clearly exploitation of the rock phosphate deposit along the lines envisaged in this project could make a very substantial contribution to economic growth.

Sensitivity analysis

51. Tests of a standard kind were carried out on the economic analysis values, to see the effect on the NPV of various departments from planned levels of some variables. The results were:

	Change in NPV (Ms million)
Increase in Capital Costs by 10%	−2.740
Increase in all Operating Costs by 10%	−5.800
Reduction in Output Value by 10%	−18.481
Investment period extended by 1 year	−10.303

52. These results are just calculations. No estimates were made of the probability of any of these deviations occurring. Individually and collectively, they were all small in relation to the large NPV at the ARI (or test discount rate), so there was no real need to carry further the analysis of risk. However, had this not been the case, it would have been important to look more carefully at the long-run prospects for the world price of rock phosphate. This project appears to be very valuable because the mine can supply phosphate of good quality to the fertiliser factory at a cost much lower than the forecast price of imported phosphate. However, in a more marginal case, forecasts for the world price would be obtained and inspected. Such forecasts may have been made by FAO, IBRD, OECD, the World Trade Centre or private interests. Analysts or consultants should check these sources, and if necessary make their own estimates of this, the most important economic feature of the project.

53. Sensitivity analysis was also carried out on the values of the Conversion Factors for two items, using CFs shown in the second column of Table I.14. The results were:

	Change in NPV (Ms million)
Buildings CF 0.64, not 0.80	+0.456
Phosphate CF 1.41, not 1.34	+9.654

Though not affecting the outcome of the analysis in this case, making such tests is good analysis practice.

Distributional Issues and Savings

54. The appraisal of every project should contain discussion of who will be the main beneficiaries. This can be assessed qualitatively, by considering the nature of the project and its financing, but a quantitative picture can also be drawn – along the lines suggested in chapters 4 and 5 – through use of the data for accounts forecasting and for shadow pricing.

55. The Rock Phosphate Project will be in the public sector. The substantial profits that will accrue will belong to the subsidiary company of the Regional Development Authority that will be set up to operate the mine. The Development Bank will recover its loan, with interest at 10%, and Central Government will obtain substantial revenue from the tax on annual profits. All of the direct financial benefits will accrue to public agencies of one kind or another.

56. Shadow Pricing shows that there will be very substantial additional benefits. What are they? Who will receive them? In the early years, government will receive taxes on the imported equipment – quite large amounts. Once the project begins, unskilled workers will be better off by the difference between the actual wage and the estimated opportunity cost. A substantial beneficiary will be the fertiliser factory that buys the powdered ore. The figures in the last section showed that imported phosphate costs the factory the equivalant of Ms 728 per tonne, whereas the output from this mine will cost it only Ms 572 per tonne (425 sale by mine, 140 transport and 7 for insurance, unloading etc.). Whether this substantial saving would be passed on as lower prices to consumers or retained as profits (and tax on profits) by the fertiliser company could be worth estimating if distributional aspects were to be handled seriously, especially as many of the beneficiaries may be small farmers who use the phosphatic manure.

57. This broad analysis suggests that a large part of the project benefits will go to agencies of the regional and state government. Some small net benefits will go to mine employees, and these may be revalued. Major amounts will go to the fertiliser factory (or possibly small farmers). Given that the government will be a major beneficiary the use of a savings premium will only make the project, with high net benefits, look significantly less valuable at the unadjusted ARI of 10% if the benefits going to the fertiliser factory are ultimately consumed rather than invested or taxed. Benefits to low income people may be so limited that distribution weighting would make little further difference to the discounted measures.

58. The dimensions of this qualitative assessment are reflected in the calculated values in Table I.15. These show in the left side who receives the net benefits of the constant market price valuation. The individual items are taken from the constant price forecast accounts, and add up to the annual value of financial net benefits at constant market prices that were shown in the last line of Table I.10.

59. The right half of the table shows the indirect benefits not accruing to the mine entity that are implicit in the shadow pricing. The labour benefits are small, but the fertiliser factory benefits are very large (although they may be passed on to consumers or taxed). Government's tax take is substantial in the first years, but it has to make a large annual payment as subsidy to the electricity authority for power sold at less than average cost.

THE ROCK PHOSPHATE PROJECT

TABLE I.15

DISTRIBUTION OF THE ECONOMIC NET BENEFITS

constant prices
Ms million

YEAR	DIRECT MARKET PRICE EFFECTS					TOTAL NET FINANCIAL BENEFITS	INDIRECT AND SHADOW PRICING EFFECTS					TOTAL NET ECONOMIC BENEFITS
	EQUITY		BANK	GOV'T			GOV'T		SCF Benefit[3]	Fert. Factory[4]	Unsk. Labour[5]	
	Annual Surplus	Financial W. CAP.		Tax on Profits	Royalties		Import Taxes[1]	Subsidy on Elec[2]				
0	-15.089		-16.000	—	—	-31.089	6.510	—	1.436	—	—	-23.14
1	-4.101	-0.083	-4.000	—	—	-8.184	0.664	-0.042	1.444	—	0.079	-6.33
2	2.750	-0.724	4.454	—	0.375	2.401	0.044	-0.315	1.176	3.510	0.316	7.08
3	2.052	-0.316	4.454	—	0.600	6.790	0.045	-0.504	1.470	6.006	0.316	14.12
4	5.646	-0.357	4.454	1.101	0.855	11.699	0.030	-0.718	1.769	8.627	0.316	21.73
5	3.728	—	4.454	3.605	0.855	12.642	—	-0.718	1.754	8.892	0.316	22.88
6	3.868	—	4.454	3.689	0.855	12.866	—	-0.718	1.697	8.892	0.316	23.05
7	3.756	—	4.454	3.801	0.855	12.866	—	-0.718	1.697	8.892	0.316	23.05
8	3.201	—	4.454	4.156	0.855	12.666	0.044	-0.718	1.705	8.892	0.316	22.90
9	2.949	—	4.454	4.309	0.855	12.567	0.045	-0.718	1.721	8.892	0.316	22.82
10	2.870	—	4.451	4.466	0.855	12.642	0.030	-0.718	1.724	8.892	0.316	22.88
11	3.861	—	—	4.650	0.855	9.366	0.770	-0.718	1.837	8.892	0.316	20.46
12	7.161	—	—	4.850	0.855	12.866	—	-0.718	1.697	8.892	0.316	23.05
13	6.925	—	—	5.086	0.855	12.866	—	-0.718	1.697	8.892	0.316	23.05
14	6.925	—	—	5.086	0.855	12.866	—	-0.718	1.697	8.892	0.316	23.05
15	9.630	1.480	—	5.097	—	16.207	—	—	-2.822	0.889	—	14.27

[1] On capital inputs where SCF has not been applied.

[2] 30% of actual amount paid.

[3] Total net economic benefits – total net financial benefits – other shadow price effects.

[4] No. of tonnes purchased × reduction in purchase price. For year 5 this equals 57,000 × (728–572) or Ms 8.892 m. Purchases in years 2 to 4 are 22,500 t, 38,500 t and 55,300 t. See paragraph 56 on ultimate beneficiaries.

[5] Change in income of unskilled labour = unskilled labour cost (w) – opportunity cost of unskilled labour (0.75 w) = 0.25 w. For every year 2 this equals 0.25 × (0.75 × 1.685) or 0.316.

Significant net benefits are attributable to applying the SCF (0.80) to all domestically-supplied inputs. Who gets those benefits? This is a well-nigh impossible question to answer. The benefit will go (in unknown amounts) to very many groups in the national society who cannot be identified. That they will go to particular groups arises as a direct result of government policy, and in this light it is convenient and partly logical to regard them either as benefits to government or as benefits to individuals of equal value as benefits to government. Because of the high economic profitability of this project and the relatively low amount of private net benefits likely, no calculations were made involving a savings premium and income distribution weighting. However, the figures in Table I.15 would provide the basis for these calculations, if they were considered useful.

Externalities

60.   It was not expected that the project would have any adverse environmental effects, though the implications of moving up to 200 tonnes of phosphate per day by road were not analysed in detail. It was noted that, since this would be the first phosphate mining project in the country, valuable experience would be obtained, which could bring benefits in the later exploitation of other phosphate deposits whose existence was known. This is a valid point, though its economic value might not be very great. The process is said to be not very complex, and foreign expertise could be obtained if necessary. There appeared to be no general lack of management expertise to join new projects if they were developed.

The Relationships between Financial and Economic Analysis

61.   This case study illustrates the differences and relationships between the two main types of analysis. Financial analysis, with its concern with money flows, is based on forecast accounts at constant (base period) prices, and later with forecast inflation allowed for. All money flows which impinge on the project sponsors are considered, both those for real inputs and outputs, and for finance payments and receipts.

62.   Economic analysis is concerned only with real inputs and outputs, and takes no account of finance flows when allocative efficiency alone is the basis of valuation. But it also includes real inputs which are outside the company accounts. It is concerned with national effects in the with/without project situations. All items are then valued at accounting prices of constant (base period) value, to show the value of net resource flows (net benefits) each year.

63.   The two types of analysis can thus be seen to differ in respect of both the items taken into account and the basis of valuation. Differences between them extend further to the types of analysis for which the data is used. Economic analysis seeks mainly to calculate discounted measures, to allow cost-benefit appraisal of the national effects of the project and cost-effectiveness of particular features within the project scheme as a whole. Financial analysis, on the other hand, pays very little attention to discounted measures. They arise only in respect of finding the rate of return to equity,[1] itself a measure of limited value in an absolute sense.

---

[1] Although this rate of return is the only one generally calculated as part of financial analysis, it is incorrect to refer to it as the Financial Rate of Return. That term is defined in paragraph 31. The equity rate of return is merely the rate of return on one type of finance. It is not a rate of return on all finance, nor is it a rate of return on the project.

Other Information derived from the Financial and Economic Data

64. The figures drawn up for financial and economic analysis can be used to indicate further information about the project that analysts may need to present. Two important sets of year-by-year values are the flows of foreign exchange and taxes associated with the project.

65. To take foreign exchange first, the direct overseas portion of imported capital costs and major inputs will normally be clearly identified in the project plans. Non-traded items will have an indirect content whose estimation calls for more detailed, general cost analysis data like those shown in Tables I.11 and I.13. Where the output is a traded item, the estimation of the border parity price will show the actual earnings or savings involved. The costs or savings between the project and the border will have an indirect foreign exchange content, but additional data for these non-traded items will be needed to allow estimation.

66. Data on flows to and from the exchequer will also be estimated on the basis of both direct and indirect sources. The actual values of taxes on direct imports and products, and the value of sales taxes on inputs, will be fairly easily calculated. However, the tax component of items in the cost of non-traded items will require secondary data for its estimation. Similarly government subsidies on items such as power or water will require secondary data. In addition, the forecast accounts will show the annual payments of corporation tax from liable revenue projects.

67. Some illustrative figures for these two flows, as they relate to the first years of the Rock Phosphate Project, are shown in Table I.16. Not all indirect flows are taken account of, so the net flow figures shown are only partial values. They understate the value of foreign exchange costs, and almost certainly understate the value of tax inflows consequent on implementation of the project. If a more detailed analysis were needed, data on other items would have to be obtained.

68. The values in both parts of the table for capital items and the one recurrent cost item included are based on the information in Tables I.11, I.12 and I.13. The tax part of the table is made from the viewpoint of government; positive values are taxes paid directly or indirectly by the project. The negative value for power reflects the fact that the indirect tax income there is less than the value of the subsidy on electricity supply. The foreign exchange and tax components of output are calculated on a per tonne basis as follows:

	%	F.E. Ms	%	Tax Ms
CIF value saved	100	516	—	—
Port costs saved	20*	7	10*	−4
Rail costs saved	67	113	22	−37
Road transport costs incurred	28	−39	37	63
Net effect		597		22

* Guessed percentage contents.

THE ROCK PHOSPHATE PROJECT

TABLE I.16

ILLUSTRATIVE FOREIGN EXCHANGE AND TAX FLOWS

constant prices
Ms million

FOREIGN EXCHANGE	YEAR 0	YEAR 1	YEAR 2	YEAR 3	YEAR 4
Capital Items					
Mining and Transport					
Machinery	−3.346	−1.443	—	−1.160	—
Grinding Machinery	−13.881	−0.270	—	—	—
Buildings	−0.998	—	—	—	—
Vehicles and Tractors	−0.129	−0.049	—	—	−0.129
Workshop Equipment	−0.047	—	—	—	—
Recurrent Costs					
Power	—	−0.077	−0.578	−0.923	−1.316
Output					
Import Savings	—	—	14.925	23.880	34.029
Net Flow	−18.401	−1.839	14.347	21.797	32.584

TAXES AND SUBSIDY					
Capital Items					
Mining and Transport					
Machinery	1.269	0.547	—	0.044	—
Grinding Machinery	5.138	0.100	—	—	—
Buildings	0.741	—	—	—	—
Vehicles and Tractors	0.045	0.017	—	—	0.045
Workshop Equipment	0.628	—	—	—	—
Recurrent Costs					
Power	—	−0.028	−0.210	−0.336	−0.478
Royalty	—	—	0.375	0.600	0.855
Output					
Net Taxes	—	—	0.550	0.880	1.254
Profit Tax	—	—	—	—	1.101
Net Fiscal Flow	7.821	0.636	0.715	1.188	2.777

69.   Quite typically, the project will absorb foreign exchange before it produces the very large net savings that can be expected. Again not untypically, central government will receive large fiscal inflows from the outset. Taxes on imported machinery are exceptionally high. Later, the fuel tax raised from road transport of the output joins the tax on profits to give large exchequer inflows. In this particular project there is no loss of import duty when local production starts because there was no duty on phosphates; and the expenditure of net income generated by the project is likely to result in extra imports.

70.   Tables of this kind can be valuable in several ways. Even though calculated at constant prices, they can give an estimate of the sign, extent and timing of flows of the parameters concerned. These are not only of intrinsic interest themselves, but also allow comparisons to be made with other projects being reviewed, and also possibly with alternative major forms of a single project.

Relationship to Other Kinds of Appraisal

71.   This case study is concerned with financial and economic analyses but the role of other kinds of appraisal should not be forgotten. The data presented above could not be derived without prior technical appraisal by geologists and engineers and their detailed design work will be vital to the project's success. Similarly institutional appraisal is necessary to ensure that the enterprise will be managed and staffed effectively; social appraisal will help to prevent human and cultural factors from impeding efficiency; and environmental analysis is needed whenever significant detriments of this type are expected.

Detailed Case Study II: The Basin Irrigation Scheme

1.   This second illustrative case covers an agricultural development scheme. It differs from the Phosphate Project in many respects, so its analysis illustrates topics covered in this Guide in different general and particular ways.

A Brief Outline

2.   This project was to develop year-round irrigation in a basin area of up to 8,000 acres, adjacent to a major river. Flow in the river is seasonal, and the basin is normally flooded to some extent, but the production of crops is uncertain, and limited to one season. A pump scheme, with a full system of distributive canals and flood protection works, would allow intensive cropping on around 7,000 acres of irrigated land. Irrigation specialists concluded that only a small drainage system would be necessary.

3.   Because of the uncertain and seasonal cropping, existing employment opportunities in the region are limited. Incomes are low, and out-migration is high and increasing. Support for the project would be directly in line with ODA's policy of assisting the poorest groups. After development, the land would be divided into uniform family holdings of 5 acres each. The land is already owned by government, but those displaced would be paid compensation. The families to be settled would mainly be those already living in the area, whose income from farming could be increased substantially, once the new cropping systems are established.

4.   The project is in a country that has extensive experience of pump irrigation schemes. The national Department of Irrigation (DOI) would be responsible for constructing and operating the irrigation works, while the agricultural aspects – from settler induction and input supply to crop marketing – would be handled by the Regional Agricultural Corporation (RAC).

5.   Since projects of this kind were well established in the country, few design alternatives arose in what was basically a 'repeat' project. The main investment would be in the pump facilities; the canal system; clearing and land levelling; and buildings, roads and services.

6.   During the operating phase, costs would arise at three levels:
   * DOI, to operate, maintain and repair the pumps and water distribution channels;
   * RAC, to supply production and marketing services; and
   * the farmers, who would independently crop the land.

The farmers were already familiar with irrigated production, and were expected to be able to adapt quickly to intensive mixed farming systems of the kind envisaged for the irrigated land, which could involve up to eight separate crops. The farming systems were based on practices that were well established on similar schemes. Although of necessity periods of fallow occur in the rotation, the new cropping index would be 150. Half the land would be cropped twice each year, the remainder once.

Forecasting Development, Output and Costs in the New Projects

7. Because developments of the kind in view are not new in this country, fairly accurate estimates could be made of the phasing of the capital works that would be required, and of their cost. As Table II.1 shows, design engineers felt that the full area could be developed within three years at a capital cost of 2.22 million Moneys,[1] Ms 317 per acre.

8. Although the investment work could be completed in the whole area by the end of year 2, not all of it would be brought into fully regulated production at once. Eventually, the scheme would contain 7,000 acres of irrigated land. It was expected that 4,000 acres could be settled and fully cropped in the first two years. Another 2,000 acres of fully administered land would be brought under command for the next two years, with the final 1,000 acres incorporated for the fifth season of operations. These rates of settlement were based on experience in similar earlier developments though, like much else in this project, the planning approach was deliberately conservative, not optimistic – unusually some may say.

9. The families would each be settled on 5 acre units. They were taken to be familiar with farming of the kind envisaged, and to understand the husbandry requirements of the range of crops to be grown. However, whilst production at a reasonable level could be expected at the outset, improvement would be expected, as both the farmers and the scheme staff became better acquainted with the environment, its possibilities and management. This might have been reflected in a programme of inputs, outputs and net production for each holding that expanded steadily each year. However, the planners of this scheme preferred to deal with this by assuming two levels of input and output only. For the first five years of cropping on any section of land, the resource employment and yields would be assumed to be constant, at a level of 'Initial Intensity'. In the sixth year of use, and continuously thereafter, production would move onto a more intensive, constant plane of 'Mature Intensity' with the same land use regime, but higher levels of inputs and considerably increased yields.

10. The year-by-year development of the land, and the area assumed to be operated under 'Initial' and 'Mature' regimes, are shown in Table II.2. This particular approach to handling what would be expected to be a gradual expansion of production has the virtue of simplifying calculation. The assumption that no further intensification would occur after year 11 could be seen as another deliberately conservative step in planning, though an alternative scheme of continuous expansion might be less realistic.

11. Experience of very similar developments in the same province allowed plans to be based on a farm size and cropping pattern that most farm families could manage, and would follow. In the somewhat regimented, uniform situation envisaged, each of the five acre farms would follow this land use pattern every year:

---

[1] As in DC I, and elsewhere in this Guide, a fictitious currency is used for this case, whose basic unit is the Money.

	Summer Season	Winter Season

Summer Season
Sorghum – 2 acres

Fodder – ½ acre
Fallow – 2½ acres

Winter Season
Legume – 2 acres
(Chick peas, haricot beans or broad beans)
Wheat – 2 acres
Fodder – ½ acre
Vegetables – ½ acre
(Tomatoes or onions)

In this standardised rotation, the small grains, sorghum and wheat would dominate land use, but fodder and the minor crops would – if successful – contribute more to net income.

12. The areas expected to be planted with each crop each year in the whole scheme are detailed in Table II.3 which shows separately the land subject to the 'Initial' and the 'Mature' levels. Fodder occupies the land for a full year, but is shown as only one crop.

13. Experience from adjacent basin irrigation projects in similar conditions allowed detailed budgets to be prepared for each crop with considerable confidence – more confidence than is common before implementation in most agricultural project planning. Per acre costs and output figures were drawn up for all of the eight crops under the two regimes. Similar figures were also prepared for the three crops that are already grown in the area which, it was assumed, would continue to be grown indefinitely in the absence of development of the kind being proposed.

THE BASIN IRRIGATION SCHEME
TABLE II.1
CAPITAL COSTS

Constant   Ms '000

	0	1	2	TOTAL
Pumping Equipment	28	250	28	306
Pump House	—	229	—	229
Buildings and Services	278	139	21	438
Canal Earthworks	83	347	69	499
Flood Protection Works	—	52	69	121
Drainage	—	—	69	69
Clearing and Land Levelling	298	24	—	322
Plant and Vehicles for DOI	73	—	—	73
Vehicles for RAC	—	—	45	45
Engineering Fees	3	7	—	10
TOTALS	763	1,048	301	2,112
Contingencies	37	52	19	108
Grand Total	800	1,100	320	2,220

THE BASIN IRRIGATION SCHEME

TABLE II.2

PHASED DEVELOPMENT OF THE AREA

Year	Area Cropped at Initial Intensity (acres)	Area Cropped at Mature Intensity (acres)	Total Area Cropped (acres)	Number of Families in Project
0	0	0	0	0
1	0	0	0	0
2	4,000	0	4,000	800
3	4,000	0	4,000	800
4	6,000	0	6,000	1,200
5	6,000	0	6,000	1,200
6	7,000	0	7,000	1,400
7	3,000	4,000	7,000	1,400
8	3,000	4,000	7,000	1,400
9	1,000	6,000	7,000	1,400
10	1,000	6,000	7,000	1,400
11+	0	7,000	7,000	1,400

THE BASIN IRRIGATION SCHEME

TABLE II.3

EXPECTED CROP ACREAGES YEAR BY YEAR

	Years	2 + 3	4 + 5	6	7 + 8	9 + 10	11 +
Sorghum	: Initial	1,600	2,400	2,800	1,200	400	—
	Mature	—	—	—	1,600	2,400	2,800
	Total	1,600	2,400	2,800	2,800	2,800	2,800
Chick Peas	: Initial	536	804	938	402	134	—
	Mature	—	—	—	536	804	938
	Total	536	804	938	938	938	938
Haricot Beans	: Initial	532	798	931	399	133	—
	Mature	—	—	—	532	798	931
	Total	532	798	931	931	931	931
Broad Beans	: Initial	532	798	931	399	133	—
	Mature	—	—	—	532	798	931
	Total	532	798	931	931	931	931
Wheat	: Initial	1,600	2,400	2,800	1,200	400	—
	Mature	—	—	—	1,600	2,400	2,800
	Total	1,600	2,400	2,800	2,800	2,800	2,800
Fodder	: Initial	400	600	700	300	100	—
	Mature	—	—	—	400	600	700
	Total	400	600	700	700	700	700
Tomatoes	: Initial	200	300	350	150	50	—
	Mature	—	—	—	200	300	350
	Total	200	300	350	350	350	350
Onion	: Initial	200	300	350	150	50	—
	Mature	—	—	—	200	300	350
	Total	200	300	350	350	350	350
All Crops	: Initial	5,600	8,400	9,800	4,200	1,400	—
	Mature	—	—	—	5,600	8,400	9,800
	Total	5,600	8,400	9,800	9,800	9,800	9,800
Land in Use	:	4,000	6,000	7,000	7,000	7,000	7,000

14. Table II.4 shows per acre budgets for the three crops that feature in both the 'without-project' situation and in the proposal. Similar figures for the other five crops at both initial and mature intensities were drawn up, but are not copied here. In summary terms, inputs and outputs for the eight crops are shown in Table II.5. Big differences exist between them, not only in the level of costs to be covered in their production, but in their labour needs, the marketing effort required, and risk. Sorghum and chick-peas are strongly-preferred subsistence foods in this area. Information on labour requirements and the returns to labour was not available or presented. Local experience was that labour needs in farming were always sufficiently met by family members and hired workers living in the area.

15. The crop budgets and planned acreage development allow projections of inputs, outputs and farming profitability to be made. On-farm labour is treated in the budgets as though it were all paid at an 'average' rural wage. However, in practice, much of the work would be performed by family labour. The 'average' family should be able to cope comfortably with the labour needs of the cropping programmes, but some farms will need to hire labour in some years, as available family work numbers swell and shrink.

16. Nevertheless, on many farms the net income to the family will include both the margin on each crop and the value of the imputed labour cost. From the aggregate value of farm income, a water charge of Ms 100 per holding would be deducted, but no other overhead charges were allowed for in the farm budgets. For each 5 acre unit, the general budget at the two levels of intensity were projected as follows:

	Initial Ms	Mature Ms
Output	576	850
Non-Labour Costs	155	184
Water Charge	100	100
Margin (1)	321	566
Labour Costs	78	96
Margin (2)	243	470

17. Operation of the scheme would require off-farm services of various kinds. These are shown in Table II.6. The main costs are those incurred by DOI to operate the pumps and the irrigation system. RAC would have to face substantial expenses for its staff who mainly advise and supervise the farmers. Other agencies (unspecified) would incur costs for sand dune fixation on the borders of the project, and for the control of common irrigation project diseases, malaria and bilharzia especially.

18. The water charges would accrue to the DOI, and would exceed that Department's annual costs from year 2. The level of the Ms 100 per holding is the normal charge levied by the Department on pump-irrigated land. At this level, DOI by itself would make a fair margin, though the charges would only just cover all operating expenses by the agencies concerned. However, it had been proposed that the ODA grant provided for capital costs in this project should be on-lent by the National Ministry of Finance to DOI, for repayment with interest at quasi-commercial terms. This would generate budget revenue for the government. As a result, DOI would need not only to take all of the water charges (leaving the operating expenses of the other agencies to be

THE BASIN IRRIGATION SCHEME

TABLE II.4

PER ACRE BUDGETS FOR THREE CROPS AT THREE LEVELS OF INTENSITY

Constant Prices

Costs (Ms per acre)	SORGHUM			CHICK PEAS			ONIONS		
	Without	Initial	Mature	Without	Initial	Mature	Without	Initial	Mature
Land Preparation	4.4	5.0	5.0	4.4	5.0	5.0	4.4	5.0	5.0
Levelling	2.0	3.0	3.0	2.0	3.0	3.0	2.0	4.0	4.0
Seeding	2.6	4.0	5.3	3.4	5.6	8.0	3.5	5.0	5.0
Transporting	—	—	—	—	—	—	4.0	4.0	4.0
Weeding	—	—	—	5.2	5.5	5.5	4.1	5.0	6.0
Spraying	—	—	—	—	2.0	2.0	—	2.0	4.0
Fertilising	4.0	2.0	3.0	—	—	—	—	15.5	20.0
Harvesting	—	6.0	7.5	3.0	5.0	7.0	8.0	10.0	12.5
Containers	—	2.3	2.5	—	1.5	2.0	12.0	15.0	16.0
Transport	—	0.6	1.2	—	0.6	1.3	4.0	5.0	7.5
Total Costs	13.0	22.9	27.5	18.0	28.2	33.8	42.0	70.5	84.0
Production									
Yield (tonnes per acre)	0.50	0.75	1.0	0.3	0.5	0.8	2.15	3.0	4.0
Price (Ms per tonne)	40	40	40	119	119	119	105	105	105
Value (Ms per acre)	20.0	30.0	40.0	35.7	59.5	95.2	226.0	315.0	420.0
Margin (Ms per acre)	7.0	7.1	12.5	17.7	31.3	61.4	184.0	244.5	336.0

THE BASIN IRRIGATION SCHEME
TABLE II.5
SUMMARY CROP BUDGETS

Constant   Ms per acre

| | | COSTS | | PRODUCTION | MARGIN |
		Labour	Others		
SORGHUM	: Initial	7.4	15.5	30.0	7.1
	Mature	9.1	18.4	40.0	12.5
CHICK PEAS	: Initial	12.1	16.1	59.5	31.3
	Mature	14.3	19.5	95.2	61.4
HARICOT BEANS	: Initial	10.6	16.4	67.8	40.8
	Mature	13.6	18.7	113.0	80.7
BROAD BEANS	: Initial	10.7	18.0	88.4	59.7
	Mature	12.9	21.7	136.0	101.4
WHEAT	: Initial	9.6	22.2	56.0	24.2
	Mature	11.9	26.4	84.0	45.7
FODDER	: Initial	20.4	49.6	210.0	140.0
	Mature	27.1	56.9	350.0	266.0
TOMATOES	: Initial	22.9	38.1	270.0	209.0
	Mature	27.8	46.2	450.0	376.0
ONIONS	: Initial	22.2	48.3	315.0	244.5
	Mature	26.3	57.7	420.0	336.0

THE BASIN IRRIGATION SCHEME
TABLE II.6
OFF-FARM OPERATION COSTS; AND WATER CHARGES

Constant   Ms '000

Year	0	1	2	3	4	5	6+
Department of Irrigation							
Operation of Pump Station	0	0	26.4	26.4	39.6	39.6	46.2
Operation of Irrigation System	0	0	16.0	16.0	24.0	24.0	28.0
Overheads	5.0	5.0	10.0	10.0	10.0	10.0	10.0
TOTAL	5.0	5.0	52.4	52.4	73.6	73.6	84.2
Regional Agricultural Corporation							
Operating Expenses	0	0	25.0	25.0	30.0	30.0	35.0
Health Control	0	5.0	5.0	7.0	8.0	9.0	10.0
Sand Dune Fixation	0	12.0	12.0	10.0	9.0	8.0	7.0
TOTAL OFF-FARM OPERATING EXPENSES	5.0	22.0	94.4	94.4	120.6	120.6	136.2
Water Charges	0	0	80	80	120	120	140

152

met from recurrent government appropriations), but the level of charges would need to be increased.

19. This issue touched on both allocative efficiency and distribution. A general principle for the former is that demand and supply in the market will not allocate resources efficiently unless users are charged full costs. On the latter, the farmers would not be among the poorest groups in the country but the DOI did not charge full costs to other tenants on its irrigation schemes. This controversy was resolved subsequently.

Economic Analysis

20. In the appraisal of this project, information on the different components was not brought together and analysed at constant market prices. As is very often the case, discounted measures were estimated only after shadow pricing.

21. The most significant point was the valuation of production from the main crops grown. They can be considered individually.

Sorghum is exported from this country, though the project is in a deficit area. The project value should be estimated from this formula:

FOB value,

minus cost of transport and marketing between the surplus region and the port,

plus saved cost of transport and marketing between the surplus region and the project.

In the absence of data, the two transport and handling costs items were assumed to be equal and with the same composition, so they cancelled each other. However, allowance was made for 15% wastage and shrinkage. With a long-run expected export price of Ms 46 per tonne, the shadow price was estimated at Ms 39.

Chick Peas are a non-traded food crop with an average price in recent years in the project area of Ms 119 per tonne. This was adjusted by an SCF of 0.85,[1] to give an economic value of Ms 101.

Haricot Beans are exported at an FOB value of Ms 140. The deduction of transport costs (Ms 20 per tonne × 0.85) and 7½% wastage gave a border parity value of Ms 114 per tonne.

Broad Beans are not traded. However internally they are a substitute for the less-preferred Haricot Beans. Because more Broad Bean production would allow more Haricot exports, the two types were both valued at the Haricot parity value.

Wheat is imported. The crop will not be consumed much in the project area, so production here will substitute in the main city for wheat that would otherwise have been imported. The long-run forecast CIF value was Ms 70 per

---

[1] The SCF used was based on an average level of imported duties on all goods of 17.5% in recent years.

Constant   Ms per tonne

CROP	'TRADE' STATUS	MARKET PRICES	ALLOCATIVE EFFICIENCY PRICES
Sorghum	Export	40	39
Chick Peas	Non-Traded	119	101
Haricot Beans	Export	113	114
Broad Beans	Substitute for export	136	114
Wheat	Import	70	77
Fodder	Non-Traded	7	6
Tomatoes	Non-Traded	45	38
Onions	Non-Traded	105	89

tonne. Home production was expected to lead to a net saving in internal transport costs of Ms 8 per tonne, to which the SCF was applied. The Shadow Price used was thus $70 + (8 \times 0.85) =$ Ms 77.

Fodder, Tomatoes and *Onions* are all non-traded. To obtain efficiency valuations, their expected market prices were adjusted by application of the SCF.

22.   The market prices and basic allocative efficiency values of these eight crop products are shown in Table II.7. Revaluation sometimes increased the nominal value, sometimes decreased, and in two cases made almost no change at all.

23.   Three types of item on the cost side required revaluation – capital items, on-farm costs and off-farm operating expenses. Analysis involved estimating the cost composition of each item, and revaluing each of the main cost groups into which the overall costs were divided.

24.   Information of the direct Foreign Exchange costs of the capital items were identified by the design engineers. Local data was used to estimate the cost composition of the construction and land works that were the main local cost elements. It was difficult to estimate the division of labour costs between skilled and unskilled categories, but for the capital works a 50:50 split was estimated. Unskilled workers of the kind envisaged were estimated to be paid wages 25% above their opportunity cost. The conversion factor for labour engaged in capital works of 0.77 was derived in this way:

$$\text{CF} = \underset{\substack{\text{Skilled workers}\\ \times \text{ SCF}}}{[0.5 \times 0.85]} + \underset{\substack{\text{Unskilled workers}\\ \times 1/1.25 \times \text{SCF}}}{[0.5 \times 0.8 \times 0.85]}$$

$$= 0.77$$

25.   Activities in the crop budgets had been built up on a process-by-process basis. Where the process was all labour, determining the cost composition was no problem. Some process costs were largely made up of material inputs, including the subsidised import elements of spraying and fertilising, and the non-traded seed used in planting each crop. Land preparation and levelling are processes that are largely undertaken by tractor, both in the 'without

project' situation and under the scheme proposals, with a relatively high import content for the tractors, implements, spare parts and fuel. Produce transport would similarly involve the widespread use of imported trucks.

26. Most of the labour involved in the farm processes would be either farm family members or unskilled workers. Local officials advised that the alternative for both would be work in traditional flood irrigation farming of the kind that this project would replace. It was estimated that average earnings for such workers over the year as a whole were only 40% of the average wage on which the farm costings were based. Recognition of this factor and use of the SCF led to a CF for on-farm labour of 0.34 (0.4 × 0.85).

27. Workers involved in mechanised farm costs with tractors and trucks were thought to be drawn from the same labour pool as farm workers. Their alternative earnings were estimated at 77% of the wage, so adjustment of their cost involved reduction for this as well as application of the SCF.

28. Individual shadow-pricing CFs for the cost items are shown, with their cost composition, in Table II.8. Characteristically where the numeraire is expressed in border price terms, all of the efficiency values are less than the market prices (ie CF <1.00) except where a subsidy applies.

29. Use of the efficiency values of output and the CFs for inputs allowed all items in the 'with-project' situation to be revalued. However, a deduction had to be made for the value of net output from the 'without-project' use of the land which would be lost.

30. Survey of the project area indicated that the development of this scheme with 7,000 acres of perennial irrigated land would displace single-season flood irrigation on 8,000 acres. The assumed cropping on the land to be taken over is as shown in Table II.9, which allows for one crop each year on the whole area and 100 acres of tomatoes as a second crop in a few parts. That Table also shows the value – at market prices and at efficiency prices – of production, costs and net output from cropping at the yield, price and input levels expected at the time the project would begin. It should be expected that the productivity of this agriculture would increase over the 40 years estimated for the life of the investment. Allowance for this was made by assuming (perhaps generously) that the net output from this traditional type of farming would increase by 5% every five years – a compound rate of almost 1% per annum.

31. The different elements of benefit costs are all brought together in Table II.10 where they are valued at basic allocative efficiency prices. Forty years of operation are provided for. Vehicles and equipment would be replaced every seven years, and the pumps in year 20. Because the project end is so far in the future, no terminal value was allowed (discounting would reduce it to a trivial sum).

32. The test rate of discount in this country is estimated at 8%. At this ARI, the NPV over 40 years operation is Ms 1,930 thousand, and the IRR is 14.8%. These figures suggest that, if the project can be operated along the lines planned, and if the estimated efficiency values have been correctly estimated and apply at that time, the project would be a competitively valuable use of the resources applied.

THE BASIN IRRIGATION SCHEME

TABLE II.8

COST COMPOSITION AND CONVERSION FACTORS (CFs) FOR THE PROJECT COST ITEMS

	Percentage of Cost Attributed to:					Item C.F.
	Traded Items	Farm Labour	Other Labour	Tax	Others	
C.F.	1.0	—	0.77	0.00	0.85	
CAPITAL ITEMS						
Pumping Equipment	95	—	—	—	5	0.99
Pump House	20	—	40	10	30	0.76
Buildings and Services	32	—	34	8	26	0.80
Land Work, Canals and Drainage	32	—	42	13	13	0.75
Vehicles and Equipment	94	—	—	—	6	0.99
C.F.	1.0	0.34	0.65	0.00	0.85	
FARM ACTIVITIES						
Land Preparation and Levelling	60	10	20	10	—	0.76
Seeding	—	10	—	—	90	0.80
Transplanting, Weeding and harvesting	—	100	—	—	—	0.34
Spraying	100	10	—	-10	—	1.03
Fertilisers	130	10	—	-40	—	1.33
Containers, etc.	—	—	—	—	100	0.85
Transport	70	—	20	10	—	0.83
C.F.	1.0	—	0.77	0.00	0.85	
OPERATING EXPENSES						
Pump Station Operation	60	—	20	10	10	0.84
Irrigation System Operation	10	—	70	5	15	0.77
DOI Overheads	10	—	60	5	25	0.77
RAC Operation, Health and Sand Dune Fixation	—	—	—	—	100	0.85

TABLE II.9

PRODUCTION, COSTS AND NET OUTPUT WITHOUT THE PROJECT

Constant Prices

	Cropped Area Acres	Value of Production Ms	Production Costs Ms	Value of Net Output Ms
Sorghum	2,500	M.Pr 50,000 Sh.Pr 48,750	32,500 20,750	17,500 28,000
Chick Peas	5,500	M.Pr 196,350 Sh.Pr 166,650	99,000 57,200	97,350 109,450
Onions	100	M.Pr 22,600 Sh.Pr 19,200	4,200 2,670	18,400 16,530
TOTALS	8,100	M.Pr 268,950 Sh.Pr 234,600	135,700 80,620	133,250 153.980

M.Pr = market price.
Sh.Pr = shadow (efficiency) price.

33.   The sensitivity of these overall project results were tested in relation to changes in some of the main parameters, with these results:

	NPV at 8% (Ms '000)	Change in NPV (Ms '000)
Base Case	1,930	—
Project life reduced by 10 years	1,696	−234
Capital costs increased by 10%	1,729	−201
Farm Output Value reduced by 10%	921	−1,009
Non-Labour Farm Costs increased by 10%	1,689	−241
Farm Labour Costs increased by 10%	1,886	−44

34.   Typically for mixed-crop agriculture, no single input or output dominates the project. Naturally, the value of discounted net benefits was most sensitive to reduction in the value of output, but the aggregate value of all production could fall from the projected levels by 19% before NPV was reduced to zero. The likelihood of a fall of this kind would depend on many factors, including:

 − the world prices of three traded crops;

 − the domestic prices of four non-traded crops;

 − the rate at which farmers are inducted, their total number, and the total area cropped;

 − the wish and ability of farmers to follow the farming systems envisaged, and the attainment by them *on average* of output at the levels envisaged in the Initial and Maturity Intensity crop budgets.

Financial Analyses

35.   The last point mentioned above − farmer incentives and abilities − is perhaps the most uncertain. Only farm families of the appropriate size and capability would be given units in the scheme, which should strengthen prospects in the early years. The farm unit budgets quoted earlier suggest incom-

THE BASIN IRRIGATION SCHEME

TABLE II.10

ANNUAL STATEMENT OF ECONOMIC COSTS AND BENEFITS AT EFFICIENCY PRICES

Constant Ms '000

Years	With the Project			Net Farm Benefits	Lost Net Benefits without Project	Net Benefits on Farms	Off farm Costs	Capital Costs	Net Benefits of Project
	Output	Non-Labour Costs	Labour Costs						
0	0	0	0	0	31	(31)	4	682	(717)
1	0	0	0	0	62	(62)	18	962	(1,045)
2	419	120	21	278	92	186	78	273	(165)
3	419	120	21	278	123	155	78	—	77
4 + 5	629	180	32	417	154	263	100	—	163
6	734	210	37	487	154	333	112	—	221
7	957	234	42	681	162	519	112	—	407
8	957	234	42	681	162	519	112	116	291
9 + 10	1,068	245	45	778	162	616	112	—	504
11	1,124	251	46	827	162	665	112	—	553
12–14	1,124	251	46	827	170	657	112	—	545
15	1,124	251	46	827	170	657	112	116	429
16	1,124	251	46	827	170	657	112	—	545
17–19	1,124	251	46	827	178	649	112	—	537
20	1,124	251	46	827	178	649	112	304	233
21	1,124	251	46	827	178	649	112	—	537
22	1,124	251	46	827	187	640	112	116	412
23–26	1,124	251	46	827	187	640	112	—	528
27 + 28	1,124	251	46	827	197	630	112	—	518
29	1,124	251	46	827	197	630	112	116	402
30 + 31	1,124	251	46	827	197	630	112	—	518
32–35	1,124	251	46	827	206	621	112	—	509
36	1,124	251	46	827	206	621	112	116	393
37–41	1,124	251	46	827	217	610	112	—	498
42	1,124	251	46	827	228	599	112	—	487

es per family with the project in the first five years of cropping of between Ms 321 and 243 per annum, depending on how much paid labour was required. Later, these incomes were expected to rise to between Ms 566 and 470 per annum. What the farm incomes would be without the project is difficult to assess. The area was farmed under traditional methods by people with land units of varying size, but it was felt an 'average' family used about 7 acres of land. The market price figures for the without-project situation (Table 11.9) suggest a value of net output from this land of Ms 117 per family. The assumed growth in output over 40 years under the traditional system would increase this by up to 50%, and if labour was not hired, family income would be Ms 56 more per annum in the early years.

36. These figures suggest the following 'average' farm income scenarios, at constant market prices.

Family Net Incomes (Ms)

	Without Project		With Project	
	First years	Year 30	'Initial' years	'Mature' years
All labour provided by family	173	221	321	566
No labour provided by family	117	150	243	470

37. If it can be explained to them convincingly, farmers already in the area would almost certainly find the prospect of an early doubling of net income persuasive enough to join the scheme and follow the proposed crop system. The 'mature' years offer a prospect of incomes between 2½ and three times the alternative, even though the average family may have less land under its control. With the project, more farmers would be in the area than before. People introduced from outside would probably have lower alternative net incomes than the families using the land at present, so they would find the prospects even more attractive.

38. This reasoning suggests that, as evidence from similar schemes in the Region indicates, plenty of families will regard joining the scheme and following the cropping regime to be beneficial on the grounds of cash flow expectations. The role of local advisers familiar with social and cultural behaviour in the area is obviously essential in forming such judgements and subsequent implementation.

39. Financial analysis of the different off-farm agencies can be based on information in Table II.6. If the Water Charges are collected, and are retained by the Department of Irrigation, its financial position should be improved as a result of this project, unless the ODA grant funds are on-loaned to it. Typical on-lending terms in this country are 5% interest over 25 years, with interest waived for the first 7 years, and no capital repayment for 7 years. Repayment of the loan thereafter in 18 equal annual amounts results in a yearly payment of 0.0855 of the capital sum. In this project, the ODA element of the capital sums listed in Table II.1 was Ms 749,000, and if these terms were applied to only this element of the capital (with other government investment provided free) the annual loan charge on DOI would have been Ms 64,000 per annum from an agreed date – year 10 say. A DOI surplus of fee income over operating costs of Ms 56,000 per annum is projected at constant market prices (Table II.11). If

159

THE BASIN IRRIGATION SCHEME

TABLE II.11

PROJECTED FLOWS OF GOVERNMENT FUNDS OUTSIDE DOI DURING OPERATIONS

Constant   Ms '000

Year	OUTFLOWS					INFLOWS			Net Out Flows
	RAC Operation	Health Control	Sand Dune Fixation	Subsidies	Total	Farm Operations	DOI Operations	Total	
2	25.0	5.0	12.0	8.3	50.3	5.1	3.9	9.0	41.3
3	25.0	7.0	10.0	8.3	50.3	5.1	3.9	9.0	41.3
4	30.0	8.0	9.0	12.5	59.5	7.7	5.7	13.4	46.1
5	30.0	9.0	8.0	12.5	59.5	7.7	5.7	13.4	46.1
6	35.0	10.0	7.0	14.6	66.6	8.9	6.5	15.4	51.2
7	35.0	10.0	7.0	18.8	70.8	9.4	6.5	15.9	54.9
8	35.0	10.0	7.0	18.8	70.8	9.4	6.5	15.9	54.9
9	35.0	10.0	7.0	20.9	72.9	9.7	6.5	16.2	56.7
10	35.0	10.0	7.0	20.9	72.9	9.7	6.5	16.2	56.7
11+	35.0	10.0	7.0	22.0	74.0	9.8	6.5	16.3	57.7

inflation were at a rate of 5% per annum,[1] the additional money surplus to DOI from operation of this scheme would probably be sufficient to cover loan terms for part of the capital on these very generous terms, if charges and costs both increased at the rate of inflation. However the question of on-lending has implications for the incentive to producers if it leads to higher levels of water charges.

40. Flows to and from Government and other public sector agencies attributable to the project can also be estimated. Outflows will include the annual costs of RAC operations, health control and sand dune fixation, together with the subsidies on fertiliser and sprays that will arise as the project involves new use of these chemical inputs for irrigated farming. However, incremental revenue inflows will arise from farming, through the tax component of land preparation work and transport (which are taxes on fuel) indicated in Table II.8.

41. The values of the different flows of government funds that are directly associated with the project (other than DOI revenues) are shown in Table II.11. The committment to extra subsidy payments will be mostly matched by tax inflows from farm and DOI operations. However, overall a negative flow will occur each year. Small though the amounts may be in national terms, the fiscal authorities, and others concerned, should be aware that implementing this project will increase the call on recurrent funds every year in the operating period. It also calls for heavy investment outflows in the development period. Finance will have to be found from exchequer sources, unless DOI surpluses can be applied to meet part of the cost.

42. Since these government flows cannot be made financially self supporting in any year, there is no need to make other projections that allow for the possible effects of inflation. Estimation of the funding deficit for each year is all the analyst needs to show.

43. The foreign exchange flows associated with this project can also be assessed from the cost and output data and the price-composition information. Currency inflows will arise from additional exports of Sorghum and Haricot Beans, and reduced imports of Wheat. ODA finance will cover much of the external portion of capital expenses. However, indirect foreign exchange demands will arise to meet the government share of capital costs, for the border price elements of farm costs, and for DOI operating expenses attributable to this project.

44. The different projected foreign exchange flows up to year 11 are shown in Table II.12. They show that, once the project gets into production, substantial foreign exchange net inflows will arise. However, as Table II.8 showed, the border price content of the 'local' capital expenses (mainly civil works and land structuring) are significant. The overall project financing envisaged leaves those costs to be covered by the government while assistance covered the direct imports. This means that government has to be able to cope with an indirect demand for quite a lot of extra foreign exchange, to meet the establishment needs. The net foreign exchange effects are however, so promising that meeting the need for these funds will be easily justified.

---

[1] A price contingency of 20% was allowed on ODA capital costs, which suggests an external inflation rate in excess of 5% per annum. Domestic inflation would probably be higher.

THE BASIN IRRIGATION SCHEME

TABLE II.12

PROJECTED FLOWS OF FOREIGN EXCHANGE

Constant Ms '000

	INFLOWS			OUTFLOWS					Net Flows
	ODA Funds	New Crop Production	Total	Capital Costs	Farm Costs	DOI Costs	Lost Farm Output	Total	
0	137.4	—	137.4	309.1	—	0.5	9.8	319.4	(182.0)
1	526.8	—	526.8	470.1	—	0.5	19.5	490.1	36.7
2	84.6	220.9	305.5	141.2	65.6	18.4	29.3	254.5	(113.3)
3	—	220.9	220.9	—	65.6	18.4	39.0	123.0	97.9
4	—	331.4	331.4	—	98.4	27.2	48.8	174.4	157.0
5	—	331.4	331.4	—	98.4	27.2	48.8	174.4	157.0
6	—	386.6	386.6	—	114.8	31.5	48.8	195.1	191.5
7	—	500.3	500.3	—	128.7	31.5	51.2	211.4	288.9
8	—	500.3	500.3	110.9	128.7	31.5	51.2	322.3	178.0
9	—	557.1	557.1	—	135.6	31.5	51.2	218.3	338.8
10	—	557.1	557.1	—	135.6	31.5	51.2	218.3	338.8
11	—	585.5	585.5	—	139.0	31.5	51.2	221.7	363.8

Other Analyses, and Overall Judgement

45. Analysis of this project suggests that the projected economic returns are attractive and fairly robust. A commitment to increased government spending both in the investment period and the long-run will arise, but foreign exchange earnings in the long-term look very attractive, once initial requirements not covered by aid grants have been met. The farming and administrative systems are well established in the region, and evidence from similar developments nearby allowed the realistic planning of attainable performance. The project should substantially improve the position of many low-income farmers and farm workers, though it is not possible to say how the net farm income will be divided between farm families and employees. Total labour absorption will be significantly increased.

46. Sand dune fixation is only a small cost item in this project, but its environmental significance could be quite large. Planting trees will not only provide a barrier to inundation by sand. This forestry should have other effects on the ecosystem of the irrigation area, by reducing the drying effect of winds and cutting down physical damage to young crops. Eventually some fuelwood and poles may be obtained, though the possible value of these products has been ignored. The opportunity will be taken for tree species trials to be carried out in the project, where farmers can observe their culture and the success of different species.

47. The other notable environmental impact expected is higher incidence of the 'classic' irrigation diseases, and cost provision has been made for their control, to the extent possible.

48. No new institutions are involved. DOI and RAC are well-established, and their performance in other projects gives confidence that this scheme could also be handled.

B.   Illustrative Case Studies

Introduction

1.   This section of the Guide contains a range of case studies which supplement the two detailed studies in illustrating various aspects of project analysis that were discussed in earlier chapters. All of these illustrations are taken from actual feasibility studies and reports that were prepared by or at the request of ODA. This does not mean that ODA was the intended financier of the projects. Many of the studies were undertaken in response to requests for Technical Co-operation assistance, where ODA provided or paid for professional services. However, all of the studies followed the approach to analysis outlined in earlier editions of the ODA Guide to Economic Appraisal.

2.   The case studies have been chosen to reflect a wide range of sectors and project types. An illustration of actual project situations, they are a limited complement to the guide to planning projects in particular sectors contained in the book *Planning Development Projects* (by G. A. Bridger and J. T. Winpenny) published by HMSO for ODA in 1983.

3.   The deliberate sectoral diversity of the cases can be seen from their grouping and titles in the list of contents. However, they differ also with respect to their 'newness'. Some (eg cases 2 and 4) were for types of development that were new to the country. Others were for new developments in the regions concerned (cases 5, 9, 13 and 14), though the type of activity involved was not new to the economy. Cases 1, 3 and 12 are for the repeat of productive investments that were already completed and well understood through successful operation. One case (10) is to augment existing systems, whilst others concern the upgrading of facilities and systems that are already in use (6 and 15). The rehabilitation of investments that are either coming to the end of their design life, or failing for other reasons, is also illustrated, in cases 7, 8 and 11. Case 16 illustrates a situation where the design of a project had to be modified to allow provision for the specific role of women in this rural development.

4.   These differences of sectoral type and degree of newness means that the cases differ in the aspects of project analysis that they feature. Each one starts with a basic description of what the project in view concerns. An indication of size and a technical outline is often accompanied by mention of ODA's possible interest in giving support in one form or another. However, the cases mainly aim to outline the important areas of economic, financial and institutional analysis that came up in each project.

5.   The particular features of analysis that were relevant varied from one case to another. No project illustrates all of the areas of analysis covered by this Guide. An indication of which aspects are featured in each of the project sketches is given in the accompanying diagram. As would be expected, cost-benefit analysis, shadow pricing and sensitivity analysis are very common major features, and demand estimation also. However, the actual cases themselves show what were their critical points, and how analysts treated them.

6. It should be emphasised that all of these project synopses come from actual working papers. Editing has been restricted to abbreviation for this format. In a few instances, some potentially interesting information (especially on methodology) cannot be mentioned here because it was not contained in the source documents. The operational nature of the project reports is also reflected in the practical way in which some analyses were handled, especially in the valuation of inputs, outputs and incremental incomes. Analysts frequently emphasised their appreciation of simplifications that they were forced to accept in their time and resource situations. However, by judging the direction (and sometimes the likely extent) of the biases that remained, they could proceed with the analysis. Situations were not uncommon where pessimistic assumptions were adopted for the 'base case' analysis, in the knowledge that, if it was crucial to the appraisal, efforts could be made to get a better estimate of a particular variable. However, if discounting showed that a proposal looked safely attractive and further refinement was likely only to increase the value of net benefits, there was no need to pursue the matter. Reflecting the general situation, none of the cases includes an attempt at applying distribution weights to expected incremental net incomes, though several studies comment on who the main beneficiaries could be expected to be.

7. Newer concerns in project appraisal are under-represented in these case studies because they are drawn from past experience. Environmental and social issues, for example, figure more prominently in current ODA appraisals.

PARTICULAR ASPECTS OF PROJECT ANALYSIS FEATURED BY THE CASE STUDIES

CASE STUDY NUMBER	1	2	3	4	5	6	7	8	9	10	11	12	13	14	15	16
DEMAND ESTIMATION	X	X	·			X		X	X	X	X	X	X	X	X	
MARKETING SYSTEM	X															
INPUT SUPPLY	X										X	X				
TECHNICAL ALTERNATIVES*						X	X	X		X	X	X			X	X
SCALE ALTERNATIVES*												X		X		
CHOICE OF LOCATION*		X													X	
ALTERNATIVE TIMING						X		X				X				
COST BENEFIT ANALYSIS	X	X	X	X	X	X	X	X	X	X		X	X	X		
SHADOW PRICING	X	X	X		X		X		X				X	X		
SENSITIVITY ANALYSIS	X	X	X	X		X		X				X	X	X		
DEPLETION PREMIUM												X				
SAVINGS PREMIUM				X												
CONSUMER SURPLUS							X	X	X	X						
BENEFICIARY IDENTIFICATION			X	X	X			X				X		X		X
GENDER				X				X						X	X	X
INDIRECT BENEFITS	X		X	X	X			X						X	X	
ENVIRONMENTAL ASPECTS	X					X					X	X		X		
FINANCIAL ASPECTS									X			X	X			
USER TARIFF POLICY							X	X	X	X	X	X	X			
FINANCIAL TARGETS								X	X	X			X			
MEETING RECURRENT COSTS			X	X	X										X	
INSTITUTIONAL QUESTIONS			X					X		X		X	X			X
PROGRAMME APPROACH					X			X						X		

* Generally, study of these aspects involved cost-effectiveness analysis.

Case Study 1:   A Fertiliser Manufacture Project

1.   This case study features these particular aspects of project analysis:
- ★ Demand Estimation
- ★ Product Marketing System
- ★ Cost Benefit Analysis
- ★ Shadow Pricing
- ★ Sensitivity Analysis
- ★ Indirect Benefits
- ★ Environmental Aspects

Description
2.   The project was to build a large nitrogenous fertiliser plant in a large coastal country. Offshore natural gas would be used to make urea, with surplus ammonia being sold to a separate compound fertiliser plant. The ODA contribution to this project was limited to financing the provision of boilers and related local costs, but the proposal was appraised in full because the boilers had no separate justification.

Analysis
3.   Several major questions were covered by the appraisal study. Most prominent was the quantitative demand for urea. Agricultural opinion was that there were limited possibilities for expansion of the area under cultivation. Consequently, increased use of fertiliser and extension of the area under irrigation provided the main prospects for output growth in agriculture. Proposals for irrigation development in the next 5-year plan period were known. A crucial factor affecting urea use was the relationship of farmer prices for crops and fertilisers, both of which were determined by government. Estimation of these factors, historic data and the low existing level of fertiliser use allowed growth rates of 9 per cent per annum to be postulated for urea consumption. From the projected figures of total national demand, deductions were made for production from existing factories and from others under construction. These suggested an effective unfulfilled demand by the time this factory would come into production well in excess of its planned capacity, so imports would continue to be required.

4.   The availability and pricing of the gas input was a second crucial area. Over a 15 year life at the expected level of capacity production, gas accounted for 57% of all discounted costs (valued at economic prices), a little more than twice the discounted value of fixed and working capital.

5.   For economic analysis, both urea and gas were valued at their world price parity values. Long-term urea price forecasts had been made by the World Bank, using their knowledge of plants in operation and under construction around the world. The value of the gas was based on projections for the value of oil, (a net import in this country), adjusted to give equivalence in calorific values.

6.   Feedstock supply through a pipeline was simple and could be relied on. Marketing was potentially more problematic. Selection of the project site gave prominence to gaining a position beside a trunk railway whose upgrading was already planned. Well established marketing and stock-holding channels for high volume fertiliser sales would be used, with confidence it was thought. Sales would not be localised to one zone: demand risk would be

166

spread by planning that sales from this plant would go to several different adjacent regions.

Results

7. Economic analysis showed a project base case IRR of 15.5%, a few points above the target level of 12%. Sensitivity analysis covered these areas:

	IRR
– delay of completion by one year,	14.0
– 10% lower capacity utilisation throughout the project's life,	14.1
– capital costs increased by 10%,	14.1
– operating costs increased by 10%,	11.7
– completion delayed by one year and capital costs increased by 10%.	12.7

Of these factors, only the increase in operating costs (mainly gas costs) had a serious effect on the IRR, bringing it just below the target level of acceptability. The price relationship between gas and urea was the most important factor. Searching analysis showed that the rate of return would be the same whether urea prices followed the IBRD projections for world prices or they maintained their existing relationship to gas (and oil) prices, for which there were relatively firm long-term world price projections.

8. Shadow pricing in detail was done only for urea, gas, and coal, another sizeable recurrent cost item that was a net export. Because only a quarter of all employees were unskilled and labour costs were only 8% of all costs, there was little point in using a shadow wage. A CF of 0.8 was applied to locally manufactured capital goods and 0.9 to other inputs – power, water, bags, chemicals.

9. Although they were not quantified, the economic analysis referred to four indirect benefits:

- higher production would allow farmers to plan (and produce) more efficiently because of the greater probability that urea would be available when required;
- substitution for the import of the bulky fertiliser would relieve pressure on ports and their facilities;
- the project would lead to the creation of around 5,000 long-term jobs in the transportation and service sectors, two and a half times the number of people directly employed by the project; and
- the project would increase the experience and general competence of local consulting and manufacturing firms.

10. Institutional aspects of the project were not scrutinised in detail. The proposed ownership of this plant by a cooperative, and the organisational structure, was similar to other cooperative fertiliser plants in the country that worked well, and which experienced no difficulty in recruiting management and skilled staff.

11. Environmental effects of this large project were carefully appraised. The site was away from built-up areas, and the prevailing wind was away from the nearby large town. Major potential pollutants were ammonia, urea, fly dust

from coal, and sulphur dioxide. Acceptable maximum levels were guaranteed by the contractors. Provision for the cleaning of gases from production was built in, in case of need, while the boilers could use gas instead of coal in case atmospheric inversion occurred or the electrostatic dust precipitators failed. Pollution monitoring stations would be installed, and a qualified environmental control officer would be employed.

12.   Some land for the factory would have to be acquired by compulsory purchase. A rehabilitation officer would help the 250 farm families affected, some of whose members the project hoped to employ.

Case Study 2: The Special Steels Project

1.   This case study features these particular aspects of project analysis:
   * Demand Estimation
   * Choice of Location
   * Cost Benefit Analysis
   * Shadow Pricing
   * Sensitivity Analysis

Description
2.   The host country was already partially industrialised. The proposed project would add to domestic capacity for producing special steels. Some output would be of types that were not manufactured in the country, and the project would generally help to reduce a forecast production deficit that would have to be met by imports.

3.   The project would have two phases. At first, an electric arc furnace and a continuous casting unit would be installed. A continuous rolling mill would soon be added, as stage two. Other developments might follow. ODA was asked to meet part of the cost of supplying equipment and services for the arc furnace and casting mill, but the whole proposal was appraised in detail.

4.   The main inputs would be scrap steel and electricity. The scrap would partly come from domestic sources, but imports would always be necessary. A variety of products would be sold, all for domestic use.

5.   The project was to be located in an area of existing industrial development, near where a small port could be built for the plant, as part of the project. The actual choice of site involved evaluation of: transportation means (roads especially); power availability; fuel and water supplies; availability of labour and other materials; and marketing requirements.

6.   Since the plant was of modest size; of standard, conventional design; and was not unique in the country, no problems were expected in finding sufficient personnel for management and skilled operation.

Analysis
7.   Market forecasting was fundamental to economic justification. Special steels have many uses, and demand fluctuates in line with the state of the economy. With some steels being produced in the country and others imported, records of actual supply and use in recent years were thought to be incomplete, and not a good basis for consumption forecasting. Reported volumes of special steel use showed them to be a much lower proportion of total steel use than would be normal for an economy of this type. Demand forecasting followed several approaches. One was to project what were thought to be realistic estimates of total use in recent years. Another was to forecast the demand for special steels for one major user, the automotive industry, whose needs could be fairly reliably forecast, and which normally took about 25% of all ouput. Demand projections from these two sources were checked against growth rates in other countries and the proportion of specials in total steel use. The 'consensus' figures arrived at, when adjusted to allow for existing capacity elsewhere, indicated the near-certain existence of a gap which this plant could meet, thus reducing the import burden. Home demand would be especially strong for the steels to be produced when stage II of the project was implemented.

8. The phase I output was an intermediate product of a kind that was not actually imported. It was valued for economic analysis on the basis of quoted selling prices in Western Europe, adjusted for shipping costs to the country and for discounts. At the time that the project was prepared, world recession was reflected in steel over-production. The border price for the base year was calculated on the basis of the list price of a major European producer. Shipping costs were added, and an allowance made for special discounts obtainable from all producers at the time. The resulting value was below what was thought to be the long-run price which, in principle, it might have been better to use. However, as a first test, economic analysis retained this minimum output value for the calculation of rates of return.

9. Similarly 'pessimistic' assumptions were made in valuing inputs. Although some scrap would be obtained from cheap local sources, it was taken that all would be imported at established market prices. Electricity was valued 30% above the negotiated contract price. Existing tariffs did not cover long-run marginal generating costs, and this major user would burden a system that was already stretched. Reflecting the surplus of unskilled labour in the region, conversion factors of 0.9 and 0.8 were applied to the civil works and erection components of capital costs, and 0.75 to the unskilled component of operating costs. However, no SCF was applied to domestic prices in general, as the country operated an almost free exchange rate regime.[1]

Results
10. No test discount rate had been established for public-sector projects. Minimal acceptability was thought to be in the range 8–12%. The base case IRR was just below 16%. Reported sensitivity analysis covered these areas:
- 20% lower capacity utilisation;
- 10% lower selling prices;
- both lower capacity and lower selling prices;
- capital costs increased 10%;
- operating costs increased 10%;
- selling prices increased 10%;
- both unit selling prices and operating costs increased by 10%; and
- start-up delayed one year.

11. IRRs below 12% were obtained in only 3 cases: with reduced selling prices alone (5.6%); reduced sale prices and lower capacity (2.8%); and increased operating expenses (6.9%). However, independent adverse movements in output values and operating costs were unlikely. The prices of scrap and special steels tend to move together, and scrap constituted 50% of the economic value of all operating costs.

12. Foreign exchange effects were calculated separately. The project would continuously be a consumer of imports, producing output for sale locally. However, over a 20 year life, savings with a present value (at 10%) of over

---

[1] This approach would not always be correct. Irrespective of the policy followed on exchange rates and foreign exchange controls, an SCF should be used wherever taxes on imports and/or exports are significant, since it is these taxes that impose a value distortion between border prices and domestic prices.

$125 million could be expected through the substantial reduction in imports of steels that this factory would allow.

13.　Studies touched lightly on institutional, social and environmental effects. Because the technologies envisaged were well established, and not new to the country, problems of delay in construction and low capacity operation were not anticipated.

Case Study 3:   District Council Development

1.   This case study features these particular aspects of project analysis:
- ★ Cost Benefit Analysis
- ★ Beneficiary Identification
- ★ Indirect Benefits
- ★ Meeting Recurrent Costs
- ★ Institutional Questions

Description

2.   This 'integrated rural development project' was to assist both the capability and the actual development work undertaken by four District Councils. Under very far-reaching new decentralisation legislation, local elected Rural Councils were amalgamated with the district administration of government departments. The new District Councils were to take over a large number of functions previously performed by Central and Provincial Government, thus achieving a very substantial decentralisation of both the planning and execution of development activities.

3.   For the District Councils to be able to carry out the extensive new responsibilities, new structures and procedures had to be established at local level. New staff needed to be appointed and trained, and experience gained in exercising the new responsibilities, and in executing the new functions.

4.   International assistance was provided in a variety of ways to assist the profound changes that the new approach would bring. The project in view mainly involved providing technical assistance to four District Councils, helping both Councillors and Officers to carry out the new responsibilities, especially for budgeting revenues and for planning the use of funds for different purposes. In addition, to allow some new development to take place, a limited amount of capital funds would also be provided under the project for the Councils to use on schemes that they formulated themselves in an annual programme that had to be acceptable to local authority and to the Regional ODA office.

5.   The project was the second phase of assistance of this kind provided by ODA in three of the Districts. Under phase I, a number of advisers had been appointed to guide and assist the Councils in planning and management work. The advisers had no executive responsibilities for the work of the Councils, it being a main feature of the reforms that national agencies and people should be responsible throughout for work and decisions. The pronounced 'institution building and strengthening' role of the advisers helped to get the new bodies launched quickly. After a few years, the first phase project had achieved a lot in respect of developing local capacity. Through financial assistance combined with local planning, substantial development of facilities had occurred, leading to increases in agricultural production that could not be explained by higher crop prices or new technology.

6.   The proposed project had three components. A team of four advisers would work with the four Councils, three from phase I and the other new. The advice would mainly concentrate on developing capacity to provide, fund and maintain district infrastructure necessary for agricultural activities, and to provide services essential for the provision of basic needs. The second project element was other advisers to help and establish a monitoring section in the

172

planning unit at provincial level, whose work would be of value to all District Councils in the Province, not just the four. Finally capital funds would be available to help cover Council-proposed maintenance and rehabilitation works, as the main priority, and a modest expansion of the economic infrastructure if this was possible.

7.   Government's long-term aim was to make the Councils as self-sufficient financially as possible, at least for them to cover recurrent costs from local revenues. Priority areas of District Council management included:
   – revenue collection;
   – identifying and mobilising income sources;
   – accounting;
   – maintenance of existing works;
   – systems for annual planning, budgeting and works programming;
   – improving links between District and Province;
   – staff training; and
   – financial and personnel management.

8.   The main realisation of development actions would be a properly prepared annual plan of revenues and expenditure that, when shown to be within the financial and operating capacity of the Councils, would attract aid funds for specific activities.

9.   The project mainly involved a team of six advisers, with a Team Leader and an Administrator. Vehicles, vehicle operating funds and some equipment would also be funded (not least for the monitoring and evaluation work), with a small provision for consultants. Training in national institutions would also be covered, for council staff. Whereas staff under phase I had been individually recruited and separately administered, the plan was for a single consultancy firm to be responsible for the whole team in phase II. This important 'institutional' feature of administration would, it was thought, lead to a better coordinated and less expensive arrangement, which also allowed greater accountability to the local Steering Committee that would oversee the project through quarterly meetings.

Analysis
10.   The main output and benefit of the technical cooperation, institution-building side of the project would be the 'intangible' benefit of a more efficient local organisation, able to realise the important national objective of decentralisation. Various unquantifiable but valuable economic and social benefits were expected to flow from this, but no meaningful economic analysis of this aspect could be undertaken. The approach of guidance by experts rather than execution by them might not lead to the quickest returns, but would be part of reaching the longer-term benefits of independent local capability.

11.   The strong emphasis would be throughout to concentrate on the proper working and expansion of facilities and services that are important for agricultural development. The capital funds would be used for works that would remove constraints. Funds would be released only against detailed, costed programmes, and when earlier schemes had been completed. Where appropriate, the proposals would be subject to economic analysis. Because of their implications to staff and operating costs, very little expenditure under

this phase would be allocated to social projects. Increasing production and the revenue base would be the priority.

12. The types of economic analysis suitable to the very small individual activities concerned would be unsophisticated. That attractive spending opportunities could be found, and crudely analysed, was illustrated by this selection of activities from phase I.

Activity	Economic Benefit
Three new small bridges allowing vehicle access to a farming area.	Costs repaid within 2 years from anticipated increase in crop production.
New crop store and link road to it.	Annual benefits in saved transport costs are four times actual project cost.
Road improvement, with six bridges, embankments, culverts, etc.	Expected increased crop production gives IRR of 25% and cost repayment over ten years.
Cattle crushes.	Reduced mortality from better stock treatment offsets the costs in one year.
Ox-training scheme.	Costs covered by extra revenue over a few years from extra area cultivated and improved transport. IRR 23%.

13. The types of scheme likely to be taken up in phase II include:

House renovations	New houses.
Well renovations	New wells.
Road rehabilitation	New roads.
Culvert construction and renovation	New bridges.
Cattle crushes	New stores for input supply and crops.

Results
14. The total level of financial assistance available for these works was such that it could be justified if output of the main (currently imported) crop increased as a result for 20 years by just less than 1% per annum (simple interest) over the present levels. Over the period of the phase I project, sales

174

of the main crop in the three districts had increased by 35%. Over the same period, gross margins per hectare for this crop had risen in real terms by only 6%, so this increase (which was higher than the national average), might be largely attributed to the improved local infrastructure. Whilst the level of increased performance from constraint removal might not be maintained, the experience of these three years appeared to indicate the scope and value of locally identified and executed development works.

15. Direct beneficiaries of the project would be the Council staff and the councillors who received guidance from the adviser team. However, the facilities developed would all be for public use. Farmers (the majority group in these land-surplus districts) would be the ones to experience the largest income improvements, certainly in the short term, as they expanded the cropped area, which could be done without environmental damage. The project was not targeted at any specific group. Eventually many sections of the community of around 350,000 people could expect to benefit from the higher level of economic activity, and the fact that it was locally controlled.

16. Successful implementation of the project would lead to the increased commercialisation of farming. In some areas, this had been thought to be associated with a decline in nutritional status. Research on the subject was in progress. If, during the project, these studies indicated effective steps to remove malnutrition that District Councils could take, selective support for these measures could be given from project funds, to assist the most vulnerable groups.

Case Study 4: The Land Settlement Programme

1. This case study features these particular aspects of project analysis:
   * Cost Benefit Analysis
   * Sensitivity Analysis
   * Beneficiary Identification
   * Gender
   * Indirect Benefits
   * Meeting Recurrent Costs
   * Programme Approach

Description

2. This project was associated with a substantial land reform programme designed to meet the aspirations of small farmers for more land, though at the same time maintaining or increasing agricultural production. Existing large holdings in a predominately agricultural country would be purchased, (providing they had water resources) in voluntary transactions, at prices based on the quality of land. Each such area would be subdivided in a planned way into individual holdings of at least 5 hectares, for families to grow arable crops of kinds that were well known in small farmer areas. Actual farm size would vary according to land category (five broad grades applied to arable land), designed to ensure that each farm family could expect to obtain a target cash income somewhere between average earnings in small farm areas and worker incomes elsewhere. While the arable land would be worked by individual families, cattle would be grazed communally on the non-arable land, contributing significantly to gross income in farms on some of the poorer soils.

3. Farm budgets were prepared for each grade of land, based on well-established knowledge of farming practice and yields in national agricultural systems of the kind to be created. Some land development and production facilities would be provided as part of the settlement process (fencing, livestock, sanitation etc.), but production credit, extension advice and marketing services would be made available by the existing national organisations. So as to minimise the need to create new facilities for the settlement areas, priority for the purchase of land would be given to areas adjacent to existing small farming divisions where these services existed.

4. A considerable amount of social infrastructure would be provided. The land purchased would be organised into separate administrative units, each with one or more villages where the farmers would live, on a house and garden plot. Roads, water, primary schools and clinics would be provided there, as well as administrative facilities, but farmers would build their own homes. Opportunity for non-farm employment would be developed in the social centres, including income-earning activities amenable to women's groups.

5. In view of the intensive production objective, the families to be settled would need to show sufficient farming experience, and to possess useful production assets like oxen or equipment. They also had to undertake to give up farmland in existing farming areas. This arrangement should ensure that the settlements would give an opportunity to able farmers who previously had access to less land than it appeared that they could cope with. In the first instance, they would occupy the land on 5-year leases or permits, although long leases or full ownership might become available. The opportunity to take up a settlement farm was open to women as well as to men, who could obtain

occupation permits in their own right, a thing that was not possible in areas where customary law obtained. Women heads of households could be admitted, whilst those who became head of the family after entry would have the same security as other farmers.

Analysis

6. Economic appraisal of the project was based on typical budgets developed for each type of land. The programme as a whole would be undertaken in a large number of individual units, each based on basic farm budgets for the various grades of land. A number of typical units were separately appraised. In each of these models, an average number of farms of only one land type was considered, associated with a typical amount of grazing land and the fixed infrastructure and administrative costs for one settlement unit. The latter excluded the educational and health components. Although these were to be provided for each unit, their provision was coincident with the land settlement programme, not part of it. The objectives that they would fulfil were not those of the land programme itself.

7. The approach of appraising 'typical' units, rather than looking at each land unit individually, was realistic. If government was satisfied that the main unit types and the programme as a whole were acceptable, there would be no need to review each unit that was similar to the studied types or some combination of them. Nor would ODA wish to inspect a large number of individual unit submissions. Its financial support was for the programme as a whole, a package of 'Sector Aid' rather than funds for individual projects. If the typical units were acceptable, finance up to an agreed ceiling could be used for specified purposes on all proposed units that were seen from simpler, outline examination to be of the general type.

8. The only shadow pricing attempted was to value the labour of the typical farm family. Their input was not costed in the budgets – the net farm income would be the labour reward. Rough estimates were made from various sources of the average income per adult worker in small farming, the activity that the settlers would engage in if there were no settlement schemes. The value of earnings per year for a stereotype family of 5 persons was added as a cost. Its value per adult worker was about half the minimum wage rate.

9. Little time was available for detailed appraisal of this programme. Not untypically with agricultural projects, early decisions by government and donors were required so that a whole farming season would not be lost. Consequently, no other shadow pricing could be undertaken. It was recognised that this approach probably understated the net value of the schemes. The output was a mixture of traded and non-traded items. In agricultural countries like this one, the economic value of traded farm products is usually well above farmer prices. Fertiliser is typically a subsidised input which can be a sizeable item of farmer cash costs, but the effect of upward adjustments of produce values generally outweighs the subsidy and other cost-increasing corrections by a wide margin. Using the market price for land could have been a separate source of error, but it was felt that land prices reflected without gross error the economic value of land in farming of the less-intensive pre-settlement kind. Cost and benefit statements combining farm and non-farm items were discounted over 30 years at the national customary rate of 10%, and cost/benefit ratios were calculated. These were highest in the units based on the best grade of land, and less than unity on the poorest grade land,

because of the high cost of infrastructure in relation to the very extensive farming systems that were possible.

Results

10. An estimate was made of the rate of return on the programme as a whole, by combining in the expected mix budgets for all of the different types of individual unit. This obviously crude measure had a good positive NPV, and an IRR of 14%. Sensitivity testing showed the following results.

	NPV (mills)	IRR
Base case	6.5	14.0
Benefits reduced by 10%	−1.2	9.2
Costs increased by 10%	−1.9	8.6
Both benefits reduced and costs increased by 10%	−9.6	3.2
Farm labour valued at minimum wage	−11.5	0.1
Health and education costs included	−8.8	3.5

11. The extreme sensitivity of the appraisal to the valuation of labour is notable though not untypical of the analysis of small farm projects.

12. In addition to the quantified benefits, the appraisal drew attention to the effects of the project in promoting social stability and in meeting political aspirations of the small farmer and rural groups. The net benefits would accrue almost entirely to low income people – the settler families. They would, on average, receive substantial increases in income, especially since only a few scheme costs would be covered by user charges. This meant that not only would capital costs not be recovered but the programme would create long-term demands for government finance to cover recurrent expenses. This aspect apart, the appraisal felt confident of the ability and motivation of local personnel to plan and implement the programme efficiently and in a cost-effective way, especially since it was intended that the productive aspects were based on established crops which were satisfactorily handled by experienced, proven institutions.

Case Study 5: A New Development Road for Agricultural Districts

1. This case study features these particular aspects of project analysis:

- ★ Cost Benefit Analysis
- ★ Shadow Pricing
- ★ Savings Premium

- ★ Beneficiary Identification
- ★ Indirect Benefits
- ★ Meeting Recurrent Costs

Description

2. This project was to construct a new all-weather motorable road in a very hilly area that had many agricultural villages. It was basically an extension, into an isolated farmers' area, of an existing road that was linked to the national roads network. The construction of a motorable way in very broken country would, it was hoped, allow agriculture and rural development projects to be formulated for the areas that would become within reach of vehicular traffic.

3. Because of the difficult terrain, design options were very limited. Specifications had to take account of what was possible, and it was inevitable that the relatively low-capacity road proposed should be fairly expensive to construct. Nevertheless in the interests of reducing capital costs, the design adopted had a narrower carriageway than had first been proposed. It was, nevertheless, an expensive road to build in an environmentally sound way. Steep slopes, unstable ground and heavy seasonal rainfall meant that major steps had to be taken to allow for the avoidance of major environmental trouble. River courses were avoided and major hairpin bends were designed only where the sub-strata was firm. Soil excavation and tipping were done with great care, good soil being dumped where it could later be terraced and cultivated. Trees, bushes and grasses were planted at once on all embankments, and bamboos, which would provide soil stability and fast growing usable products.

Analysis

4. Appraisal of the road project put particular emphasis on two points.

(i) The importance to the success of the new road of adequate maintenance and periodic rehabilitation of the existing road, which was an indispensible link. The ability of government, through the appropriate authority, to provide recurrent funds for this was raised, especially since the limited revenue-raising power of the authorities had led to poor road maintenance elsewhere.

(ii) Estimating the value of benefits from this new road. Rough estimates existed of farming systems and productivity in the valleys that would be affected by the new means of transport. However, the newness of the situation being created prevented any estimates being made of how production would change in response to the new opportunities for selling produce out of the area. Cost savings would be realised on the small amount of existing exports from the region affected, which were carried out by porters, but the volumes were small. No guesses could be made of the net value of the induced traffic that the road would bring. Consequently, analysis approached the question from the other direction. From a knowledge of the expected capital and maintenance costs of the road, and an estimate of the required discount rate, it was possible to calculate that

179

the road would be economically justified if, through the opportunity of relatively cheap transportation, the road induced a rate of growth over twenty-five years of 1% per annum in the value of net agricultural output throughout the area affected. This would need to be additional to any net benefits from other investments in agriculture and rural development. Appraisers of the project thought that this necessary target of 1% per annum would be reached or exceeded in these areas, where access was a major constraint. However, sustained development of this kind was not assured. Consequently, plans for construction of the road were associated with proposals for technical assistance to survey the productive potential of the area, and the need also to develop output packages; input and marketing facilities; and institutions. Development of these aspects would increase the likelihood of the necessary production benefits being realised.

5. Shadow-pricing focused on the valuation of labour and agricultural output. Construction over five years, would follow labour-intensive methods, and would be relatively expensive, and unskilled labour wages would be more than double estimated alternative incomes for the local people employed. However, account was taken of the national lack of savings and government's difficulty in raising revenue in this very poor country. Incremental income to the workers was thus valued at only half its nominal value. (In the Little–Mirrlees formula $SWR = c' - \frac{1}{s}(c{-}m)$, s was given a value of 2). An SCF of 0.89 was applied, to reflect the observed divergence between international and local prices.

6. Only the SCF was applied to estimates of the value of farm output. Production in the area affected – food, grain, vegetables, fruits, livestock products – would be consumed within the country. As they would not directly affect imports or exports, they could be regarded as non-traded agricultural produce.

Results
7. The increases in agricultural output needed to justify the cost of the road were considered to be reasonably likely. Appraisal of the project also took note of the time-savings for pedestrians that the road might allow. The motorisation of many thousands of journeys was expected to generate productive benefits of very little value, at border prices, and ODA's practice is not to place any value on leisure savings. The existence of these benefits, and of the other social and political advantages of opening up a new important area, were mentioned but not given weight in the calculation of possible net benefits from the construction of this new road.

8. Because of the remoteness and site difficulties, a tender-contract approach to implementation could not be considered. Instead, a management team was envisaged, working to an agreed budget and controlled by an agency with previous experience of road construction in the country. Only major bridges would be handled through separate contracts. Local experienced engineers were expected to be available for the work, which would be reviewed annually by joint teams from ODA and the national government. The road was designed to require limited routing maintenance, but assurances were sought on the availability of adequate funds each year during the operation phase.

Case Study 6:   The Road Improvement Project

1.   This case study features these particular aspects of project analysis:

* Demand Estimation
* Cost Benefit Analysis
* Technical Alternatives
* Sensitivity Analysis
* Alternative Timing
* Indirect Benefits

Description

2.   The project was to bring to a Class II bitumen standard 196 Kilometres of an existing road. Most of it was sand-sealed, but around 41 Km was bitumen which had become pot-holed and deteriorated. Because of swamps, escarpment and a lake, the terrain allowed few options for realignment. A few small horizontal changes would be made, but in particular it was assumed that existing Bailey bridges would be used at river crossings.

3.   The entire road was divided into 6 sections, differentiated on the basis of traffic characteristics. Major agro-industrial developments were planned at two points along the route. These would generate local traffic, with raw materials brought for processing and the removal of produce. They would also lead to the development of small towns, for which additional road traffic would be generated.

Analysis

4.   Underlying the design and analysis of the project was quantitative modelling of the forecast traffic. The first step was estimation of the traffic likely to be generated by development of the two new towns. Data from Origin and Destination Surveys in the country concerned allowed a gravitational model to be estimated that was based on populations in different zones, and the operating cost of vehicles on the different routes. Physical plan estimates of the population sizes of the two new towns, and regression analysis, allowed forecasts to be made of traffic between these towns and various destinations, that would use the 6 sections.

5.   The second step was to estimate a growth model for existing and generated traffic. This model took account of growth in both population and incomes. The basis for the incomes part was a household expenditure survey which provided data on daily vehicle trips per person for nineteen income groups. Again, regression analysis was employed to establish an income–journeys relationship. For estimation of the growth of traffic along the road, different rates of growth of population and per capita income were taken for the rural areas and the two proposed towns. Both variables were slightly higher for the towns.

6.   Taken together, these estimates implied annual traffic growth rates from the base period of 8% for existing traffic and between 11 and 12% for the generated traffic. Estimates of total traffic were thus made which combined these two types with special traffic directly associated with the two proposed agro-industrial projects. The different categories were shown separately, to allow the data to be separately assessed if the two projects were cancelled or delayed.

7.   The estimates of traffic flows were further refined into their component volumes of six different categories of vehicle. Special adaptation for vehicle

flows associated with the new projects allowed the number of commercial vehicles each year to be estimated separately for each of the 6 stretches of road. Using empirical data derived by the UK Transport and Road Research Laboratory, the volume of commercial vehicles were converted into a given number of 'equivalent standard axles' of 8,200 kilograms each. The wear on a road depends on the number of 'standard axles' that use it over its life. Design of the road base will vary according to the expected number of standard axles over the life of the road.

8. This analysis showed that two stretches of the road should be constructed to a higher specification than the others, because of expected high levels of commercial traffic volumes. On the basis of this knowledge, and detailed engineering studies, construction costs for each stretch could be estimated. These were major elements of the cost side of the project. The other cost feature was maintenance cost savings. Routine, recurrent and periodic maintenance needs and costs were separately estimated for both the existing road and the proposed improved one. Despite the 6-yearly cost of resealing the bitumenised roads (which were converted to an annual basis by use of the appropriate Capital Recovery Factor), the new road would have lower maintenance costs.

9. Against these main costs would be set the principal benefit of vehicle operating cost savings. The project study involved a major survey of vehicle operating costs on roads of different kinds for each of the 6 vehicle categories used. Detailed work allowed the calculation, year by year, of cost savings for each group of vehicles according to the traffic models used.

10. The cost-benefit appraisal of this project took account of only these elements:
   * Vehicle Operating Cost Savings (including crew costs), the main benefit;
   * Road Maintenance Cost Savings, a lesser benefit; and
   * Construction Costs.

11. A number of other possible minor benefits that could arise with such a large road were not included, because data and data-gathering resources were not available. The study mentioned that no account was taken of:
   * diverted traffic: for a short while the improvement of this road might attract a little traffic, but other new road developments would make this only a temporary phenomenon;
   * agricultural development benefits outside the two new projects;
   * passenger time savings;
   * accident reduction savings;
   * savings from reduced damage to goods in transit; and
   * consumer surplus from private journeys. Most traffic was expected to be commercial. Better access to health, education and social amenities would become possible, but leisure benefits from this or any other source would be given no value.

Results
12. In the knowledge that some net benefits had not been estimated, economic analysis of the costs and benefits of each section went ahead. The main

shadow pricing adjustment made was to remove the tax element of costs in each of the 3 elements. In the case of labour, it was felt that the wages paid to both skilled and unskilled labour reflected opportunity costs. Regarding foreign exchange, since policy was to operate flexible exchange rates, there was no large discrepancy between the official rate of exchange and the scarcity value. A small adjustment to the import component of costs was required. A discount rate of 12% was used, this being the minimum rate acceptable in the country.

13.   Using a desk-top computer, the analyst calculated the NPV and IRR for each of the road sections. Sensitivity Analysis looked at 25% variation in the three main variables – construction costs, traffic growth rates and vehicle operating cost savings. In IRR terms, the results were these:

ROAD SECTION	CENTRAL ESTIMATES	CONSTRUCTION COST + 25%	TRAFFIC GROWTH RATE – 25%	VOC SAVINGS – 25%
	%	%	%	%
A	28	24	25	24
B	13	11	12	11
C	14	11	12	11
D	14	12	13	11
E	32	27	30	25
F	35	30	33	30

14.   These results were interpreted as justifying reconstruction of all parts of the 196 Km route. Substantial adverse variations of 25% pushed the IRR on some sections just below the test rate, but some benefits had not been taken into account.

15.   Results of the economic analysis were also used to indicate what the sequence of construction should be – judged from the purely economic viewpoint, disregarding engineering, management and financial factors which might in practice be of overwhelming importance in allowing minimum cost construction. The method used was to rank the sections according to their 'first year rate of return', a measure that expresses net benefits in the first year as a proportion of costs, including an annual value for capital costs. As the figures above suggest would be the case, sections A, E and F were preferred.

Case Study 7: Rehabilitation of a Thermal Power Station

1. This case study features these particular aspects of project analysis:
   - ★ Technical Alternatives
   - ★ Cost Benefit Analysis
   - ★ Shadow Pricing
   - ★ Consumer Surplus
   - ★ User Tariff Policy
   - ★ Programme Approach

Description

2. Power consumption in a middle-sized country was growing rapidly, especially in the central belt where most economic activity was concentrated. New generating capacity was being constructed through a long-term plan that included the rehabilitation of existing power stations; new generators; and the extension and rehabilitation of the grid. Nevertheless, demand was still ahead of supply. Hydro-stations contributed most, but the seasonality of water availability and demand meant that deficits always occurred in a few months each year.

3. The core of this project was completion of the rehabilitation of a thermal station built 30 years earlier. Steam generating boilers, steam turbines and diesel generators would be replaced quickly. The new plant would have a capacity in excess of the existing station, which was unable to work close to its theoretical potential. The provision of equipment was essential. However, ODA provided assistance to the power station as programme aid. Provision of capital would be accompanied by funds for supervising consultants and a 3-year programme of assistance with operation and maintenance that included equipment and personnel. This was hoped to raise effective capacity of the power station from 18 MW (10% of existing demand) to 48 MW (28%) very quickly.

4. Even after rehabilitation, the generators in this station would be relatively expensive to run, as their design allowed a lower thermal efficiency than modern equipment. When completed, generation from this plant would come fairly low in order of merit. It would provide stand-by capacity that would certainly be called upon at some seasons of peak demand and deficit. Steam generation would be more expensive than diesel, but a lower need for maintenance would allow steam to supply power more continuously than diesel at times of peak need. Over a year, however, the diesel plant would be used most. Because it would provide only stand-by capacity until new stations were completed, this project was envisaged to have a life of only ten years.

Analysis

5. Economic appraisal in formulating and reviewing the plan for this project featured cost-effectiveness and cost-benefit analyses. Cost-effectiveness focused on questions of whether rehabilitation of this plant was the best way of providing stand-by capacity. All other major stations were either in reasonably efficient operation or were being renewed. The only alternative for a quick increase in capacity was new gas turbines. Cost comparisons between steam, diesel and gas turbines were made on the basis of cost per KWh. Discounting was done at 10%, and assumed a life of 20 years for gas turbines. In all cases, fuel was overwhelmingly the main input (90% of costs), and both it

and capital costs were relatively easily valued at border prices. This analysis gave the cost ranking per KWh: diesel 4.14; steam 5.31; gas turbine 6.24.

6.   The cost-benefit question was whether any generation was justified at these cost levels. This could not be measured through tariffs. They had been held down for a long time, and at the time of project formulation were less than half the cost of incremental production. Tariff increases were planned, as part of a new policy for financing and managing the power sector, but the new tariffs would probably not cover the costs of marginal stand-by capacity.

Results

7.   A proxy for the value of consumer-willingness-to-pay was the cost of independent stand-by generation that many firms were installing, to meet their needs during power cuts in the deficit months. Whereas both steam and diesal plants in the project would use furnace oil, these other plants used expensive distillate. Even after allowance for distribution cost savings, the independent generators were much more expensive, from the national view-point as well as in terms of financial cost to users. On these grounds, rehabi-litation of the steam and diesel plant was regarded as the cheapest quick means of meeting peak power demand for a few years.

8.   Since it would rehabilitate existing plant, with no new building or types of emission, the project raised no new environmental issues. The only social effects were benefits associated with a more reliable supply.

9.   The project was formulated during a time of institutional change in the power sector. The national corporation responsible for power was being sub-divided along regional lines. This change, and alteration of the tariff poli-cy, would, it was thought, give a better chance of full benefits being obtained from this project. This was especially important, since capital aid funds were being associated with technical assistance in this power station for a few years. Some unspecific money would also be provided for equipment, that could be drawn on as needed during this period for minor essential items.

Case Study 8: The Hydro-Electric Rehabilitation Project

1. This case study features these particular aspects of project analysis:

- ★ Demand Estimation
- ★ Technical Alternatives
- ★ Alternative Timing
- ★ Cost Benefit Analysis
- ★ Sensitivity Analysis

- ★ Consumer Surplus
- ★ Beneficiary Identification
- ★ User Tariff Policy
- ★ Financial Targets
- ★ Institutional Questions

Description

2. Electricity supply in this country came mainly from a large hydro-electric project which had been inaugurated over 30 years before. At that time, the concrete dam was constructed and four turbines and 15 MW generators were commissioned. Gradually the number had been increased to the full complement of 10 generators. However, all of them were now old, at or approaching the end of their design life, as was much of the transmission and distribution system that was built at the same time. Due especially to severe national economic difficulties in recent years, maintenance and repair work had been grossly neglected. With the prospect of stability, a major scheme of rehabilitation was envisaged. This included several components, which included these:

- ★ Repair to the dam and water passages, to rectify wear and deterioration over the years;
- ★ Strengthening the power station structure, to rectify cracking initiated when a rapid rise in the water levels in the lake required much larger volumes of water to be passed than had been anticipated;
- ★ Rehabilitation of the turbines;
- ★ Rehabilitation of the generators, especially rewinding them;
- ★ Rehabilitation where necessary of the transmission lines and substations; and
- ★ The supply of many items of equipment, vehicles, stocks of parts, etc., to allow rehabilitation and proper maintenance.

3. A major feature of the rehabilitation was that the use of modern insulators would allow each generator's capacity to rise to 18 MW. In association, technical assistance would be given to the electricity authority, to modernise operations and management, and to the Ministry of Energy, etc., for long-range sectoral planning. All this implied a very expensive project, (over $70 million) with a lot of design and supervision engineering. Three foreign donors were in prospect to share the predominating offshore costs, with government and the authority meeting most local costs.

4. The work to be undertaken was fairly easily specified, but the exact detail and cost for some items could not be determined until work began: examples were underwater work on the dam; power-house foundation strengthening; and transmission line rehabilitation. Consequently, generous provision (10 to 15%) for physical contingencies were made for these items, and flexibility was allowed for in the work tender documents, not only to increase the work but (for unsurveyed transmission lines) possibly to reduce it.

Analysis

5. Economic analysis of the project considered first whether rehabilitation was the cheapest form of power supply. For domestic users, the alternatives were kerosene and charcoal. For large users, various forms of large thermal generation were possible, but all would take many years to plan and implement, too long for them to be realistic alternatives for the plant, which was thought to be likely to lose one of the remaining 8 functional generators every 6 months. The same time objection would apply to a second large hydro-project. Gas turbines and diesels were the only quick alternatives. However, they were shown to be much more costly than rehabilitation. Investment costs per KW were estimated to have the following relationship:

Rehabilitation of turbines and generators	100
Replacement of turbines and generators	150
Gas turbines	250
Diesels	800

6. Operating costs – fuel especially – would be overwhelmingly higher also for the last two options. The manufacturers of the original machinery were still in business, and could rehabilitate without difficulty.

7. A separate calculation considered optimal timing. The consequences of delay for 1 and 2 years were calculated. The costs were the value of energy not supplied, and the benefits were the lower discounted costs of rehabilitation. Delay would undoubtedly lead to shortages. The value of cost savings per KWh lost from the postponement (discounted at 12%) were much less than the existing tariff levels. It would be more valuable to undertake rehabilitation at the first opportunity, not to wait.

8. This part of the analysis depended on demand projections. These were made in a segmented way, based on the electricity authority's records of sales. Electricity was very cheap by international standards, and was thus treated as price-inelastic for most users. Slow growth during the coming years of economic recovery indicated an expansion of domestic use of only 5%. Large commercial users were projected individually. Minor commercial user demand was projected on the basis of a historic-based relationship between growth and consumption. In aggregate, these calculations suggested a growth in overall consumption of 9% annually from the existing recession-depressed levels, but a growth in maximum demand of only 5%. At these levels, the rehabilitated plant would reach full capacity operation in about 10 years. This would allow time for a second major hydro project to be planned and constructed, if detailed preparatory work for it began soon and confirmed that it was the best form of new supply.

9. The calculation of an IRR for the rehabilitation required estimates of the 'true economic value' of electricity. This involved the always-speculative assessment of consumer surplus. Willingness to pay was estimated separately for domestic consumers and for other users. For domestic users, the alternatives were kerosene or charcoal, valued at $0.2 per KWh. Taking the average income per connected household of $1,000, average consumption per household (3,000 KWh) and a willingness to pay up to 10% of income on electricity, it was estimated that they would be willing to purchase 500 KWh at the replacement cost. These calculations produced an estimated average value of actual consumption of $0.093 per KWh, 6 times the present domestic tariff. Other

users were assumed to be price elastic for 25% of power used, but willing to pay the full alternative cost for the remainder. Diesel sets would give costs of $0.2 per KWh for small users and $0.128 for large consumers.

Results

10.   The weighted average value of electricity for all consumers was $0.164. This value was applied to the incremental sales of electricity that would arise as rehabilitation avoided decline. These were set against the capital and increased operating costs attributable to the project. Discounting over 25 years gave an IRR of 75%!

11.   When the benefits were valued at existing tariffs, the IRR was 21.6%. Sensitivity test results were:

Capital costs 10% higher	19.8%
All system operating costs charged to project, not just incremental	18.1%
All benefits deferred one year	18.6%

In view of the very high rates of return, no shadow pricing was undertaken. Most investment items and many operating costs were traded items. Use of the SCF and other adjustments would not have brought the IRRs anywhere near the test rate of 12%.

12.   Financial analysis showed that present tariffs were only about one-third of long run marginal costs. The need for a second hydro project was in view, for which reserves should be built up, and a much higher tariff would then be required. It was agreed that all project finance would be on-lent to the electricity authority at 9 and 10%, over 20 years with 5 years grace. Financial targets should produce a tariff that would cover all costs (including loan charges) and give a return of at least 8% on the net value of assets employed, revalued from time to time to allow for future inflation. This would require an increase in tariffs by completion of the rehabilitation of 70% in real terms.

13.   These financial points apart, the analysis expressed confidence in the electricity authority. It had an effective structure and a good training policy, and had come through recent extremes better than most parastatals. In project negotiation, realistic physical performance targets had been fixed and agreed. While contractors would carry out the new capital work on the dam and in the power station, the authority should be able to handle the other capital work (under supervising engineers) with existing skilled staff. It should also be able to absorb an updated computer for operations control, user billing and other work.

14.   As a final point, the analysis noted that none of the direct beneficiaries would be poor people. This is typical of power projects. However, all people in the cash economy would benefit to some extent from the continued production and service provision that rehabilitation would allow. The effects to everyone of collapse of the power system could be very costly.

15.   The study from which this illustration is taken also quoted values for tariffs to different users, the long run incremental costs of supplying each type, and the difference (which could be regarded as the premium actually being charged).

16. The figures in Ms per unit were:

User Type	% of gas	Tariff	LRIC	Balance
Bulk	59	13.05	15.74	−2.69
Industrial	27	36.00	19.29	16.71
Commercial	7	45.20–51.00	40.12	5.08–10.88
Domestic	7	34.00	51.97	−17.97
Weighted average	100	23.16	20.94	2.22

These figures indicate the high potential value and significance of the premium. Although sales revenue exceeded long run costs, the average margin was 35% less than the lowest estimate of the correct premium in Year 1. Estimates of the premium in Year 1 ranged from 15 to nearly 100% of LRIC.

17. During negotiation of the project for which this analysis was made, it was agreed that the tariff levels would increase in real terms by an average of 14% in each of two years, and that a depletion premium would be an element in all future price formulae.

Case Study 9: The Village Electrification Project

1. This case study features these particular aspects of project analysis:

- ★ Demand Estimation
- ★ Cost Benefit Analysis
- ★ Shadow Pricing
- ★ Consumer Surplus
- ★ Gender

- ★ Indirect Benefits
- ★ Financial Aspects
- ★ User Tariff Policy
- ★ Financial Targets

Description

2. This project was to allow the supply of electricity to villages in a district where the towns, a few nearby villages, and other main users were already supplied from the national grid. The (autonomous) district electricity company (DEC) could expect to continue purchasing all its power needs in bulk from the national authority, so no local generation was involved.

3. Two donors – ODA and another – had indicated a willingness to consider meeting the offshore capital costs of electrifying different sections of the district. For technical planning reasons, the entire district system had to be studied, not just parts of it. Following first installation in a village, the consumption of electricity tends to increase very rapidly for a few years, as new connections are made, and at quite high, steady rates thereafter. For a 20-year life, the installations would need to be capable of meeting high future demand, as the staged development of electricity distribution systems is prohibitively expensive. The forecasting of load was thus a crucial starting point.

Analysis

4. Bulk requirements for the whole district were forecast separately for four major types of use – villages; other rural uses; the district capital; and other major towns. Each group was divided between existing users and new users. As in all power studies, the forecasts had to show both actual use of power (in KWh or GWh) over each year and the maximum demand (MD) at any time. The system must be designed to meet both needs.

5. To forecast village demand, a study was made of recently electrified villages. This indicated the rate of connections to individual houses, and consumption per household, initially mainly for lighting. It was recognised that women would benefit from domestic connections. Demand for the connected villages was thus projected, assuming no change in the real cost of power.

6. Other rural loads were of several kinds. Two main pumping stations for potable water were already operating, and their needs were ascertained without difficulty. The same was true of three smaller pump installations. An established soap factory was expecting to expand, and growth patterns were similarly projected for some agricultural users, a university campus and various camps and other sites.

7. For the district headquarters, the establishment of new industries was being encouraged, so supply provision was made for anticipated new projects and for unknown new loads, together with the expansion of existing users' consumption. A similar approach was followed for the other three towns.

190

8.   To forecast the load for the new village connections, a sample of the unconnected villages was studied. Population, levels of prosperity, the degree of scatter/compactness, and the different levels of industrial, commercial and other non-domestic activities were all used to categorise the 127 villages involved into 6 groups, each of which had different assumed initial consumption levels and rates of growth of consumption and MD.

9.   Consolidating all this information (with a computer) allowed full projections of needs for the new villages, individually and in aggregate. To these were added quite substantial amounts for prospective new 'other rural loads', including a radio transmitter, several more pumps, a cement factory and a new college.

10.   All of these individual forecasts were brought together to allow composite demand to be estimated for 18 years. With the addition of system losses (expected to be lower than before due to improvements in the network) total needs in the district system could be assessed. The projected development over 18 years was dramatic – more than 9 times as much MD capacity would be needed in the end than in the base year.

11.   These aggregate forecasts allowed district needs to be fully assessed, and the overall system of grids and transformers to be designed down to the level of sub-unit supplies. Part of the cost of the total system would be attributable to the villages, but not a lot – about 23% over 18 years in this relatively diverse district.

12.   The pattern and cost of the supply connections to the villages (which the aid would cover) was separately worked out. Standard types of overhead line, posts and transformers would be used, imported in the main from the two donor countries. It was evident that, due to limitations in the supply of some inputs, (skilled labour and concrete posts especially), it would take over 4 years to connect the 127 villages in a cost-effective programme.

13.   A schedule was thus required. A priority ranking was first made on the basis of the discounted value of net benefits (estimated sales less the cost of generator fuel, operation and maintenance charges) in relation to the capital cost of connecting each village. 'Cost-benefit ratios' were calculated by dividing capital costs by net benefits. The ratio values, which ranged from 0.6 to 2.3, allowed comparisons of the merit of electrifying any village compared to others. The priority sequence of work thus established was modified to make the whole process cost-effective, but from this basis a rational sequencing of the work in the two donor zones was planned over 4 years.

14.   The district electricity company was expected to be financially self-sufficient, paying dividends on equity, so its financial position needed to be analysed. Review of its past figures showed a poor level of return on fixed assets at first, but as sales increased, expenses per KWh fell. This improvement had allowed dividend provision to be made in the last two years, though payment was delayed.

15.   Estimation of the future financial position involved making provision not only for the village electrification, but for other developments of the grid, including some new installations as well as reinforcement in towns. (Connections for all other new works apart from the village would be paid for by them,

not by the district electricity company.) Tariffs also had to be assessed. They varied for different users in relation to costs of supply. The highest charges were paid by rural users (including villagers). Urban users paid a little less, with much lower charges on the high-consuming and relatively constant load radio transmitter and water pumping agencies.

16. The off-shore capital costs of the village electrification was to be met by soft loans from the two donors, which would be on-lent to DEC by government on more commercial terms. In calculating the cost of this work, the equipment cost quotes were inflated to the year of project planning by 10% for domestic costs and 8% for off-shore items. Before this, 7% was added for engineering and 8% for physical contingency. The two loans would be on-lent at slightly different terms. Interest would be capitalised during construction in both cases. One would be repaid over 12 years at 5%, and the other at 5% over 20 years.

17. Onshore costs would be partly funded from consumer connection charges. It was proposed that the remainder be met by equity from government. Following local practice, dividends at a rate of around 7.5% would be required from an agreed date. However, because of the time-lag between investment and returns in rural electrification, and because of general uncertainty, it seemed best that this part of financing take the flexible form of equity rather than more loans.

18. Economic Analysis concentrated on four features – the cost of imported capital items; the cost of concrete poles, the main local capital cost item; the cost of electricity generation; and the value of power in the villages. The discussion of shadow pricing concluded that no value adjustments were called for. The economy was growing rapidly, with shortages of labour of all kinds, so there was no case for a shadow wage. Regarding foreign exchange, high import duties existed on imported consumer goods, but the overall average tariff level on imports was 12%. The deficit on the current account of the balance of payments was readily financed by transfers and other capital account inflows. An SCF of 0.89 reflected the differential between domestic and international prices.

19. The test discount rate of 8% had been established over a number of years.

20. The economic cost of bulk supplied power was taken to be quite substantially above the actual tariff price charged to DEC, more than double. Although most power is generated with residual fuel oil, obtained at prices well below free market prices under a bilateral arrangement with an oil-exporting country, it was expected that generating costs to meet increased demand would be higher in the future. The economic cost was estimated in full, eliminating subsidies.

21. Concrete poles could also have been revalued upwards because the manufacturers (the national electricity authority) obtained cement at a concessional rate. However, this would affect the unit cost of poles by less than 5% so it was ignored, and market prices accepted, even though (underpriced) electricity was also an important input into cement production. Forecast costs for distribution and administration by DEC allowed for the scale economies that would obviously arise.

22. Overall appraisal looked not just at NPV and IRR, but also at what consumer value per KWh would have to be assumed to give an 8% IRR at efficiency shadow prices.

Results
23. The financial projections (at fixed prices) showed that the village electrification sections of the accounts would take a few years to get into a profit situation, while loads and tariff revenue built up. However, DEC should make profits at that time from supply to the new large consumers, and so will be able to meet its outlays.

24. Although the village sector would contribute 21% of DEC income a couple of years after completion, it would never be a major source of profits. However, provided tariffs were allowed to increase with costs, the DEC financial position should be secure, with dividends paid at the required rate.

25. In the base case of the economic analysis, taking the combined value of power charges at actual tariff plus connection charge and deposit, the average consumer charge was 88% of the 'required' value, and the IRR was only 6.8%. A 10% increase in capital costs increased the required tariff by 7%. Using the existing actual oil price in the cost of power, rather than the free international price, pushed the required tariff below the actual level.

26. Typically for such studies, indications of consumer surplus were sought. It was found that existing electricity supply costs in unelectrified villages (from batteries, small generators, a small private scheme) were all far in excess of the proposed actual tariff. Furthermore, most of the villages were 'visibly prosperous', which suggested that many people would be willing to pay more, with the price elasticity of demand estimated at between -0.3 and -0.8. The analyst's view was that consumer surplus benefits valued at 20% of the tariff would arise. This would carry the rate of return to about 10%. On these grounds, without quantifying other benefits of different kinds, (lower rural-urban migration; regional income equality; tax on electrical goods; stimulation of local industries; etc.), the project was recommended for financing.

Case Study 10:   Water Supply for a Coastal Town

1.   This case study features these particular aspects of project analysis:

- ★ Demand Estimation
- ★ Input Supply
- ★ Technical Alternatives
- ★ Cost Benefit Analysis

- ★ Consumer Surplus
- ★ User Tariff Policy
- ★ Financial Targets
- ★ Institutional Questions

Description
2.   This project was to allow very substantial expansion of potable water supply to a port town. The need for a new development arose partly from failure of the existing system to meet the needs of an urban area (population 20,000). The town was growing, and was projected to continue expansion up to 50–60,000 people, especially through manufacturing, port expansion and tourism. However, a substantial new industrial development was being planned at a site a few miles along the coast. The fresh water needs of this plant would be about as great as requirements for the town and all its users.

3.   Existing supplies were pumped from an alluvial area a few kilometres away, but the facilities were insufficient to meet the existing need, let alone major expansion.

Analysis
4.   The fundamental basis for planning by consultants was demand estimation on the assumption of charges to consumers which met the full cost of supply. Consumption records existed, but because of water shortages at times, they understated demand. For major existing users (industries, port, hotels), each was projected separately for 25 years. A separate composite projection for all other uses (domestic, commerce, construction, small industry, government, etc.) was made on the basis of future levels of population and per capita consumption amounts. To this was added the separate estimates of the comparatively massive needs of the new industrial plant. Considerable uncertainty surrounded the timing and volume of its needs, and the requirements of other users.

5.   At first, ten separate sets of alternative projections were made. These were later reduced to five, but consultants felt unable to choose between them or to attach probabilities to them, so there was no probability-weighted expected estimate. The importance of avoiding any need for further early expansion of whatever water supply system was installed meant that one of the higher demand estimates was the one mainly used, though it was realised that there was a certain probability that even this could be exceeded.

6.   Estimates of user demand, expanded to allow for system losses, showed total supply needs. These covered both annual needs and peak demand. For the bulk transmission pipeline, a peak factor of 1.3 was used (ie peak = 1.3 times average), but for the distribution system, the factor was 2.0.

7.   The annual needs thus estimated over 25 years were the basis for assessing available sources of supply. The port is in an arid zone, and a wide search had to be made, involving quite extensive hydrogeological and other studies. The existing source could be expanded, beyond the present level, but its upper limit would soon be reached. Other sources considered were:

194

* a seasonally-dry river bed nearby, which had an insufficient catchment;

* another aquifer a few kilometres away, where the water was deep, limited and brackish;

* desalination of sea water, which was feasible but very expensive;

* meeting some water needs by using sea water, but these uses were very limited;

* recycling sewage effluent, which could meet 50% of needs, but was risky on health and salt build-up grounds; and

* development of a group of aquifiers some 75 kms distant.

8. The last was the preferred alternative. Quantities and quality looked adequate. A pilot pump-irrigation farming scheme was there already, but it was not very successful, and government agreed that, in the case of conflict, the port needs would prevail.

9. Capital works were planned in four parts. *Development at the well field* covered boreholes, mains, reservoirs, a power generating station, housing and administration buildings. Up to 14 boreholes might be needed, each with two electric pumps. Seven would be put down immediately, with the others phased to match the growth of demand. Other elements were: a *trunk main* from the wellfield to a new terminal reservoir near the town; a *second trunk main* to the site of the new industry; and an *expanded distribution system* in town. Each of these was the subject of detailed consideration of alternatives to find the most cost-effective solution, bearing in mind the need to meet forecast demand over 25 years with facilities expected to have a 40 year life. The same approach was applied to technical alternatives such as pump sizes, borehole development programmes, trunk pipeline alignments and capacities, reservoir sites and distribution system capacity.

10. Generally, where size was a factor, technical analysis indicated that it was best to install at one time systems able to meet the highest long-term need, rather than develop the system in stages, either by replacing pipes with bigger ones after some years, or by putting in parallel systems.

11. Capital costs of the system designed were estimated from unit rates and quantities, based in large part on manufacturers' quotations. Pipes and pipe-laying were the main cost. Quotations for pipes of various materials were obtained from twelve suppliers, and many contractors gave civil engineering estimates. Actual capital cost estimates were made by using inflation adjustment factors. Available ODA funds could only meet part of the cost of this quite big water scheme, so eventually three donors would be involved. ODA preferred to avoid 'joint financing', with all donors sharing the cost of everything in fixed proportions. 'Parallel financing' allowed ODA funds to be used for the total costs of specific items, while all other donor items would be met by the other two, jointly.

12. Economic appraisal noted that the town supply would not need such major expansion if the proposed industry was not to be catered for. Part of the water scheme could thus be seen as a necessary component of the industrial project, which had an expected IRR at efficiency prices of 15%. Since the industry could not be located elsewhere in the country (it had to be near the coast and a port) the only alternative source of its water needs was desalination.

13. Studies showed that the present value of costs to meet that plant's requirements through desalination was less than the present value of costs for the entire proposed town and industry water supply project. On these grounds alone, the water project was justified, given that the industry project was acceptable in economic terms with water costs included. The test discount rate used was 8%.

14. In the economic analysis, little shadow pricing was done. Duties and taxes were removed, and the price of fuel for the wellfield generators was raised, to take account of a subsidy. In the port area, and in the country as a whole, labour of all kinds was scarce, so no shadow wage was justified. Because of a relatively open exchange rate policy, only a small conversion was made of domestic prices to border prices. Import tariffs averaged 10% or more, and the SCF used was 0.91.

Results
15. For independent assessment of the water project, analysis sought to calculate the average tariff needed to ensure an 8% IRR. This could be compared with consumers' ability and willingness to pay. High and low minimum price estimates were made, corresponding to the extremes of the different demand forecasts in view. Even at the high cost per cubic metre (low quantity) estimate, the projected expenditure per family at the assumed (fairly high) average level of per capita consumption was, for almost all families, less than 5% of average income, the upper limit (in the view of the World Bank) of what households are likely to be prepared to pay for water.

16. Given the significant amount of consumer surplus that would exist at this tariff level, the NPV of the project would be substantially positive at 8%, though no value of this surplus was calculated. No distributional benefits could be claimed. Incomes in the port were already higher than the national average, and likely to remain so. Few people in the town could be regarded as poor.

17. Financial analysis looked at the position of the whole port water-supply entity. Analysts from all the donors felt that the tariff fixed should allow the coverage of: operating costs; interest and capital repayments on the loans from the three donors involved; and an annual net return of not less than 8% on fixed assets employed, from 2 years after the completion of construction. The tariff actually used in the forecasts involved prices that increased with consumption, with most future users on the highest rate, especially the new industry. Some increase over current tariff levels would be needed each year to meet the financial objective, but over time these increases could be less than the rate of inflation, as the real financial burden of the loans decreased. Government policy towards water was that industry and commercial users should not be subsidised, and that the national water tariff should be reviewed every year. These policies allowed analysts to believe that if the policies were properly applied, financial viability of the project could reasonably be achieved.

18. The main risk to the project and its success was postponement or cancellation of the new industry, but neither was thought to be likely. Commitment to development of the full water system need not be made until the industry project was assured.

19.   Important questions arose over the institutional arrangements for implementation and operation. Although the water supply system for the port stood on its own, all water supply systems in the country were to become the responsibility of a national corporation. This corporation was experiencing problems during establishment. Separate from the port water project, but with obvious relevance to it, ODA were providing short-term and long-term technical assistance to the corporation, to support its planning and operations in some areas.

20.   Expansion of the water supply system has obvious implications for the waste water disposal arrangements. Parallel expansion of the sewage system was to be undertaken, though as a separate project.

Case Study 11: The Water Distillation Replacement Project

1. This case study features these particular aspects of project analysis:
   * Demand Estimation
   * Technical Alternatives
   * Scale Alternatives
   * Environmental Aspects
   * Financial Aspects
   * User Tariff Policy

Description

2. This project was located in a very small Dependent Territory where rainfall and groundwater did not supply enough potable water to meet demand. The desalination of sea-water had for a long time been a major source, though in recent years importation had been necessary, in small tankers from a nearby larger country. This had partly become necessary because of poor performance of the two existing distillers. One was near the end of its technical working life, 15 years. The other, newer plant was experiencing corrosion problems which could have been overcome, but only at the cost of more down-time and new materials.

3. In the light of this situation, the water department called for tenders for the installation of one or two new plants, each of fairly large capacity. Project analysis reviewed many relevant questions in the light of the quotations received.

Analysis

4. The starting point for planning and analysis was projection of demand. This related to only one of two water supply systems. Because clean potable water was expensive and scarce, a sea-water system had been developed for use wherever possible, especially for sanitation and fire fighting. This supply system would continue, and the need was to project the demand for fresh water only.

5. The general structure of this demand was:

Households	63%
Hotels	17%
Shipping	9%
Commercial and Industrial	11%

In recent years, aggregate demand had been almost static. Almost all households had been connected up to the system, and further demand growth with increasing incomes was not expected to be large, especially as water was relatively expensive to all users. No general increase in demand was expected.

6. However, a substantial new manufacturing development was possible, which could increase total demand by 5%, while wider regional developments could lead to an expansion in tourism which might lead to an increase in aggregate water demand of about 2% per annum. It was not felt that the availability of more water would increase consumption given its cost to users. There had never been rationing, though occasionally ships had been refused replenishment when stocks were low.

198

7.   Demand study thus envisaged three possible future scenarios: no increase from present levels; an increase of 2% per annum; and 5% annual
growth.

8.   Supply in the most recent year had come from:

Rainfall and Wells	22%
Distillation	40%
Imports	38%

The latter source was unusually prominent in that year because a succession
of dry seasons had diminished natural sources, while the age and corrosion
problems with the distillation plants had led to low capacity working.

9.   Before tenders were obtained, various technical approaches to purifying
sea-water had been considered. Reverse osmosis had not yet been shown to
be reliable or economic at the scale required here. The vertical tube effect
process was regarded as unsatisfactory (it was used in the failing, newer
existing plant), so technical design concentrated on the multi-stage flash process. A particular feature of the renewal situation was that the new unit(s)
would be located on newly-recovered land adjacent to a new diesel power
generating station, and considerable scope for fuel economy would exist in
the use of waste heat from this power plant. This site had no other obviously
beneficial use.

10.   The tenders received were dominated by one offer which appeared to
be technically as sound as the others, but was at much lower cost for a single
unit. However, the same supplier offered to construct an identical second
plant at much lower unit cost than the first, but the two had to be done together
to get this cost advantage, and naturally the offer price was good for only a
limited period.

11.   The analytic approach was to look at the cost per cubic metre of supplies
from different sources. Estimated costs in the year of project preparation of
supply from different sources were:

Rainfall	0.48
Wells	0.69
Imports	2.91
Newest existing distiller	2.96
Oldest existing distiller	3.16

These figures suggest that it would have been better to import than to continue distilling water, but the import source was not considered to be fully
reliable, and part of the distillation costs was fixed expenses (labour especially) which could not be curtailed quickly.

12.   In calculating the expected cost of production with the new distillers, the
capital costs were discounted over an expected life of 18 years, using a relatively low discount rate, which reflected the limited opportunities for new
projects within the territory. No shadow pricing was attempted. Almost all
goods and service in the dependency were traded, and labour prices were
not effectively fixed.

13.   Projected future costs were made for two sets of assumptions: (1) that one or two new distillers would be installed, and (2) that demand would follow the three courses outlined earlier, namely annual increases of zero, 2 and 5%.

Results

14.   These were the calculated figures of cost per cubic metre in constant market prices.

	Rate of increase in demand		
	Zero	2% per annum	5% per annum
One new distiller			
Initial capacity level	85	85	85
Years to full capacity	1	1	1
Average lifetime cost	2.53	2.53	2.53
Two new distillers			
Initial capacity level	62	62	62
Years to full capacity	—	16	6
Average lifetime cost	2.52	2.24	2.12

If only one new unit were installed, it would have to operate at full capacity from the outset. By itself it could not replace both the existing plant and imports, but production costs would be substantially cheaper than both.

15.   If two new units were built together, all imports could be stopped and both existing distillers could be retired at once. There would be surplus capacity initially, and this would persist for some years even if demand grew at the higher of the two projected rates. However, even at the outset, the cost of water would be the same as with only one unit, and less than the alternatives. This outcome, despite the lower level of operation, arises from two sources, (1) the much lower capital cost of the second distiller unit as quoted by the tenderer, and (2) the fact that many capital and operating costs that would have to be met for one distiller could largely or entirely be shared by two – the sea-water intake and outfall; electrical installations; pipework; civil works; and many minor items.

16.   This analysis indicated the value on economic grounds of taking up the offer of installing two new distillers at the new site, retiring the others as soon as the new ones were operational, and dispensing with imports. The spare capacity created would be effectively free, and would provide a safeguard against breakdown, interruptions in imports and possible increases in demand. The alternative of tendering for a smaller second unit was not investigated, since there seemed no possibility that it could be obtained at less cost than the offered price of the second large unit.

17.   The study also looked at the financial policy of the water department. Until a few years before, tariffs had been less than average costs, and deficits accrued. However, charges had recently been raised, and a surplus was being made. The tariff structure set the highest levels for commercial users, while domestic consumers paid charges which, on average, were less than the average cost of supply, although they were the most expensive to deliver water to, and to administer. A separate study of tariff policy was being undertaken, but this analysis felt that the pattern should be altered to encourage commerce. The effect of higher domestic tariffs on the poorer consumers

could be met through specific targeted measures, not a general consumption subsidy. However, this point apart, there was no need for a general increase in charge levels beyond inflation-related adjustments. The new distillers would offer cheaper water in future, so charges might be able to fall in real terms, especially if total consumption increased.

18.   This point apart, the appraisal saw no other causes for institutional concern. Construction of the new installation would be done by the suppliers on a turnkey basis, supervised throughout by consulting engineers and the water department. The latter had adequate staff for operation, and a good performance record, reflected particularly in the reduction of distribution losses in recent years from 25 to 9%. Training their personnel would be part of the installation contract.

19.   As a final point the analysis noted that, as a straight replacement of existing facilities, the project would create no new social or environmental problems.

Case Study 12:   The Natural Gas Project

1.   This case study features these particular aspects of project analysis:

- ★ Demand Estimation
- ★ Technical Alternatives
- ★ Alternative Timing
- ★ Cost Benefit Analysis
- ★ Sensitivity Analysis

- ★ Environmental Aspects
- ★ Depletion Premium
- ★ Beneficiary Identification
- ★ User Tariff Policy
- ★ Institutional Questions

Description

2.   This project, for the development of natural gas, associated infrastructure and institutional development, was located in a large country where existing natural gas fields were already supplying energy. The Natural Gas Corporation (NGC) controlled a fairly large industry, exploiting the only major indigenous fuel source and supplying several users. In a recent year, main consumer groups were fertiliser 39%, power 38%, industry 13%, commercial and domestic 10%.

3.   Demand had been growing at 14% annually in recent years, and future growth when this investment was completed was projected at 7–9%. Three major gas fields were already in production, and reserves were known to exist in other areas. The planning question for this part of the energy sector was to schedule the timing of expansion of production from existing areas, and the exploitation, appraisal and development of new gas fields. In general, production costs were low, and the full economic use of this domestic form of energy was a major opportunity for valuable import substitution. The country was typically short of foreign exchange, and fuel imports were absorbing around 40% of export earnings.

4.   The project in view involved a large investment (over £170 millions) for the development of production in a new area. In addition to the construction of facilities in the gas field, a pipeline of over 100 miles had to be built, bringing supply to a major consumption area. This was a second main feature, but the project also had provision for training of various kinds, and for consultancy for various purposes, including assistance with the appraisal of the gas field before the completion of detailed design; supervision and management of the capital investment over four years; and changing and strengthening the organisation and management of NGC. ODA was only one of five parties assisting the Government to finance the project. The World Bank was the main financier but a UN agency and two other bilateral donors were involved. ODA expected to pay for certain specific parts of this co-financed project, but it conducted a detailed analysis of the project as a whole.

5.   This project envisaged meeting increased demand by the development of a new field and associated pipeline, rather than expanding production from existing areas. The chosen approach was obviously more expensive, but opening up a new source was thought to be justified on the grounds that the gas from the prospective area contained condensates not present in the gas from other fields. These could be used to produce significant amounts of petroleum and kerosene, additional import substitutes that might be obtained efficiently if the costs of the enterprise were justified.

Analysis

6. Existing seismic data and tests from exploratory drilling indicated that development of the field would be worthwhile. However, the best size of the development was not evident during pre-decision planning. Analysis of the project was based on specific proposals, but final design and costings would not be completed until detailed appraisal of the gas field had been undertaken, as a first element of the project. To permit appraisal, relatively pessimistic assumptions were made. A 20 inch pipeline was allowed for, although a 16 inch diameter might prove to be adequate, while a 20% physical contingency was allowed for surface installations at the gas field, a higher contingency than normal for constructions of this kind. Another area of provisional costing was the extent of minor connections from the main pipeline for small users who would be able to take gas at reasonable cost. Although potential users along the route could be identified, it was not evident that connections to them all would be justified. Guidelines and decisions on this would derive from further study to be made as part of the project.

7. In the economic analysis of this investment, little shadow pricing was required beyond valuation of the gas. Almost everything in this capital-intensive development was traded, and the only significant adjustment was the removal of duties and taxes where these arose.

8. A crucial feature of the analysis for this particular form of expanded gas supply was the justification of undertaking this project so as to obtain the condensate, a second product not obtainable from other fields. Investigation of this question involved estimating separately all of the elements of cost in this plan attributable to the development of this new gas field, including especially the cost of a new pipeline and works associated with recovery and handling of the condensate.

9. Cost-effectiveness analysis of this particular means of meeting the expanding demand for gas was more important than the general question of justifying further exploitation of the national energy resource. There really was no question that supply from this source would be at a lower cost than the import of alternative fuels.

10. The costing of units within the project could be undertaken on a secure basis, drawing on known cost information from the development and operation of similar works in this well-established major national industry. Good international cost data was also obtained, and World Bank forecasts of international fuel prices were available. However, a novel feature of the analysis of this kind of project was the incorporation of a cost element to reflect the eventual need to replace the diminishing asset in the natural reserves by fuel supplies from more expensive sources. This 'opportunity cost' element, additional to actual production costs, is the Depletion Premium that was described in paragraph 3.96.

11. Reserves of natural gas are an especially clear case of non-renewable natural resource for which a depletion premium should be allowed. As MI4 brings out, firm estimation of the premium can be difficult, but estimates were obtained and used in the analysis of this project for two products – both the gas itself and the condensate, a constituent of gas in this field that was of specially limited availability.

Results

12. For analysis of the condensate elements of the project, estimates of the separable costs in this project were related to the expected output, which was first estimated at relatively modest levels of production, especially the availability of wells (80%) and the load factor (68%). Sensitivity analysis considered delays of one and five years in the development of the field, and alternative levels of depletion premium. All of these analyses gave economic IRR's of between 13 and 15%. Interpretation of these results against the test rate of 15% took note of the conservative production estimates used and of omission from the calculations of the cost of new wells in other fields that would be needed if this project did not go ahead. The judgement was that the value of the condensate justified the extra costs of developing this gas field earlier than would otherwise have been necessary, ahead of more full exploitation of already-producing areas.

13. Analysis of the main project for gas supply was undertaken in cost benefit terms, though it was recognised that this 'partial' approach might not have been altogether appropriate for the analysis of such a large project, that could have widespread ramifications. The development and its repercussions were distinctly non-marginal to the sector and the economy as a whole. However, a simple calculation indicated an economic rate of return of 70%. Clearly using locally available natural gas in preference to imported fuels would be a very efficient use of national resources. Even at financial prices, with no adjustment for taxes or depletion, the rate of return was calculated to be 32%. Understandably, no sensitivity analysis was undertaken on this aspect of the investment.

14. The consideration of social effects raised few points. The developments envisaged were of a kind that had already been undertaken and accepted. In such a capital-intensive project, with low operating expenses, few if any benefits could go to poor people, who were unlikely to be gas consumers. However, the main benefits would take the form of the proposed large revenue surpluses to NGC and the large foreign exchange savings. Analysts surmised that, since these benefits were so great, the 'trickle down' value of benefit from this investment to the poor groups could be as great as those accruing from projects more obviously geared to benefiting the poor.

15. Environmental factors were also considered carefully. A new feature of this particular gas development would be the production of water and water solubles as part of the condensate. Special plant for their handling was provided for. However, a much more significant factor was the general risk of a major fire or explosion. The risk was not specific to this development, and NGC had handled its system so-far without major difficulty. However, the project involved a major expansion of the network and the risk. Provision was included for training and new procedures directed specially at safety, crisis aversion and emergency procedures.

16. The project as a whole contained significant provision for consultancy and training. These related in part to appraisal of the gas field, and assisting with management of implementation. However, they also related to the reform and strengthening of NGC. In association with this project, NGC subsidiaries would be reorganised from a geographic to a functional structure, distinguishing gas field operations from pipelines, and both from distribution and sales. This change would be assisted with training and consultancy. Various

associated changes would also be made, but special emphasis was put on the questions of tariffs and finance. Donors had insisted that a depletion premium should be an element in pricing. This would have the effect that increasingly price would direct the use of this diminishing resource to those processes that would use it most efficiently. Charges that merely covered costs could lead to wasteful and sub-optimal use in the short and long terms.

17.   Although NGC had for several years earned a fair return on assets employed, it had been agreed that tariffs should be increased at once, and continuously pushed up gradually in real terms to recognise dwindling reserves. The progress of this depletion premium over time would have to depend on review of total estimated reserves, and estimates of production costs. However, it was established that this principle should apply. Even with this premium, gas would be a very attractively priced form of energy for all users. As a result, NGC should earn very large financial surpluses, and their monitoring and management would require planning and control. This valuable project would not only have distinct balance of payments and efficiency effects – it also provided a substantial opportunity, through tariff management, for domestic resource mobilisation on a significant scale.

Case Study 13:   The New Port Project

1.   This case study features these particular aspects of project analysis:
  * Demand Estimation
  * Scale Alternatives
  * Cost Benefit Analysis
  * Shadow Pricing
  * Sensitivity Analysis
  * Financial Aspects
  * User Tariff Policy
  * Financial Targets
  * Institutional Questions

Description
2.   This project is located in a large country that had only one port – Old Port. Despite the on-going construction of additional berths there, traffic growth will exceed available capacity. Port congestion is already evident, with freight surcharges and increased charter rates being applied to compensate for long ship waiting times. New port capacity for general cargo is required. However, a new steel mill is also to be constructed, using large quantities of imported coal and iron ore, for which new berths and facilities will be required.

3.   Old Port could be expanded to meet the need. However, it could never be dredged to allow ships of more than 20,000 tons dead weight (TDW) to enter. This handicap did not apply at an alternative port site along the same coast, where dredging would allow ships of up to 50,000 TDW to be accommodated. Consequently, plans were made for New Port to be developed. The site had considerable long term potential capacity, once the approach channel had been dredged, but development in stages was proposed. The project in view was Phase 1.

Analysis
4.   Estimation of the volumes of materials to be imported and exported were basic to the design of Phase 1. Various categories were forecast individually: semi-bulk and bulk goods, grain, general cargo, coal and iron, as required for the developing steel mill. Various combinations of types of berth and cargo handling facility were considered for New Port, but eventually it was decided that Phase 1 would consist of one iron ore and coal berth (the essential feature) and seven semi-bulk cargo berths. No bulk, grain or oil terminals were proposed at this juncture. Associated with the planned berths would be floating craft, navigational aids, cargo handling equipment, dredging of both the approach channel and the inner channels and ancillary facilities, including road and rail connections, utilities, offices, etc. Development of all this would require considerable engineering inputs. A new authority would be established to manage the construction and operation of the New Port.

5.   The capital costs were estimated at £123 million (excluding taxes and duties) at constant prices. Overall Foreign Exchange costs were 60%, and local costs 40%. Dredging was 21% of costs; the iron and coal berth 26%; and the other seven berths 30%. Operating costs were around only £4.7 million per annum. Dredging was the largest item, followed by the operation of floating craft and the berths. The proposal was that ODA and two multilateral agencies would each finance specific parts of the capital cost.

6. Project benefits were estimated separately for the coal and iron berth, and for the semi-bulk berths. Coal and iron facilities would have to be constructed somewhere. The alternative to building them at New Port was to have them at Old Port, so a first benefit was the avoided cost of building and operating an equivalent installation at Old Port. These were estimated year by year. However, substantial additional savings would arise because the coal and ore could be carried to New Port in larger vessels. Freight rate quotations allowed these transport cost savings to be estimated for the two categories. For the semi-bulk berths, the benefits would be the savings in ship waiting costs that arise from relief of the congestion at Old Port. These were estimated on the basis of the number of ship days saved and an average cost per ship-day. Some inland transport cost savings might also arise, but these were not thought to be large enough to justify the effort of estimation.

7. Beyond the removal from costs of all taxes and duties, no other shadow pricing could be undertaken. An SCF of 0.9 had been estimated, which could have been applied to local costs, but the cost composition (between FE and local currency) of many items was not known. SWR estimates for the country were around 0.8, but any adjustment for the opportunity cost of labour would have been very small. During construction and operation, most labour costs would have been for skilled labour, which it was thought there would be no difficulty in recruiting. On balance, the absence of shadow pricing meant that costs were overstated, though the same would apply to part of the benefits – the costs saved by not building the coal and iron berth at Old Port. The other two benefits were all foreign exchange. The country had no significant mercantile fleet, and virtually all trade was in foreign vessels.

8. Costs and benefits were estimated over 30 years. Congestion at Old Port was already such that the Phase 1 semi-bulk berths at New Port would reach 70% utilisation (the 'optimal' level for a small port) in the third year of operation. If the steel mill was ready on time, the coal and iron berth would reach normal full capacity operation after five years.

Results
9. The calculated IRR was 20%, well above the 12% rate normally used in the country. Sensitivity analysis showed that a 30% increase in New Port capital costs, or an 18% reduction in benefits, would be required to reduce the IRR to 12%. On the basis of these figures, and bearing in mind that costs were probably a little overestimated, the Phase 1 proposal was judged to be economically attractive. The need for further shadow pricing did not arise.

10. Economic analysis looked also at the question of the number of semi-bulk berths envisaged. Was seven the correct number? More or fewer could have been planned. The optimisation point here would be when the marginal cost of constructing and operating an additional berth was equal to the saved reduction in ship waiting costs. Zero waiting time was not necessarily the objective. This calculation was complicated by the fact that the new berth was at New Port, while the ship waiting time costs were incurred at Old Port, where ships of a different size were involved. Rough calculation suggested that, in the second year of planned operation, only about 6 berths would be needed at New Port at normal levels of utilisation. However, this limited over-capacity would soon be taken up: Phase 2 of New Port development was expected to be justified in less than ten years after the completion of Phase 1.

11.   As with all projects for transport improvement at an international border, the question arose of who would get the benefits. In the first instance, the value of lower transport costs in newer ships might accrue to foreign shippers, though it was confidently expected that lower freight charges would apply almost at once, so those benefits would accrue to the steel mill or its customers. The ship waiting cost savings would also largely accrue to foreigners.

12.   The removal of waiting surcharges is a domestic benefit, but would shipping rates for semi-bulk cargo fall? In the long-term, probably they would, but perhaps not at once. Some of this benefit may be captured through changes in the charges raised at Old Port, and in the New Port tariff policy, which depended in part on the policy and management of the new authority. In addition to ODA's capital input, they agreed to supply TC advisers for up to 3 years, who would especially help to plan and implement organisational structures, administrative procedures, accounting and management information systems and staff training, in addition to giving advice on port management and operation.

13.   Financial policy in the New Port Authority (NPA) was a matter of concern to all financing donors. It was agreed with government that:
   ⋆ NPA would be financially self-supporting;
   ⋆ donor grants and loans would be on-lent to NPA at 8½% interest, with repayment to the National Ministry of Finance over 20 years, but five years grace;
   ⋆ each operating unit would have to cover its own operating costs and make a contribution to overheads;
   ⋆ government could not enforce tariffs for some customers that were not sufficient to cover all costs, including finance and overheads;
   ⋆ fees for the use of transit storage would penalise importers and exporters using them for more than a few days; and
   ⋆ financial performance targets would be set, including rate of return on investment, debt–equity ratio, and self-financing ratio.

14.   These minimal requirements should ensure financial self-sufficiency, though NPA could make significant surpluses if it were policy to do so. Forecast accounts for 10 years (based on preliminary estimates of port use tariffs) showed profits in the first year of operation, and useful cash surpluses from the second.

Case Study 14:   The Woodlots Project

1.   This case study features these particular aspects of project analysis:

- ★ Demand Estimation
- ★ Cost Benefit Analysis
- ★ Shadow Pricing
- ★ Sensitivity Analysis
- ★ Gender

- ★ Beneficiary Identification
- ★ Indirect Benefits
- ★ Environmental Aspects
- ★ Programme Approach

Description

2.   This project was located in a land-locked country that had no fossil fuels and little forest. The fuel needs of the predominantly rural population were met to the extent possible by the direct collection by users (and some local sales) of fuelwood, brushwood and dung. Large amounts of fuelwood were imported from a neighbouring country, as well as paraffin and coal.

3.   The project in view was a 3-year phase in a continuing programme to establish plantations throughout the country on land blocks of 10 ha or more offered by local communities. The provision of fuel for local use (fuelwood and brushwood) from these woodlots was the main objective. Building materials would be a valuable by-product in some areas. Tree planting would also contribute to water and soil conservation. Within this phase, the project would also assist the development of a national forest policy; the establishment of a self-reliant Forest Service; and training nationals at all levels for positions in the Forest Service. The main inputs were for continuation of an expanding planting programme, the maintenance of existing plantations, and some re-planting.

4.   Different species would be grown at various altitudes, under varying regimes. In lower areas, eucalyptus types would be established and coppiced every 8 years. At intermediate levels, pines would give output from thinning after 8 years and felling in year 12. Cypress would be grown in the small amount of high land, thinned after 9 years and felled after 14. Seedlings for all woodlots are grown in eight countrywide nurseries.

Analysis

5.   Demand estimates for fuelwood were based on localised demographic projections and surveys in different climatic zones of consumption per household. These indicated that, in the yield period of the trees to be planted under this project (ie starting about 10 years hence), a very substantial need would have to be met for imports of fuelwood or other fuel substitutes like kerosene. The main output (fuelwood), was thus regarded as a traded good, valued at its border parity price in villages, where the main substitution was expected to take place. The established woodlot sale price of fuelwood was quite a lot less than the border parity value, making it cheaper in calorific terms than all other substitute fuels available – kerosene, imported wood, manure, coal and brushwood. Although some timber usable for fence posts, poles and building would be obtained from the pine species at felling, there was no system for getting local production into the market – all timber was imported. For the basic economic analysis, the value of this lumber output was ignored. Thus, all production was valued as fuelwood, even though the timber might have been more valuable.

6.   The approach to economic analysis was to appraise a model of 1 hectare planted to each species. Direct costs were easily established, but care was needed in allocating fixed project costs to each hectare over the life of an expanding programme, of which this project was just one phase. The land offered by the communities was likely to be the least productive and its opportunity cost was therefore ignored.

7.   In the shadow pricing of inputs, the border price of imported items was taken to be 84% of their local cost, reflecting the average level of import taxes of 16%. The project would employ large amounts of casual manual labour. Average returns to farm labour were carefully estimated to be 54% of the actual daily wage, so a CF of 0.5 was applied to those employed by the project. However, the project would also use labour provided under the World Food Programme (WFP). Although numerically many more people would be WFP employed than were to be directly engaged by the project, they worked fewer hours per day and their productivity was less, so they were valued separately, in terms of full-term worker equivalents.

Results
8.   Analysis using uniform shadow pricing showed that the eucalyptus and pine models had ERRs of 22 and 12%, above the 10% opportunity cost that was used. Cypress had a return of only just over 4%, but the weighted average for the mix of trees envisaged for this three year project was over 15%. It was argued that the use in all models of the same product prices underestimated the value of the cypress output. Highland areas are less accessible, and transport costs on imported alternative fuels are higher than normal, while timber from those woodlots might have a value higher than fuelwood.

9.   Sensitivity analysis focused on two main points, lower yields than expected, and higher establishment costs that would arise if planting targets were not met and fixed costs became a larger burden. A 20% increase in costs or a 20% fall in yields would still leave eucalyptus very attractive. Either factor brought pine woodlots to just below 10%, but the weighted average remained safely above the acceptable level.

10.   Analysis of the project drew attention to some social aspects. The woodlots are a type of community forest. Communities would donate land, and would protect the trees from damage and interference. In return, they will share in the revenue from wood sales. 20% of all revenue will be made available to the communities that donated land. This element, and special training, will (it was hoped) give local leaders a good incentive to seeing that the planted woodlots were protected from fire and livestock. It was also observed that the availability of cheap local fuelwood would especially help the poorer households, while it would particularly release women from the task of gathering brushwood. Many of the project employees were expected to be women.

Case Study 15:   The Island Secondary School

1.   This case study features these particular aspects of project analysis:

* Demand Estimation
* Technical Alternatives
* Choice of Location
* Indirect Benefits
* Meeting Recurrent Costs
* Gender

Description

2.   This proposal related to a very small island, a dependent territory. At the time, there were four secondary schools, two of them in adapted temporary buildings. Schooling was compulsory between 5 and 15 years. At age 11, a competitive entrance exam determined which children should go to the one selective school. The remainder went to non-selective schools.

3.   In their last year, all the children took a school leaving exam. A few children did 'O' levels, but very few took 'A' levels. Some school leavers went on to a poorly equipped trade school, but there were no specific training programmes or tests there. Reform of secondary education was the top priority for resource allocation for the island government. Low educational attainment, resulting in a poorly qualified workforce, was a major problem. Partly as a reflection of this, but also recognised as a contributory cause, the secondary teaching staff were poorly qualified and trained; and facilities at all the schools were limited, especially for science teaching.

4.   The proposal was to build a single secondary school to accommodate all pupils, which would allow a broader curriculum and better schooling in academic and vocational subjects. Selection between schools at 11 would be discontinued. Science and craft facilities and teachers would be available for all pupils. This would allow a broader curriculum for all of the children. For a few years, additional expatriate teachers would be required, especially for the new subjects. At the same time, overseas training awards would be given for the upgrading of selected teachers, and the full education of new ones. The provision of recurrent costs for these and related purposes over 5 years were combined with capital costs in the overall project proposal, as integral parts of the change package.

Analysis

5.   Demand estimation in this case looked at the opportunities for employment that called for school-acquired skills. An increased supply might find work in expanding local small enterprises; in employment outside the island; and in government service, the main form of employment.

6.   If the secondary stage of education was improved, scope also existed for school leavers to go on to tertiary education and then to take up senior government positions otherwise filled by expatriates. However, it was evident that not all qualified school leavers could expect to find employment unless, as seemed unlikely, more could take up jobs outside the island. Thus, the 'planned capacity' of the educational system was likely to lead to oversupply of grade-awarded leavers, especially in years when large batches left school at the same time. It was recognised that this situation might work to the particular disadvantage of girls. Outside the project, moves to reduce sex discrimination in job opportunities were already in progress, but despite the improved

skills that girls would acquire, special steps might be needed to provide work opportunities for women school-leavers, so that their employment prospects were not worsened through the improved education of boys attending the new school.

7.   The proposal for a single non-selective school was only one of 6 alternatives considered for upgrading the secondary education system. Others included:

* upgrade all facilities at the four existing sites;
* have a new selective industry and trade school; and
* have a new comprehensive centralised trade school.

All of these had lower finance costs than the new school alternative. However, the island government and ODA advisers were agreed that the social and educational benefits of the single comprehensive proposal outweighed the disadvantages of higher costs and over-supply. Significantly, because of the remote situation and limited resource base, it was not expected that a better general level of education would lead to measurable growth in the local economy. The budget and trade balances were covered only by fiscal transfers from the UK. With the project, expatriate costs would be reduced in the long term with localisation, and remittances from abroad might increase, but the value of these benefits were reckoned to be small.

8.   Termination of the selection exam, and its divisiveness, was seen as a major benefit. The availability of science and technical subjects for all would also be a general benefit. Furthermore, the large central building would be an asset to the whole community, additional to its use for schooling.

9.   Conventional economic analysis extended to consideration of where the new school might be located. Without any shadow pricing, several possible sites were considered. The one chosen was judged to be the most suitable with respect to the relative cost of transporting children and staff to and fro, topographical suitability of the site, climatic suitability, the provision of services and scope for expansion. It was noted that this development allowed an opportunity for improving infant and pre-secondary schooling in the released buildings.

Results
10.   Although the new school was the most expensive of the options considered, its advantages over the alternatives were thought to justify the extra cost. These advantages were largely non-quantifiable – social and educational gains – and certainly they could not be valued in allocative efficiency terms.

11.   The project proposal envisaged that the new school would be built by the PWD of the island government to designs consistent with the distinctive local style. To the extent possible, it would employ local materials and labour, though some skills and site management personnel might need to be imported. The school would be the biggest construction project for several years and there was no basis for costing the civil work accurately. Costs from the nearest similar situation were used, and higher than normal physical contingency was allowed.

Case Study 16: Redesigning a Rural Development Project to Reach Women Farmers

1. This case study illustrates the relevance of gender in project design and implementation. In particular the case study features these particular aspects of project analysis:

* Gender
* Beneficiary Identification

* Technical Alternatives
* Institutional Questions

Description

2. This project was part of a national rural development programme aimed at providing a package of services such as extension, credit and marketing together with improvements in infrastructure, roads and health facilities, to enable people in rural areas to raise their agricultural output and standard of living. The project area covered 12,800 square kilometres and contained, when it began, an estimated 38,979 farming families.

3. The objective of the agricultural programme of the initial project was to increase the production of food crops, such as maize (which accounted for 80% of the cropped area), sorghum, cassava, rice, pulses and groundnuts, and other crops including tobacco, cotton, green grams, chickpeas and sunflowers. The main emphasis of the project was to promote the use of high yielding composite and hybrid maize varieties, supported by fertilisers and chemicals for pest control to use with that crop.

4. The number of front-line field extension workers was to be increased to a ratio of one to seven hundred farmers. The area was divided into six Extension Planning Areas (EPAs) each managed by a Technical Officer with eight to fifteen Technical Assistants working as Field Assistants. Each EPA was to have a credit supervisor and a Farm Home Assistant (a female extension/ home economics worker). The field staff was backed up by specialists based at the project headquarters.

5. An important part of the extension effort of the original project was the provision of seasonal credit to enable farmers to cover the short-term inputs required to support the hybrid varieties. Credit was administered through credit groups who were responsible for repayment. Failure to repay barred the group from receiving further credit.

6. Other project components would complement the extension and credit package. The existing road network would be upgraded and a main all-weather road built. Five sub-markets would be established to provide inputs and buy produce from the farmers. Additional dip tanks were to be built to improve disease control for the 24,000 head of cattle in the area. A tree planting component was included to provide firewood supplies, principally (in the initial project plans) for the curing of tobacco. Finally, a small health component was included consisting of the provision of a maternity clinic, two health posts and the renovation of some old houses.

Analysis

7. At appraisal the project was justified on the basis of increased production brought about by the use of inputs and improved crop husbandry. But it was

213

agreed that the project should be reviewed after the first agricultural season to determine whether any modification would be desirable.

8.   In the course of project appraisal a number of questions had been raised relating to the likely impact of the project on women and their involvement in it. A survey carried out two years after the project began found that 35% of the households were headed by women. As a result of this, and because men from male-headed households were often engaged in off-farm employment, the women did the majority of the agricultural work.

9.   The majority of farmers in the project area were semi-subsistence small-holders who suffered from considerable land pressure and produced low yields of maize. One particular finding was that only one out of twenty-four unmarried, female household heads interviewed was self-sufficient in maize. These household heads relied on a range of off-farm activities to support their families.

10.   The original project proposal made no specific mention of women, however, and did not differentiate by gender on the reported ratio of exten-sion workers to farmers. Nor did it comment on the cultural feasibility of male staff working with women. The project extension records revealed that during the first two years of the project the women's importance as agricultural producers was not reflected in their participation in agricultural extension activities. Only 5% of seasonal credit borrowers were women. Only one or two women had attended agricultural classes and few women attended agricultu-ral meetings in the villages. The few female Farm Home Assistants giving home economics classes to women's groups were doing little to solve the women's farming problems.

11.   In the light of these findings this project was redesigned to take particu-lar account of the needs of women farmers. A female agriculturalist was employed who helped to change the general extension approach and set up a women's progamme within the project.

12.   A pilot programme was started in sixteen villages. The aim was to en-courage women to participate fully in discussions and in decision-making so that the agricultural development programme could be directly related to their situation. Village meetings to which all farmers were invited were orga-nised at times convenient to women with heavy domestic duties. The women set up women-only or mixed credit groups which met once a month with the extension workers.

13.   A new extension approach was formulated, the 'problem-solving' approach, which involved Field Assistants and farmers discussing the prob-lems faced by farmers and deciding how best they could be overcome rather than simply telling the farmers what they should be doing. A wide range of programmes was developed in response to the problems identified in the villages.

Results
14.   When the original project was designed it was expected that the pro-duction of maize would be increased by the adoption of new maize technolo-gies. The review showed that these technologies had not been adopted. Most farmers introduced by the project to the new maize varieties decided not to grow them.

15. The initial project submission had seriously over-estimated the amount of local maize grown in pure stands. The local maize was often grown with legumes, not in pure stands, but the hybrid and composite varieties were not as suited to intercropping as local maize. Intercropping had a number of advantages for the farmers: it involved the intensive use of scarce land, the spread of labour peaks, provision of a balanced diet and reduced risk of crop failure, all of which was particularly important to the poorer, female-headed households.

16. As a result the review showed that the area turned over to improved maize was less than 25% of appraisal estimates. The yields per hectare achieved by those who had adopted new technologies had not matched expectations. However, cotton, tobacco and livestock production had increased in line with appraisal estimates.

17. Credit was originally only available for packages of inputs for 0.4 hectares of maize and fertiliser for maize could only be obtained through credit if improved maize seed was also purchased. As a result of the redesign of the project and the adoption of the 'problem-solving' extension technique, a minicredit package was introduced which allowed farmers to buy enough fertiliser for 0.2 ha of maize and did not include the purchase of improved maize seed as a condition.

18. The credit package could, therefore, be used to purchase one or two bags of fertiliser which could be applied to local maize which the women, in particular, preferred because it was reliable, less likely to suffer pests, easier to pound and had a better flavour.

19. The revised project has had a beneficial impact on the maize production of the poorer farmers, particularly the female headed-households. They have been able, through the mini-credit package to produce more than their subsistence needs and their welfare has consequently improved.

20. On average the women taking part in the programme had double the yields of those not taking part. More intercrops were planted and tree seedlings were established in many of the villages, not only to supply wood for tobacco curing but also to ease the burden on women of fuelwood collection.

21. Male support for the women's programme within the project was shown in the way male leaders helped the women's groups. It was not practicable to recruit large numbers of women workers but, after training, male extension workers became sensitive to the needs of women. Some husbands are helping their wives repay their loans with the proceeds of their own off-farm employment or crop sales.

22. This project has had a positive impact on production through an intensified extension effort. Some of the weaknesses of the original project design were offset by the extension agents helping to solve the identified problems of the farmers.

23. The main lessons to emerge from the project are:

   a. determined efforts had to be made to enable women to benefit from the project's activities;

b. when a high proportion of farmers are women, agricultural projects are unlikely to achieve production objectives unless the particular needs of women are appreciated;

c. support was gained from the whole community by addressing women's needs as an integral part of the overall development package.

C. The Methodology Illustrations

Introduction

1.   The four illustrations which follow are designed to provide detailed guidance on four particular aspects of valuation in economic appraisal: agricultural output, long-run marginal cost, the standard conversion factor and the depletion premium for non-renewable natural resources. The first three of these are commonly encountered; the last is a more specialised aspect of appraisal but it is included here because the answer to the analytical problems it presents may not be immediately apparent from general principles.

2.   All four illustrations are selected from projects investigated by ODA in recent years so both the problems and the solutions devised are real-world examples. These cases show how the analytical principles can be applied under the pressures imposed by the need to take decisions, when data are less than perfect and the time available to the analyst is constrained.

Methodology Illustration 1

The Estimation of Border Price Parity Values for Agricultural Produce

Different situations regarding three products
1.   This example comes from a project for irrigation development in a Distant Province in a large country. Distant Province is remote in the sense that traded produce moving between it and the Port has to be consigned through Central Province.

DISTANT PROVINCE→CENTRAL PROVINCE→PORT
DISTANT PROVINCE←CENTRAL PROVINCE←PORT

Three products were involved: faba beans, wheat and sorghum. Each of these crops was for consumption within the country, but there were differences between them regarding the direction of trade (imports or exports) and the areas where the new produce substituted for alternatives (Distant Province or Central Province).

2.   *Faba Beans* are imported, for consumption in all parts of the country. Distant Province produces a surplus, which goes to Central Province. Extra production by the project allows less to be imported for consumption in Central Province. The value of the beans in Distant Province is calculated as:

The cif value of saved imports
PLUS
The saved cost of moving imports
from Port to Central Province
MINUS
The new cost of moving the extra produce
from Distant Province to Central Province.

217

3.   *Wheat* is also imported. Even with the project, Distant Province will have a deficit. Extra wheat from the project will reduce the need for alternative quantities to be imported and carried all the way to Distant Province. The value of the project's wheat is estimated from these components:

The cif value of saved imports
PLUS
The saved cost of moving avoided imports
from Port to Central Province
PLUS
The saved cost of moving this imported wheat
from Central Province to Distant Province.

4.   *Sorghum* is an Export. However, Distant Province consumes more than it produces, so it imports from other parts of the country, by way of Central Province. Extra production by the project allows less to be brought into the Province. Instead, exports can be increased. The components of the value of extra sorghum produced in Distant Province are these:

The FOB value of the extra exports
MINUS
The new cost of moving more sorghum
from Central Province to Port
PLUS
The saved cost of moving sorghum
from Central Province to Distant Province.

Calculating the Project Values
5.   In the analysis, all values were expressed in Sterling Pounds. Costs within the country were divided by the analyst into traded and non-traded categories:

Traded	*Non-Traded*
Shrinkage and Losses	Port Charges
Bagging	Port Handling
Transport between Port and Central Province	Trader Margin between Port and Central Province
Transport between Central Province and Distant Province	Trader Margin between Central Province and Distant Province

These particular cost categories were chosen by the project analyst, and their values estimated, according to what proved possible at the time, especially the form of data that was readily available or easily obtained.

6.   The traded items were expressed directly in Sterling. Although they were incurred in National Moneys, they could be expressed in Sterling by application of the Official Exchange rate of 3.125 Ms = 1.00 Sterling. Non-traded values were presented in local currency. Their translation into numeraire units – border prices expressed in Sterling – required both currency conversion at the Official Exchange Rate and the application of conversion factors. Individual CFs for the non-traded items were not available, and could not be estimated in the time available, so a Standard Conversion Factor was applied as a second-best approach to all of them. The SCF value used was 0.60, a figure taken from a recent World Bank project appraisal.

THE ECONOMIC VALUATION OF THREE TRADED CROPS GROWN IN DISTANT PROVINCE

Economic Prices per ton

| | FABA BEANS Import Substitute | | | WHEAT Import Substitute | | | SORGHUM Export | | |
| | MONEYS | | STERLING | MONEYS | | STERLING | MONEYS | | STERLING |
	TRADED	NON-TRADED		TRADED	NON-TRADED		TRADED	NON-TRADED	
Border Price	+891		+285	+481		+154	+328		+105
Port Charges		+18	+3		+10	+2		−7	−1
Port Handling		+36	+7		+19	+4		−13	−2
Losses	+9		+3	+6		+2	−4		−1
Bagging	+19		+6	+19		+6	−19		−6
Transport, Port to Central Province	+72		+23	+72		+23	−72		−23
Trader Margin, Port to Central Province		+95	+18		+51	+10		−35	−7
Transport, Central Province to Distant Province	−54		−17	+54		+17	+54		+17
Trader Margin, Central Province to Distant Province		−110	−21		+62	+12		+44	+8
Distant Province Farm-gate Value			+307			+230			+90

Conversion to Sterling – equivalent Values.
  Traded Items: × ⅓.125 = 0.32
  Non-Traded Items: × ⅓.125 × 0.60 = 0.192

7. The figures used in the actual calculations are shown in the table. The resulting crop output values used in the allocative efficiency analysis of the irrigation project were:

Faba Beans	£307 per ton.
Wheat	£230 per ton.
Sorghum	£ 90 per ton.

Methodology Illustration 2

The Calculation of Long Run Marginal Costs

The principle
1. It is necessary for economic analysis in appraising some projects, and for the fixing of product prices, to calculate the cost of supplying inputs where the needs of the project will have to be met by the supplier of a non-tradeable increasing production by a significant volume. It there is spare capacity in the supplying industry, so that project requirements can be met without new investment, then only operating costs need to be taken into account in valuing this input – short run marginal costs. But if the needs of the project are large, or total capacity is already fully utilised in the supply industry, meeting them will call for new investment in productive capacity. The cost of supply must then take account of the cost of creating this additional capacity – its capital cost – as well as the operating costs of the output. Estimates which include both capital and operating costs for extra (ie marginal) production are Long Run Marginal Costs (LRMC).

2. The LRMC that should be taken into account in valuing an input for a project should include on the capital side only the actual extra cost of creating increased capacity required to meet the needs of the project in view. It is possible that not all capital costs necessary for production will need to be incurred to allow increased supply – some existing capital facilities may be able to cope with new productive capacity. Only the extra costs should be taken into account – the marginal costs. Frequently LRMC will be less than average total costs.

3. To illustrate, a project may call for increased supplies of an input, for example glass bottles. The needs of the project might be met by the supplier adding another set of bottle-producing machines. Possibly no new buildings or glass furnace may be required. The capital element of LRMC in this case would include nothing for buildings, furnace, etc. No new cost for them would be required. Only the new equipment needed to meet this particular need should be included. The same applies to the operating costs to be included. If no additional management is required (the existing team can cope with the extra work without any new cost), then LRMC should include nothing for management. Management will of course be required, but no new expense will arise in providing it.

An Illustration
4. The method and some special features of calculating LRMC are illustrated in the following example, where an economic analysis needed to assess the LRMC of supplying electricity for a number of different new users.

5.   In the country concerned, the national grid was supplied by three main types of generator: hydro turbines associated with irrigation dams; gas turbines using natural gas from national sources; and steam turbines, also using natural gas.

6.   In the situation studied, capital costs for gas turbine and for steam turbine generation was taken to be the cost of completely new plant, both of which were provided for in the relevant 5-year plan. However, in the case of hydro, extra generation could be obtained by installing and operating new turbines in the existing power houses associated with existing dams. Needs for irrigation had determined the scale of the dams. The associated generating potential was very large. The plan was to install and operate new turbines over several years, as the need arose. At the time of calculation, scope existed for adding new generators at two large dams. Consequently, in this situation, incremental capital costs (for additional turbines and generators only) were relatively low, much less than they would be for completely new hydro capacity, even if much of the civil works of a new dam were charged against irrigation.

7.   Figures for the cost of installed capacity at allocative efficiency values were:

	Capital Cost per KW (Moneys)	Life of Plant (years)	Annual Capital Charge (at 10%) per KW (Moneys)
Steam Turbines	9,000	25	992
Gas Turbines	4,500	15	591
Hydro	4,000	30	424

These figures are the cost of the new installed capacity. The cost per unit of electricity generated will depend on the expected level of utilisation of each type of plant, which will vary according to technical and operating cost considerations. Because they are the least efficient users of energy, gas turbines are used only to meet peak demand, and were found to be used to the extent of only 20% of theoretical capacity. Steam turbines had been found generally to operate at 50% of capacity. The capacity level taken for hydrogeneration was 45%. This was less than the average capacity utilisation of the existing turbines. Because of absolute limits in the flow of irrigation water that can be allowed to pass through turbines – especially at particular seasons – the maximum extent to which hydro turbines can be used declines as their number increases. In this case, 45% was the utilisation level thought possible for the additional turbines envisaged.

8.   Estimation of operating costs turned mainly on the marginal cost of gas for the thermal stations. Although in principle this should have been based on the opportunity cost – the value of the gas to other users – this could not be estimated for this study. (A detailed study of this and the optimal use of existing generating capacity was to be undertaken over a few months, starting a little while after the LRMC calculation.) Consequently, actual gas sale tariff prices were used. These were complex. Not only were they stepped, so that average cost was higher than marginal cost, but they varied between power stations, according to distance from the gas field, which would affect pipeline and pumping costs.

9. Generating costs per unit were estimated at these levels:

	Capital Cost per KWh (Ms)	Operating Costs per KWh (Ms)	Total Costs per KWh (Ms)
Steam Turbines	0.226	0.09	0.32
Gas Turbines	0.337	0.21	0.55
Hydro	0.108	0.002	0.11

These figures represent the estimated LRMC per KWh generated that is available outside the power house. The figures allow for losses of 3.5% in the power house after generation.

10. The cost of power delivered to any user must take into account transmission losses between the power house and the consumption point. These are always present and can be substantial. In addition to technical losses, supply to consumers is often associated with bad metering and theft, which lead to the use of supplied power that is not paid for.

11. The cost of supplying electricity must also take account of the costs of the system of getting it to consumers. There are the costs of transmission (in bulk at high voltages), and of distribution to end users at lower voltages. The latter also includes the cost of metering, billing and collection.

12. Estimating the capital cost of transmission facilities raised some complex points. A simple approach would have been to start from the annual capital charge shown in the electricity authority's accounts, but these were based on historic cost. Some equipment was quite old, and estimation in this way would substantially understate future costs. However, it was apparent that the existing system could carry much more power. For a few years, no new investment was envisaged, but new transmission lines would then be installed, which would reduce losses. Because early increases in supply now would bring forward the date of new transmission investment, its cost (in allocative efficiency terms) was discounted back to the present (at 10%) to give an incremental capital cost per KWh of Ms 0.13. The accounts showed operating costs of 0.01 in transmission, and these were added.

13. The capital cost of the distribution system was obtained by attributing planned new investment to expanded consumption over 30 years. Discounting gave a capital cost per discounted KWh of Ms 0.08. To this was added Ms 0.05 for operating costs, including especially overheads, billing and collection.

14. In the power cost study, losses and costs outside the power house were estimated as follows:

	Losses, as percentage of gross power generated.	Costs per KWh (Ms)
Transmission	6.5%	0.14
Distribution	9.5%	0.13
Theft, etc.	7.5%	—

15. From all this information, the following aggregate estimates were made of the Long Run Marginal Cost of power generated in different ways. Apart from gas supplies these costs are at allocative efficiency values and are expressed as Moneys per KWh.

	Steam Turbines	Gas Turbines	Hydro
Cost ex power house	0.32	0.55	0.11
Transmission losses	0.02	0.04	0.01
Transmission costs	0.14	0.14	0.14
Total cost of power available for distribution	0.48	0.73	0.26
Distribution losses	0.06	0.09	0.03
Distribution costs	0.13	0.13	0.13
Total cost of power delivered to consumers	0.67	0.95	0.42
Theft, etc.	0.07	0.09	0.04
Cost of net power paid for	0.74	1.04	0.46

16.   These calculations give the LRMC for the three important forms of power generation. They could be used in the economic analysis of power using projects – especially for major potential uses, like electrification of the railways. They can also be used to value the savings of power-reducing projects, like improved transmission and distribution, which could reduce losses.

17.   But which of the three types of generation is marginal? An 'average' LRMC could be calculated by combining the figures for each method in the proportion of actual use in recent years, but not all would, in future, be expanded together.

18.   The analysis took it that steam turbines would be the realistic marginal source. Hydro power from existing dams would generally always be used up to the limit of available capacity because of its low cost. New major schemes could not come into production for at least 10 years. Gas turbines were so expensive that they would generally be used only as standby, in peak periods. New base load capacity would be met from increased construction of steam turbine stations, using natural gas, reserves of which were expected to last for several decades at least. LRMC at the point of domestic consumption was thus taken to be Ms 0.74 per KWh, in constant prices at the time of estimation. For large consumers, taking power directly from the transmission network, the cost ex power house would be Ms 0.48. These figures were, respectively, double and three times the tariffs being charged at the time.

Methodology Illustration 3

The Estimation of a Standard Conversion Factor
1.   This example is taken from work done to estimate a set of national parameters (ie basic Conversion Factors) for a country. These parameters were used in the economic appraisal of a fairly large project that called for relatively rigorous analysis.

2.   The SCF was estimated separately using both of the equations presented in paragraphs 3.42 and 3.43. Data for four years only was used, to obtain estimates of the historic value of the SCF, as a basis for projection into the

period of the project. The data used, taken from published sources, was as follows:

Millions of currency units	Year 1	Year 2	Year 3	Year 4
Imports	973	1,647	2,377	2,325
Exports	767	1,022	978	1,100
Taxes on Imports	184	276	433	560
Taxes on Exports	106	188	116	121

Standard Conversion Factor values were calculated to be the following:

	Year 1	Year 2	Year 3	Year 4
SCF (Imports Only)	0.84	0.86	0.85	0.81
SCF (Imports and Exports)	0.96	0.97	0.91	0.89

3.   In this case, the analyst considered the second equation to be the most relevant. For analysis of the project, the SCF value used was 0.90.

4.   The use of the historic formula-based value was justified firstly on the grounds that no major changes were expected in the economy which were likely to substantially alter the pattern and balance of imports and exports. Secondly, severe controls on the availability and use of foreign exchange were not in operation or expected. Import quotas and licensing were not major constraints, and a black market operated for few imported goods. Had any of these facts been very evident a rounding down of the SCF value might have been justified, by an amount that the analyst (or the central agency responsible for establishing shadow prices) would have to judge.

Methodology Illustration 4

The Depletion Premium for Non-Renewable Natural Resources

The basic idea
1.   The Depletion Premium is an amount over and above conventional costs that should be included in the economic value and in the market price of non-renewable natural resources. It is a significant factor in both the economic analysis and the fixing of tariffs for agencies and projects that consume the resource in question.

2.   Appraisal of a project that uses a non-renewable resource is conventionally carried out at opportunity cost prices such as its import substitution value in the case of the rock phosphate project (DC 1) or LRMC when it is a non-tradeable input (Methodology Illustration 2). That approach is correct when it is safe to assume that the resource will not be in short supply for a very long time to come so that its relative real price will not change much. The cost of this potentially endless supply will be the opportunity cost of the resources required to produce it. However, the situation is different when the supply of the resource is not endless. For a finite resource, we know that the supply from a particular place will one day run out. The cost of using it up now is the cost of not having it available when the source is exhausted. At that time, users will have to switch to other, more expensive sources of supply. So, the cost of exploiting the resource today, as an input or output, is the discounted extra cost of having to use the more expensive substitute in the future, or the higher

value output foregone in the future. This discounted value differential is additional to the long run incremental cost of extracting the resource. It should be added to the cost-based price as the 'Depletion Premium'.

3.   The value per unit of resource J of the premium (DJ) in any particular year t is indicated by the expression

$$DJ_t = \frac{PA_{t+n} \quad - \quad CJ_{t+n}}{(1+r)^n}$$

where n is the number of remaining years over which the resource will be exploited,

   PA_{t+n} is the price of the equivalent amount of the substitute resource which will be available in period n,

   CJ_{t+n} is what the long run cost of extracting a unit of the resource would be in the future period n, if any of it remained to be extracted, and

   r is the opportunity cost discount rate.

4.   The case for a Depletion Premium for the valuation of what is thought to be a limited stock of a non-renewable resource is appealing, but estimation is difficult. The date of exhaustion (period t + n) is far in the future – 15 years, twenty, perhaps more. It is necessary to determine what amount of what alternative input would be used then, by the marginal remaining user, and what its costs will be. Furthermore, it is necessary to estimate what the extraction costs will be – will they be constant, as might be the case in the quarrying of homogeneous material, or will they increase over time, as it became more difficult to extract the remaining quantities of oil say, or gas?

5.   Not all of these variables are independent of each other. In particular, the value of the premium may influence the time to exhaustion. Its value will increase as t approaches n. If the premium is incorporated in the price, the increasing cost to users over time will reduce demand. The value of the premium will therefore have an influence on the parameter n. To estimate n at all involves taking a view of the shape and behaviour of demand for the resource over the life period of the stock. Obviously an iterative series of calculations would be the best way to estimate demand each year, and thus determine the life of the fixed reserve that is thought to exist.

6.   Uncertainties of this kind may be no greater than project analysts have to handle elsewhere, knowingly or unknowingly. If a domestic non-renewable resource is thought to be rather limited in extent, a depletion premium should be estimated. Of course, alternative values can be considered before it is decided what premium to apply. Operationally, the need is to estimate the value of the premium in the base year. Thereafter, it will increase in real terms at the rate of discount used and in money terms at that rate plus the rate of inflation.[1]

An Illustration
7.   The need to estimate a Depletion Premium arose in a project to determine the tariff policy for exploiting a natural gas field that was thought to be limited in extent. A number of different studies looked at the question, and

---

[1] The depletion of energy resources is discussed in the book 'The Economics of Energy' by M. G. Webb and M. J. Ricketts, Macmillan 1980.

four different estimates of the premium were developed. They illustrate the different views and assumptions that can be made in estimating variables of this kind.

8.   Basic features of the four estimates were as follows:

		Case 1	Case 2	Case 3	Case 4
Years to exhaustion (n)		28	35	26–31	33
Year assumed when price should equal alternative cost		n–15	n–15	n–15	n
Alternative fuel		coal	oil	coal	oil
Discount rate (r) %		12	12	15	15
Premium	: Year 1	15.23	16.89	20–12	3.41
(Ms per unit	: Year 2	18.08	20.59	24–15	4.16
of gas.)	: Year 3	21.47	25.10	30–18	5.07

9.   All estimates were based on the same presumed size of natural gas reserve. Three studies took the view that the tariff should equal the cost of alternative fuels when the ratio of reserves to annual extraction was 15:1. No new users should be induced after that, but all remaining users were expected to continue to buy gas at the same constant level each year until all switched to another fuel simultaneously. The fourth estimate – made by an ODA economist – was prepared after the others, and rejected this view as too simplistic. A price that rose steadily up to the exhaustion year would allow users to switch to other fuels gradually, a change they could easily prepare for if the pricing system was made known to them, and was adhered to consistently.

10.   Another source of difference was the assumption about what would be the alternative fuel. Two studies were based on coal, which was a lower-priced future alternative than oil. However, coal was not a feasible alternative for some uses (fertiliser manufacture was an example), so the ODA analysis based its estimates on the cost of the alternative to the user that would value the gas most highly.

11.   The differences in substitute cost and the time until gas prices should reach their peak in real terms account for the differences between cases in the period to exhaustion. The third study recognised the great uncertainty of this variable, and so made a range of estimates, spanning 6 years. Finally, two different discount rates were used. The ODA estimate used the figure recommended at the time by the National Planning Commission.

12.   The wide range of premium value estimates reflect its sensitivity to all of the others. Time to price parity with alternatives is clearly the main cause of the big difference between estimate 4 and the others, though the higher discount rate also separates this one from the first two.

TABLE 1: DISCOUNT FACTORS FOR IRREGULAR FLOWS

Rate Year	0	2	4	5	6	7	8	9	10	11	12	13	14	15	18	20	25
0	1.000	1.000	1.000	1.000	1.000	1.000	1.000	1.000	1.000	1.000	1.000	1.000	1.000	1.000	1.000	1.000	1.000
1	1.000	.980	.962	.952	.943	.935	.926	.917	.909	.901	.893	.885	.877	.870	.847	.833	.800
2	1.000	.961	.925	.907	.890	.873	.857	.842	.826	.812	.797	.783	.769	.758	.718	.694	.640
3	1.000	.942	.889	.864	.840	.816	.794	.772	.751	.731	.712	.693	.675	.658	.609	.579	.512
4	1.000	.924	.855	.823	.792	.763	.735	.708	.683	.659	.636	.613	.592	.572	.516	.482	.410
5	1.000	.906	.822	.784	.747	.713	.681	.650	.621	.593	.567	.543	.519	.497	.437	.402	.328
6	1.000	.888	.790	.746	.705	.666	.630	.596	.564	.535	.507	.480	.456	.432	.370	.335	.262
7	1.000	.871	.760	.711	.665	.623	.583	.547	.513	.482	.452	.425	.400	.376	.314	.279	.210
8	1.000	.853	.731	.677	.627	.582	.540	.502	.467	.434	.404	.376	.351	.327	.266	.233	.168
9	1.000	.837	.703	.645	.592	.544	.500	.460	.424	.391	.361	.333	.308	.284	.225	.194	.134
10	1.000	.820	.676	.614	.558	.508	.463	.422	.386	.352	.322	.295	.270	.247	.191	.162	.107
11	1.000	.804	.650	.585	.527	.475	.429	.388	.350	.317	.287	.261	.237	.215	.162	.135	.086
12	1.000	.788	.625	.557	.497	.444	.397	.356	.319	.286	.257	.231	.208	.187	.137	.112	.069
13	1.000	.773	.601	.530	.469	.415	.368	.326	.290	.258	.229	.204	.182	.163	.116	.093	.055
14	1.000	.758	.577	.505	.442	.388	.340	.299	.263	.232	.205	.181	.160	.141	.100	.078	.044
15	1.000	.743	.555	.481	.417	.362	.315	.275	.239	.209	.183	.160	.140	.123	.084	.065	.035
16	1.000	.728	.534	.458	.394	.339	.292	.252	.218	.188	.163	.141	.123	.107	.071	.054	.028
17	1.000	.714	.513	.436	.371	.317	.270	.231	.198	.170	.146	.125	.108	.093	.060	.045	.023
18	1.000	.700	.494	.416	.350	.296	.250	.212	.180	.153	.130	.111	.095	.081	.051	.038	.018
19	1.000	.686	.475	.396	.331	.277	.232	.194	.164	.138	.116	.098	.083	.070	.043	.031	.014
20	1.000	.673	.456	.377	.312	.258	.215	.178	.149	.124	.104	.087	.073	.061	.037	.026	.012
25	1.000	.610	.375	.295	.233	.184	.146	.116	.092	.074	.059	.047	.038	.030	.016	.010	.004
30	1.000	.552	.308	.231	.174	.131	.099	.075	.057	.044	.033	.026	.020	.015	.007	.004	.001
40	1.000	.453	.208	.142	.097	.067	.046	.032	.022	.015	.011	.008	.005	.004	.001	.001	.000
50	1.000	.372	.141	.087	.054	.036	.021	.013	.009	.005	.003	.002	.001	.001	.000	.000	.000

TABLE 2: DISCOUNT FACTORS FOR REGULAR FLOWS

Rate Year	0	2	4	5	6	7	8	9	10	11	12	13	14	15	18	20	25
1	1.000	0.980	0.962	0.952	0.943	0.935	0.926	0.917	0.909	0.901	0.893	0.885	0.877	0.870	0.847	0.833	0.800
2	2.000	1.942	1.886	1.859	1.833	1.808	1.783	1.759	1.736	1.713	1.690	1.668	1.647	1.626	1.566	1.528	1.440
3	3.000	2.884	2.775	2.723	2.673	2.624	2.577	2.531	2.487	2.444	2.402	2.361	2.322	2.283	2.174	2.106	1.952
4	4.000	3.808	3.630	3.546	3.465	3.387	3.312	3.240	3.170	3.102	3.037	2.974	2.914	2.855	2.690	2.589	2.362
5	5.000	4.713	4.452	4.329	4.212	4.100	3.993	3.890	3.791	3.696	3.605	3.517	3.433	3.352	3.127	2.991	2.689
6	6.000	5.601	5.242	5.076	4.917	4.767	4.623	4.486	4.355	4.231	4.111	3.998	3.889	3.784	3.498	3.326	2.951
7	7.000	6.472	6.002	5.786	5.582	5.389	5.206	5.033	4.868	4.712	4.564	4.423	4.288	4.160	3.812	3.605	3.161
8	8.000	7.325	6.733	6.463	6.210	5.971	5.747	5.535	5.335	5.146	4.968	4.799	4.639	4.487	4.078	3.837	3.329
9	9.000	8.162	7.435	7.108	6.802	6.515	6.247	5.995	5.759	5.537	5.328	5.132	4.946	4.772	4.303	4.031	3.463
10	10.000	8.983	8.111	7.722	7.360	7.024	6.710	6.418	6.145	5.889	5.650	5.426	5.216	5.019	4.494	4.192	3.571
11	11.000	9.787	8.760	8.306	7.887	7.499	7.139	6.805	6.495	6.207	5.938	5.687	5.453	5.234	4.656	4.327	3.656
12	12.000	10.575	9.385	8.863	8.384	7.943	7.536	7.161	6.814	6.492	6.194	5.918	5.660	5.421	4.793	4.439	3.725
13	13.000	11.348	9.986	9.394	8.853	8.358	7.904	7.487	7.103	6.750	6.424	6.122	5.842	5.583	4.910	4.533	3.780
14	14.000	12.106	10.563	9.899	9.295	8.745	8.244	7.786	7.367	6.982	6.628	6.302	6.002	5.724	5.008	4.611	3.824
15	15.000	12.849	11.118	10.380	9.712	9.108	8.559	8.061	7.606	7.191	6.811	6.462	6.142	5.847	5.092	4.675	3.859
16	16.000	13.578	11.652	10.838	10.106	9.447	8.851	8.313	7.824	7.379	6.974	6.604	6.265	5.954	5.162	4.730	3.887
17	17.000	14.292	12.166	11.274	10.477	9.763	9.122	8.544	8.022	7.549	7.120	6.729	6.373	6.047	5.273	4.775	3.910
18	18.000	14.992	12.659	11.690	10.828	10.059	9.372	8.756	8.201	7.702	7.250	6.840	6.467	6.128	5.273	4.812	3.928
19	19.000	15.678	13.134	12.085	11.158	10.336	9.604	8.950	8.365	7.839	7.366	6.938	6.550	6.198	5.316	4.843	3.942
20	20.000	16.351	13.590	12.462	11.470	10.594	9.818	9.129	8.514	7.963	7.469	7.025	6.623	6.259	5.353	4.870	3.954
25	25.000	19.523	15.622	14.094	12.783	11.654	10.675	9.823	9.077	8.422	7.843	7.330	6.873	6.464	5.467	4.948	3.985
30	30.000	22.396	17.292	15.372	13.765	12.409	11.258	10.274	9.427	8.694	8.055	7.496	7.003	6.566	5.517	4.979	3.995
40	40.000	27.355	19.793	17.159	15.046	13.332	11.925	10.757	9.779	8.951	8.244	7.634	7.105	6.642	5.548	4.997	3.999
50	50.000	31.424	21.482	18.256	15.762	13.801	12.233	10.962	9.915	9.042	8.304	7.675	7.133	6.661	5.554	4.999	4.000

This table shows the discount factors to be used to derive the present value of a stream of uniform values over a number of years. For example a uniform annual flow £y from years 1 to 10 will have a cumulative PV at a discount rate of 8% of £y multiplied by 6.710. If the flow is uniform from years 5 to 15 the PV (discounting at 8%) will be the annual flow multiplied by 5.248 (ie 8.560 minus 3.312). The discount factors in this table are the factors in Table 1 cumulated over the years from Year 1.

Glossary of Terms Relating to Economic Analysis as Used in this Guide

Accounting Price
The basic allocative efficiency (ie opportunity cost) value of a good or service. Sometimes referred to as the Shadow Price.

Accounting Rate of Interest (ARI)
The Discount Rate used in Economic Analysis. The rate by which the project's annual costs and benefits are discounted to produce the project's Net Present Value. The value of the ARI used for basic allocative efficiency may be different from the ARI used where a savings premium is also taken into account.

Basic Economic Allocative Efficiency (Basic Allocative Efficiency)
The efficiency with which resources (in particular uses) generate domestic benefits which are valued in terms of opportunity costs. These valuations do not differentiate either between beneficiaries or between consumption or savings uses of net benefits.

Appraisal
The examination of a project before it is undertaken. (See also Evaluation below.)

Base Case
The set of figures used for economic analysis, for financial analysis and for other analyses, in which each value is the one that the analyst thinks is the most likely that the variable will take. Generally base case values will be shown at constant prices, though they can also be presented at forecast current prices.

Base Period
The time period (month, quarter, year) for which a set of relative prices and values is determined for use as the basic set of prices and values in Constant Price and Constant Value projections of finance and economic worth.

Border Prices
The Prices of Traded Goods and Services at the point where they enter or leave the national economy. Generally this is the cif or the fob price. The border in this sense is the point at which conversion takes place between foreign and domestic currencies. Also called International Prices.

Border Price Parity Values
The Economic value of a Traded Good at the project (or at another internal level) which corresponds with its Border Price. This value is based on the Border Price and the resource cost of all the relevant cost savings or expenses which arise between the Border and the project (or other level of valuation).

cif
Cost, Insurance and Freight; the import price of a good (or service) which includes these costs. (See also fob below.)

Consumer Surplus
The benefit over and above what is paid that is obtained by a consumer who

is prepared to pay more for a good or service than is actually charged. When a benefit is obtained free of charge, all of its value is consumer surplus.

Consumption Rate of Discount (CRI)
A notional rate at which 'society' might discount the future value of consumption. Although unmeasureable, it lies behind the idea that a savings premium is justified because the opportunity cost rate of return on investments is a lot higher than the CRI.

Consumption Weights
Weights that are applied to extra consumption arising from a project that vary according to the level of consumption of the beneficiaries. For poor people the weight would exceed unity, for the rich it would be less than one. The scale of weights can be determined only subjectively, and would usually be determined by the Government.

Contingency Allowance
Financial provision which is made to meet costs which are not certainly expected to arise, but which have a fairly high likelihood of occurring. Physical Contingencies for possible extra work or resource needs are distinguished from Price Contingencies for possible increases in price.

Conversion Factors (CFs)
Coefficients that are used to transform the market price value of traded and non-traded goods into numeraire units – border price equivalent values. They are the ratio of the true accounting price (the world price or value in terms of foreign exchange) to the domestic market price. They can be estimated for single commodities; for whole sectors; or for the whole economy. (See also Standard Conversion Factor.)

Cost Benefit Analysis (CBA)
A broad term covering analysis which compares the costs and benefits of a particular action. Its form can vary according to the range of agencies affected (eg an individual company or an entire country) and type of effect (eg financial only or non-quantifiable effects also). The most comprehensive form of CBA measures all types of effects within (usually) a national boundary and is termed 'social cost benefit analysis'. Discounting will normally be involved in all forms.

Cost Effectiveness Analysis
A mode of analysis which compares alternative input combinations on the basis of their overall costs. In project analysis, this generally means calculating and comparing the greatest value of all costs over the relevant period, the costs being valued at basic allocative efficiency values and discounted at the ARI.

Depletion Premium
A premium to be added to production cost in pricing non-renewable natural resources whose volume is known and is limited. It takes account of the eventual opportunity cost to users of having to switch after exhaustion to higher cost sources of supply.

Discount Rate
See Accounting Rate of Interest, above.

Domestic Income
Income accruing to individuals, organisations and government in a country. Domestic income, valued at border prices, is the basis of the numeraire for

use in the analysis of a project from the viewpoint of basic allocative efficiency.

Evaluation
The examination of a project after part or all of it has been undertaken. (See also Appraisal, above.)

Expected Value
The value of a variable that is the sum of all the different possible values of that variable, each multiplied by the probability of its occurrence.

Externalities
The net costs and benefits for the economy, which will arise from the execution of the project under consideration but which do not impinge in parties directly involved in the project itself.

Financial Rate of Return
The IRR of the flow of direct net benefits to a project when all costs and benefits are valued at constant market prices.

fob
Free on Board; the export price of a good or service, at the domestic point of departure (border, port or airport). (See also cif above.)

Internal Rate of Return (IRR)
The discount rate which gives a particular set of annual net benefits an NPV of zero.

International Prices
See Border Prices.

Linkages
Forward linkage effects are externalities (see above) occurring in industries which process or use the project's outputs. Backward linkages are external effects which occur in agencies which supply inputs to the project. Linkage benefits generally take the form of extra profits, taxes and surplus labour incomes.

Little-Mirrlees Method
The approach to the economic analysis of projects that is based on methods developed by I. M. D. Little and J. A. Mirrlees, and contained in books written by them and others. (See bibliography.) It uses as the numeraire 'uncommitted social income, measured in terms of convertible foreign exchange', where uncommitted social income is equated with savings.

Multipliers
Externalities (see above) in the form of short-run increases in income which are generated when surplus capacity in an economy is activated by additional rounds of spending resulting from the expenditure on a project.

National Parameters
The central shadow prices which are used to derive basic allocative efficiency values of key resources. They are: the Standard Conversion Factor (SCF); the Shadow Wage Rate (SWR); the value put on Taxes and other Transfer Payments, which is zero by definition; and the Accounting Rate of Interest. Sometimes the term is extended to include main sectoral conversion factors.

Net Present Value (NPV)
The sum of the discounted annual values of the net benefits of a project, or of any other type of separately analysed activity. There will be a different NPV

value for every discount rate used, and for every different set of annual net benefits.

Non-Tradeable Goods and Services
Goods or Services which are not imported or exported and (strictly) would not be imported or exported even if the country had pursued policies which fully took into account the possibilities of trade (ie the country's long-term comparative advantage). (See also Tradeable Goods below.)

Non-Traded Goods and Services
Goods and Services which are not actually imported or exported.

Numeraire
The unit of account for any economic analysis in terms of which all values are measured. (See Domestic Income.)

Opportunity Cost
The value to the economy of a good, service or resource in its best alternative use. (See also Accounting Prices above.)

Producer Surplus
The additional benefit received by a producer when paid more for the product than is necessary to induce him or her to sell it.

Risk
Situations where the range of possible values that a variable could take is known, and a probability of each value occurring can be estimated. Different from **Uncertainty**.

Savings Premium
The extent to which the value placed on a unit of income uncommitted to consumption (or saved) exceeds the value placed on the same unit of income used for consumption.

Sensitivity Analysis
The process of changing the values of selected variables in an analysis, to determine the effects on the overall position. Particularly used in cost benefit analysis, to see how Net Present Value may change with variation in some key variables.

Shadow Prices
See Accounting Prices above.

Shadow Wage Rate (SWR)
The Accounting Price of those types of Unskilled Labour where the wage exceeds the value of alternative earnings. The cost of the economy (in terms of forgone net output) of diverting such labour from its alternative occupation. It is usually expressed as a fraction of the market wage rate, ie the Conversion Factor for Unskilled Labour.

Skilled Workers
See Unskilled Workers.

Standard Conversion Factor (SCF)
A general Conversion Factor which is applied to domestic prices whose cost composition is not known, to convert them approximately to numeraire units. It adjusts only for price distortions due to average taxes on imports and should be used only for small items where no specific or sectoral CF is available, and for the revaluation of Non-Traded Output.

Tradeable Goods and Services
Goods and Services which are actually imported or exported, and also domestically produced goods which would have been imported or exported if the country had followed policies which fully took into account the possibilities of trade (ie their long-term comparative advantage).

Traded Goods and Services
Goods and Services which are actually imported or exported.

Transfer Payments
Payments made by a project or any other agency which are not associated with the use of real resources. Taxes are the main category (subsidies are negative taxes), but other types are surplus profits, excess rents, etc.

Uncertainty
Situations in which probabilities cannot be estimated for a variable to take any particular value. Different from **Risk**, where these probabilities can be calculated.

Uncommitted Income
That income which is not committed to consumption or earmarked for particular expenditures. It is more-or-less equivalent to savings created as the result of a new activity.

UNIDO Method
The approach to the economic analysis of projects that is based on works commissioned and published by the United Nations Industrial Development Organisation (UNIDO). (See bibliography.) It uses the numeraire 'net present-consumption benefits in the hands of people at the base level of consumption in the private sector in terms of constant-price domestic accounting rupees'.

Unskilled Workers
Workers, both male and female, who carry out tasks for which no training is needed, or which can be learned on the job. Generally such workers are in surplus supply. In the Organised sector, their wage may be higher than their alternative output, so a Shadow Wage Rate CF may need to be applied. Differentiated from **Skilled Workers**, who require prior training or experience; are generally in short supply; and are generally paid wages equal or close to opportunity cost.

Selected Bibliography

A. Introduction to Cost-Benefit Techniques

Henderson, P. D., 'Investment Criteria for Public Enterprises', in Turvey, R., ed. *Public Enterprises*. Penguin: Modern Economic Readings 1986.

HM Treasury, *Investment Appraisal in the Public Sector: A Technical Guide for Government Departments*, HMSO 1984.

Mishan, E. J., *Cost-Benefit Analysis:* An Informal Introduction. Allen and Unwin 1971.

Ray, A., *Cost-Benefit Analysis:* Issues and Methodologies, World Bank 1984.

B. The Little and Mirrlees Method of Project Analysis

'Cost-Benefit Analysis and Income Distribution in Developing Countries: A Symposium'. *World Development*, Vol. 6 No. 2 February 1978.

Little, I. M. D. & Mirrlees, J. A., *Project Appraisal and Planning for Developing Countries*. Heinemann Educational Books 1974.

Little, I. M. D., 'Nuffield College Research on Project Analysis in Agriculture'. *Journal of Agricultural Economics*. Vol. XXII No. 3 September 1971.

Squire, L. & Van der Tak, H. G., *Economic Analysis of Projects*. World Bank Research Publication 1975.

'Symposium on the Little-Mirrlees Manual of Industrial Project Analysis'. *Bulletin Oxford University Institute of Economics & Statistics*. Vol. 34 No. 1 February 1972.

C. Case Studies using the Little and Mirrlees method

Little, I. M. D. & Scott, M. FG., *Using Shadow Prices*, Heinemann Educational Books 1976.

MacArthur, J. D., 'Appraising the Distributional Aspects of Rural Development Projects', *World Development*, Vol. 6 No. 2 February 1978.

OECD Development Centre Studies, Series on Cost-Benefit Analysis:

Case Study Number One. Lal, D., *Wells and Welfare*. An explanatory cost-benefit study of the economics of small scale irrigation in Maharasthra 1972.

Case Study Number Two. Stern, N. H., *An Appraisal of Tea Production on Small Holdings in Kenya* 1972.

Case Study Number Three. Little, I. M. D. & Tipping, D. G., *A Social Cost-Benefit Analysis of the Kulai Oil Palm Estate*. West Malaysia 1972.

Case Study Number Four. Seton, F., *Shadow Wages in the Chilean Economy* 1972.

Porter, R. S. & Walsh, M. R., 'Cost Effectiveness Analysis in Practice: A Case Study of Domestic Water Supplies', *World Development* Vol. 6 No. 2 February 1978.

Scott, M. FG., MacArthur, J. D. & Newbery, D. M. G., *Project Appraisal in Practice*, Heinemann Educational Books 1976.

Squire, L., Little, I. M. D. & Durdag, M., 'Application of Shadow Pricing to Country Economic Analysis with an illustration from Pakistan', World Bank Staff Working Paper No. 330, 1979.

D. Sets of Accounting Prices for Particular Countries

Adhikari, R., *National Economic Parameters for Nepal.* University of Bradford, Project Planning Centre, Occasional Paper No. 9, 1986.

Lal, D., *Prices for Planning: Towards the Reform of Indian Planning.* Heinemann 1980. (*India*)

Powers, T. A. (Editor), *Estimating Accounting Prices for Project Appraisal.* Inter-American Development Bank 1981. (*Paraguay, El Salvador, Ecuador, Barbados*)

Scott, M. F. G., MacArthur, J. D. & Newbery, D. M. G., *Project Appraisal in Practice*, Heinemann 1976. (*Kenya*)

Weiss, J., *Practical Appraisal of Industrial Projects.* United Nations (UNIDO) 1980. (*Pakistan*)

Weiss, J., *National Economic Parameters for Jamaica.* University of Bradford, Project Planning Centre, Occasional Paper No. 7, 1985.

E. The UNIDO Method of Project Analysis

Dasgupta, P. S., Marglin, S. A. & Sen, A. K., *Guidelines for Project Evaluation*, United Nations (UNIDO) 1972).

UNIDO, *Guide to Practical Project Appraisal*, United Nations 1978.

UNIDO, *Practical Appraisal of Industrial Projects*, United Nations 1980.

F. Other Main Texts on Economic Analysis

Commonwealth Secretariat, *A Manual on Project Planning for Small Economies.* Commonwealth Secretariat, 1982.

Gittinger, J. P., *Economic Analysis of Agricultural Projects.* Johns Hopkins University Press 1982.

Harberger, A. C., 'Basic Needs versus Distributional Weights in Cost-Benefit Analysis', *Economic Development and Cultural Change*, Vol. 32 No. 3 April 1984.

G. Environmental Analysis

Baum & Tolbert, *Investing in Development: Lessons of the World Bank Experience.* OUP 1985.

Dixon, J. A. et al., *Economic Analysis of the Environmental Impacts of Development Projects.* Asian Development Bank Economic Staff Paper No. 31. 1986.

Hartwick, J. M. & Olewiler, N. D., *The Economics of Natural Resource Use.* Harper and Row, 1986.

H. Risk and Uncertainty

Reutlinger, S., *Techniques for Project Appraisal Under Uncertainty.* World Bank Staff Occasional Paper Number Ten. IBRD 1970.

Wagle, B., 'A Statistical Analysis of Risk in Capital Investment Projects'. *Operations Research Quarterly.* Vol. 18 No. 1.

I. Financial Analysis

Bierman, H. & Smidt, S., *The Capital Budgeting Decision.* 2nd Revised Edition. Collier-Macmillan 1967.

Harvey, C., *Analysis of Project Finance in Developing Countries.* Heinemann 1983.

Institution of Civil Engineers, *An Introduction to Engineering Economics.* Institution of Civil Engineers, 1969.

Merrett, A. J. & Sykes, A., *The Finance & Analysis of Capital Projects.* Longmans 1965.

Rockley, L. E., *Finance for the Non Accountant.* Business Books Ltd., 1986.

Simons, L. *Basic Arts of Financial Management.* Century Hutchinson Ltd., 1986.

J.   Institutional Analysis

Handy, C. B., *Understanding Organisations.* Penguin Business Library, Third Edition, 1985.

Woolf, E., Tanna, S. & Singh, K., *Organisations and Management,* Pitmans Publications Limited. 1986.

K.   ODA Publications

Bridger, G. A. & Winpenny, J. T., *'Planning Development Projects'.* HMSO 1983.

Cracknell, B. E. (Editor), *The Evaluation of Aid Projects and Programmes.* HMSO 1984.

Cracknell, B. E. & Rednall, J. E., *'Defining Objectives and Measuring Performance in Aid Projects and Programmes'. ODA* Evaluation Department Report EV384, 1986.

Manual for the Appraisal of Rural Water Supplies. HMSO 1984.

Telecommunications Sector Manual. HMSO 1986.

Index

(Numbers Relate to Paragraphs)

Printed in the United Kingdom for HMSO
Dd 294688   C70   5/93   8206